BOOK TWO

PRACTICING SAINTHOOD

BOOK TWO

PRACTICING SAINTHOOD

Walking the Path of Your Ascension

REV. SIDNEY W. BENNETT

GOLDEN EAGLE PRESS

GOLDEN EAGLE PRESS

Book Two
Practicing Sainthood
Walking the Path of Your Ascension

Some materials used by kind permission of
The Summit Lighthouse,
www.SummitLighthouse.org
ISBN: 979-8-218-41960-8

Editing: Carol Anderson
Transcribing: Diana Good
Book Design: James Bennett Design

Preface to Book Two

It is a joy to offer Book Two of Practicing Sainthood with thirteen new sermons, each containing deep mysteries of the Path that encourage and enlighten us on our journey Home.

In the four years since the publication of the first book, I have had the privilege of not only working on these sermons, but also experiencing the profound effect of striving to incorporate them into my life. To read, study and implement these ascended master teachings can bring powerful progress on our path of personal Christhood.

As I shared in the Book One preface (which follows), each sermon is unique, and they are not in any order of importance. It can be a great blessing to reflect, pray and incorporate key teachings from each one before moving on to the next. If you desire to delve more deeply into their meaning, page 301 has a list of the dictations that were played after the sermons.

As El Morya says, "Tempus fugit," time flies. We are on a magnificent path that will take us all the way Home. As we put these precious teachings into practice, we are forging our eternal victory. It may be closer than we think!

Rev. Sidney W. Bennett
April, 2024

Preface to Book One

For me, as for so many others, the search began before I even knew what I was searching for. It started as a vague uneasiness and a desire to understand my life at a deeper level. As a young teen I was trying to make sense of why things were the way they were. Why was I born into my family? Why in America and not India or somewhere else? Why did I sometimes feel lonely and out of place, even when I was surrounded by family and friends? Was there a bigger purpose to my life?

My father, who was a doctor, was a lifelong spiritual seeker, and I remember him reading one book after another in his quest for the truth. As I grew older I often talked with him about my questions. One day he shared with me that he believed in reincarnation because it seemed so logical. I was intrigued with the possibility that I had lived before—something I had never heard about in church.

The next day, instead of feeling sleepy in my 10th-grade study hall after lunch, I was wide awake and absorbed in a book he had suggested on karma and reincarnation. It was exciting to have discovered a teaching that answered so many of my questions! Though I loved aspects of the Christian church my family attended each week, I often left services feeling unsatisfied or confused, believing that there was much more to learn. Suddenly I saw my life from a different perspective because the teachings on reincarnation and karma helped explain so much more than the orthodox Christian view. Many of my questions remained unanswered, but I knew I was on to something and I determined to continue searching.

That was only the beginning. I eagerly continued my spiritual quest throughout high school, ever seeking a deeper wisdom and understanding. As I was nearing graduation from high school in southern California, my plan was to attend college in Oregon. At the urging of a friend, I changed my mind at the last minute and decided to attend the University of Colorado in Boulder.

College was a challenging time, as I tried to integrate my spiritual interests with a social and academic environment that often pulled me in other directions. I was always looking for people to talk with about the spiritual path but very few seemed interested.

One Saturday afternoon while I was browsing in the religious section of the university library, a book caught my eye and seemed to "jump off" the shelf at me. It was the *I AM Discourses* by Godfre Ray King. Something about the book clicked with me, so I checked it out and started reading. I vividly remember sitting on the grass several days later, staring at the book and pondering what I was supposed to do with it and the teachings it contained. I finally decided to go back to the library and check out the first two books in the series, *Unveiled Mysteries* and *The Magic Presence*. These three books introduced me to my divine identity and the world of the ascended masters—the saints and sages of East and West who had won their eternal victory. I was never the same again.

I read and re-read those books and told everyone who would listen about Saint Germain and the other masters. At that time I was working in a dormitory snack bar and one quiet Sunday morning I told a co-worker about the books and the masters. She said, "Wait a minute! I just read something in the classified ads about a store in Denver that carries books about the ascended masters." I eagerly went to the store the following week and found out about an upcoming conference in Colorado Springs.

I wasn't sure what to expect upon arriving at the headquarters of The Summit Lighthouse that Saturday in April 1971. After paying the $5 student rate for the conference, I soon found myself seated in what was originally the mansion's living room that was now being used as a chapel. I was handed a small binder with a few pages of decrees. Since I had no idea what they were, while others said them I just looked around and wondered what in the world I was doing there! Even so, something felt very right to me.

At the conclusion of the decrees, Mark and Elizabeth Prophet entered the room. Mark had a powerful presence and I listened intently as he talked about his life as Longfellow and read one of Longfellow's poems. Then Elizabeth shared a beautiful teaching and meditation on the song "God, God, God!" that affected me profoundly and has stayed with me to this day.

Very shortly it was announced that Elizabeth would be delivering a dictation from Mother Mary. I wasn't raised Catholic and I had never thought much about Mary except at Christmastime. After a musical meditation, I began to hear Mary's words telling us about our path home to God:

> *All of heaven stands waiting and watching... to assist you. But none will ever do it for you, beloved ones; for the joy is so great to do this oneself that no angel or Cosmic Being would be so selfish as to deprive you of that opportunity and that joy. Therefore in rejoicing we cheer you on as though in a grandstand, a cosmic amphitheater. And so it is your time; it is your place.*[1]

I pondered what she said and felt excited without fully comprehending what had happened. But I have never forgotten her teaching that it was *my* time and *my* place.

As I left that day, Mark and Elizabeth were at the door saying goodbye to everyone. At the time I didn't think much about shaking Mark Prophet's hand, but I do believe it created a heart tie that has been a great mercy and help to me these many years since.

Driving home to Boulder that night, I felt more than a little overwhelmed. Nonetheless, something resonated within me, and I was sure of one thing—these teachings were true! An inner soul memory stirred within me, deeply comforting, but just out of reach of my conscious mind. In any case, I *knew* my search was over and my path home to God lay before me. I was filled with profound gratitude and anticipation.

As I learned more about the masters' teachings and applied them, I marveled at their very practical spirituality. I discovered the journey home to God is a path of striving and testing, not to perfect the human, but to become our Higher Self. I began to appreciate that the master-disciple relationship (in the East, the guru-chela relationship) is one of deepest love. The path the masters teach is the greatest adventure of all; it is, indeed, "the sacred adventure," as the Ascended Master El Morya has called it.

In the almost fifty years since that day in Colorado Springs, my outer life has unfolded in many ways much like others'. After graduating from college, I traveled the world, worked in Africa and began a lifelong career in banking and finance. In other ways, my life has largely been a reflection of my spiritual journey. I met my wife as our independent search for God brought us together unexpectedly and almost miraculously. Since our marriage, we have continued to study and apply the masters' teachings and have served in many capacities within our international spiritual community.

Over all these years my love for the masters and their teachings has only increased. They explain the equation of life on planet Earth. They teach us who we are and—surprisingly important—who we are not! They help us understand that the ascension is the goal of life and that our destiny is to walk in the footsteps of Jesus and the saints of East and West. The teachings are filled with the profound mysteries of God, yet are simple enough for a child to understand. My greatest joy is talking about them, sharing and reflecting on their meaning, and helping to make them an integral part of our daily lives until ultimately we *become* them.

In 1987 I became a minister in the church arm of The Summit Lighthouse—Church Universal and Triumphant. The sermons in this book are selected from Sunday services I delivered over a seven-year period. In reviewing them, I discovered many of the same themes are shared in different ways, focusing on key teachings the masters have emphasized on the path to our ascension. And although the sermons have been edited to make them more readable, please keep in mind that they were delivered before a live congregation and therefore have a more personal and informal style.

I enjoy doing sermons because it is often like solving a puzzle: What teaching will God inspire me to explore and share with others? Sometimes the subject comes out of my reading or from a comment I heard; other times it is in response to a difficult initiation that someone shared with me in counseling or that took place in my personal life. Such things make me want to understand what the masters have taught about these tests and the ways that we can master them. I've endeavored to make the teachings understandable, relevant and workable no matter where one is on the Path.

The order of the sermons is not chronological. As a result, *Practicing Sainthood* does not read like a "how-to" book with each chapter building on the previous one. It may be helpful to read the sermons as if you had heard them in a weekly service, giving yourself time to pray, reflect and consider the most important keys for your life before reading another one.

I am reminded that in the East a chela or student of a master may only receive one new teaching to guide them through an entire lifetime. Many of the direct quotes from dictations or from the messengers included in this book could fulfill that premise.

Our journey home to God begins with searching and finding the truth, and then the work begins in earnest! Gautama Buddha admonished us to "Practice sainthood daily."[2] This path of practicing sainthood—of striving, being tested and giving loving service—is our joyous sacred labor as we work to out-picture our individual God-identity. That's what becoming a saint is really about—putting on our Christhood and becoming the fullness of our true identity while we yet walk the earth. This doesn't happen all at once! But as we apply the masters' precious teachings day by day, our Christhood will increase incrementally until, through many trials and testings and with great love and God's help, we *become* the truth of Being.

It has been a blessing to prepare these sermons, and my prayer is that the masters' teachings in this book will help you pass every test on your journey home to God. As our dear master El Morya has said, "The trek upward is worth the inconvenience!"

Rev. Sidney W. Bennett
April, 2020

Note to the Reader

While the sermons in *Practicing Sainthood* are geared toward those who have been practicing the Teachings of the Ascended Masters for some time and are familiar with the terms and concepts they contain, the book can be helpful for anyone seeking a deep spiritual path. Here are a few brief explanations for those new to these teachings.

The ascended masters are our elder brothers and sisters on the spiritual path. They are our teachers, mentors, examples and friends. Having balanced their karma and fulfilled their unique mission, they have graduated from earth's schoolroom and returned to the heart of God in the ritual known as **the ascension.** Through this ritual, the soul reunites with the Spirit of the living God, also known as the **I AM Presence.** This reunion with God in the ascension signifies the end of the rounds of karma and rebirth and is the goal of life for all sons and daughters of God. Prior to the ascension, we are called to follow in the footsteps of Jesus and other saints in the alchemical marriage of our souls to our **Christ Self.**

The ascended masters have emerged from all races and

nationalities, all walks of life and all religions. Collectively they are called **the Great White Brotherhood** (white refers not to race, but to the white light that is seen in the aura of the saints). Many of these masters are familiar to us, having walked among us throughout the ages. These include **Jesus Christ, Moses, Gautama Buddha, Lord Maitreya, Mother Mary, Kuan Yin, Zarathustra, El Morya, Saint Francis, and Saint Germain.** (El Morya is quoted extensively in the sermons. He was embodied as Abraham, one of the three wise men, Thomas Beckett, Thomas More and many others.) *Practicing Sainthood* includes teachings from many ascended masters whose names may be unfamiliar, but who are close to us and desire to help us toward our ascension.

God has always sent **messengers** as wayshowers. **Mark and Elizabeth Prophet** (Prophet was Mark's family name) were two such messengers and their mission was to bring forth the masters' teachings and revelations for the Aquarian age. Mark founded **The Summit Lighthouse** in 1958 and Elizabeth served with him from 1961 to 1973. They married, had four children, wrote many books, and lectured worldwide.

Mark passed on and ascended in 1973 and is now known as the Ascended Master **Lanello.** Elizabeth continued teaching, writing and ministering for decades. She was affectionately called "**Mother**" by students worldwide because of her devotion to the flame of God as Mother. Elizabeth passed on and ascended in 2009. Both are now working from spiritual realms to assist mankind.

Mark and Elizabeth Prophet were trained over many lifetimes to be messengers of the ascended masters. Through the power of the Holy Spirit in the manner of the apostles and ancient prophets, they received thousands of **dictations**— messages from the ascended masters for the upliftment of mankind in this age. Each dictation is a gift of the Holy Spirit and is not something the Prophets made happen themselves. Dictations contain the light and energy of the masters released from the highest spiritual levels as opposed to channelings from lower, psychic realms.

Each of us is created in the image and likeness of God. This **Divine Self** includes the I AM Presence and Holy Christ Self— the Higher Self or Real Self of every man, woman and child. The Holy Christ Self is each one's personal teacher, guardian, friend and the voice of conscience. Your Christ Self is also the mediator between God manifest in your mighty I AM Presence and your soul evolving in time and space.

The ascended masters teach the **Science of the Spoken Word**, a step-up of all prayer forms East and West. It combines prayer, meditation and visualization with what are called dynamic **decrees**, placing special emphasis on affirmations using the name of God—I AM THAT I AM. The masters teach that this form of devotion is the most effective method known today for spiritual resolution, the balancing of karma and soul advancement.

The violet flame is the energy of freedom, mercy, justice, ritual and alchemy. It transmutes negative energy and restores it to positive energy, and is a missing key to vitality, health and inner wholeness on our spiritual path. You can access the transmutative power of the violet flame through the Science of the Spoken Word in mantras, decrees and songs.

Our spiritual work includes overcoming the not-self or synthetic self, also called the **dweller-on-the-threshold**. The dweller is the antithesis of the Real Self and includes the negative energies a soul has created through misuses of free will. It stands in the way of the soul bonding to her Christ Self and it must be overcome for the soul to have her victory.

For more information on the path of personal Christhood, decrees, the violet flame and many other teachings by the ascended masters and the messengers to assist your spiritual journey, see www.SummitLighthouse.org.

Table of Contents

CHOOSING JOY

Beloved ones, there is joy in this path as no other joy you have ever known. ...verily I ask you, how can the Path that leads to perfect joy be without that joy?

—ARCHANGEL GABRIEL

Joy is indeed the motor of life!

—SAINT GERMAIN

ONE

Choosing Joy

Is the path of the ascension the Via Dolorosa (the sorrowful way) or the fullness of joy? The answer can profoundly affect how we live every day of our life.

The book *The Life of St. Teresa*, a 1912 translation taken from the French, relates the following story about our beloved Florence Miller, the Ascended Lady Master Kristine, in her embodiment as St. Teresa of Avila. Our excerpt begins:

> *In January of the last year of her life, 1582, she left Ávila to establish convents in Burgos and Grenada, and this befell her along the way:*

> *Teresa describes the journey thus: "We had to run many dangers. At no part of the road were the risks greater than within a few leagues of Burgos, at a place called Los Pontes. The rivers were so high that the water in places covered everything, neither road nor the smallest footpath could be seen, only water everywhere, and two abysses on either side. It seemed foolhardiness to advance, especially in a carriage,*

*for if one strayed ever so little off the road (then invisible),
one must have perished." The saint is silent on her share of
the adventure that follows, but her companions relate that,
seeing their alarm, she turned to them and encouraged
them, saying that "as they were engaged in doing God's
work, how could they die in a better cause?" She led the way
on foot. The current was so strong that she lost her footing,
and was at the point of being carried away when our Lord
sustained her. "Oh, my Lord!" she exclaimed, with her usual
loving familiarity, "when wilt Thou cease from scattering
obstacles in our path?" "Do not complain, daughter," the Divine Master answered, "for it is ever thus that I treat My
friends." "Ah, Lord, it is also on that account that Thou hast
so few!"* [3]

Can't we identify with encountering obstacles along the
Path? Hopefully we will meet them with faith and a sense of
humor like Teresa did!

Author Thomas Wolfe wrote: "*Man is born to live, to suffer,
and to die....*" [4] Not a very happy thought, is it? But perhaps at
some level we tie into that idea and view the Path as mostly
suffering that will hopefully lead to our ascension someday.
And perhaps we view joy as just a fleeting feeling that soon
yields to the difficult path of karma yoga.

The title of today's sermon, "Choosing Joy", implies that joy
is a choice. If it is a choice, why *wouldn't* we choose it? Do we
believe that joy is only in our future? Or do we think we can
have it now? Can we have joy and still walk the fourteen sta-
tions of the cross? Can joy and sorrow exist at the same time in
our world?

Let us ponder together what the masters have taught about
the path of joy.

The Ascension is a Path of Joy

Archangel Gabriel makes some very clear statements about joy and the Path.

Beloved ones, there is joy in this path as no other joy you have ever known. ...verily I ask you, how can the Path that leads to perfect joy be without that joy?[5]

That's a logical question, isn't it? After hearing Gabriel's words there can be little doubt in our minds that the path of our ascension *should* be a path of joy. Lanello dispels any remaining doubts we might have when he says:

Joy is the very first principle of the ascension. Take two individuals—one who fulfills his assignments without joy and one who fulfills them with joy. The one without joy, beloved, may lose his ascension for want of joy, and the [one with joy] may make it even though some elements are lacking.[6]

Now, if we accept that this is a joyous path, then why isn't joy a bigger part of our lives? And if this is a joyous path, then what about the via dolorosa? Does it have to be one way or the other or can they exist side by side? We will get to the question of joy and sorrow later. But first let's consider how we find joy and how we can choose joy.

Finding Joy

Henri Nouwen reflects that "*Joy does not simply happen to us. We have to choose joy and keep choosing it every day.*"[7] That sounds easy, doesn't it? But if it's easy, why don't we have the joy we want? Well, maybe Henri doesn't have the karma we have! While that might be a part of the reason, we know there's much more.

The popular evangelist Billy Graham made a very astute comment that may help us understand how to find joy. He had a different perspective than Henri: "*Joy cannot be pursued. It comes from within. It is a state of being. It does not depend on circumstances, but triumphs over circumstances.*"[8]

Think about that statement: "It does not depend on circumstances, but triumphs *over* circumstances." Are there circumstances in our personal lives or in the world that have led us to think we should deny ourselves the feeling of joy? Maybe we have forsaken joy because we see people all around the world in so much pain. Or maybe we have fallen into the common misunderstanding that joy and sorrow are mutually exclusive.

I have often thought about the attainment of Gautama Buddha. As Lord of the World, his aura envelops the planet. He holds a balance for the planet while he feels everything that is happening in his aura. Yet amidst all the pain and suffering of the world, he is perpetually meditating on the Divine Mother, even as he does other tasks. The "Ode to Joy" from Beethoven's Ninth Symphony directly attunes us to him, and we can undoubtedly learn by his example of maintaining joy in spite of everything happening to the contrary. How would we feel if Gautama Buddha did not have joy? I for one would be pretty concerned! Well, perhaps he's concerned that we don't have all the joy that *we* can have.

If we wait until everything is right in our lives and in the world, we will never find joy. We'll always be putting it in the future, thinking, "Well, if I only had this problem solved, I could be happy and joyous today." Or "If this world situation would resolve itself, then I could feel joy." But if we wait, it's *never* going to happen.

Maybe we harbor subtle resentment about our karma and our lot in life that resists joy, thinking, "Well, I can't be joyous. Look at my life. Look at my karma. Look at my health. Look at my finances." Or does a sense of unworthiness shut out joy and prevent us from accepting it? At some level of consciousness are we choosing *not* to have joy in our lives?

We need to ask ourselves, "Do I really want joy?" We might think, "Well of course I do!" But we need to also ask, "Am I sabotaging myself by my choices?"

Jesus explains what some people do.

> Blessed hearts, you may not be able to convert others to joy, for so many, so many enjoy the indulgence in sadness, in self-sympathy and self-pity. So many are so accustomed to nonjoy that allows the complaining and the self-indulgence that they would not know what to do with themselves if life were perpetually joyous.[9]

For whatever reason, nonjoy has become part of their identity, and joy would ironically mean they wouldn't have anything to complain about!

We have all encountered people who are habitual complainers. The Elohim Peace reminded us in his dictation played several weeks ago that there are still people who have a gripe against Moses and how he treated them![10] They complained about him then, got in the habit of complaining and never moved on. And how many thousands of years ago was that?

Of course, that doesn't mean that everyone who complains was with Moses. But it does alert us to the dangers of habitually complaining about something. It could be anything.

Oftentimes a complaint is almost the first thing out of a person's mouth when they see someone else. It's really an issue of their psychology, and they may not be aware of what they are doing and why they are doing it. If they understood it, I'm sure they would want to stop.

So we can ask if our complaining could be denying us our joy. Perhaps we should ask God to show us if we are sabotaging our own joy by our unresolved psychology and wrong habits.

Now, what do you think is one of the biggest opponents to joy in our lives? It's our dweller, isn't it? Our dweller doesn't want us to be happy. It has had a good thing for a long time, reigning supreme in our temple until we started recognizing what it was doing. So our dweller will no doubt manifest the force of anti-joy. We must choose joy over any circumstance that is manifesting in our world. And for those of us who may fall prey to complaining, let's try beginning our day with a feeling of joy and greeting others with that joy!

There is a price to be paid for joy. It includes striving to resolve problem areas of our psychology (including indulgence in sadness, self-sympathy and self-pity), the surrender of our human self, our dweller and any resentment and non-forgiveness of others, including God.

Joy and Laughter

Finding joy is not just about battling with our negative psychology or our dweller. It is also about taking the time to look for joy and finding it in the world around us.

Author Eileen Daspin tells us: "*Many Egyptians believed that after death they would be asked two questions by the gods and that their answers would determine whether they could continue to paradise...The first question...was, "Did you bring joy?" and the second was "Did you find joy?"*[11]

During the height of the Covid pandemic, our family made the decision to get a second dog. At the time, I was not terribly enthusiastic about the idea. Our older dog was approaching thirteen and I had envisioned that we might not replace her when she passed and that the household would be quieter. However, despite my various misgivings, we soon had a mini aussie puppy on our doorstep.

As you all know, training a puppy is fraught with challenges on many levels, largely physical. For example, we used to have a nice swivel rocking chair in our family room (emphasis on *used to*). Actually, it's still there, but clearly a victim of the puppy's chewing phase.

But something else happened besides the trials of training a puppy—she brought tremendous joy to our home! Her love of life, her unbridled enthusiasm, her greeting each day as a new adventure, and what's more—she made us laugh! In the middle of the pandemic, we were able to laugh. I laughed more than I had for years. We didn't forget Covid or the challenges and pain that came with it, but we were able to deal with it much better because of the joy this dog brought and continues to bring.

Joy can also come in the form of laughter. You may recall the lecture excerpt with Mark Prophet when he was using a laughing bag. Perhaps the most important spiritual teaching in that was that it's good to laugh and not take yourself so seriously! In fact, Jesus reminds us:

> *...there is a point of joy, there is a point of laughter in every day. And I speak of the joy and the laughter of you who are my disciples as I have known you and shepherded you in my own heart as we have gathered together over the centuries...* [12]

I love that vision—all of us together as disciples of our Lord, always doing the work at hand but enjoying friendship, camaraderie and laughter at the same time. To be with Jesus and share in his joy and laughter *every day*—such a gift!

Don't you always feel better when you really have a laugh of sheer joy, the pure laughter of God? There's a saying that "Laughter is the best medicine." The bible says, *"A merry heart doeth good like a medicine."*[13] And Norman Cousins made medical history in the 1970s when he was given a diagnosis akin to a death sentence. He took things into his own hands, watched funny movies, read funny books and laughed himself back to health! A great example of how joy and laughter can help heal not only our soul but our body as well.

"As Good as Gold in a Grim World"

A recent article in the Wall Street Journal entitled "Finding Joy Is as Good as Gold in a Grim World" states that positive emotions are linked to: *"longer life, stronger immune function, lower blood pressure and lower levels of the stress hormone cortisol."*[14] The author gives examples of how to find joy, including taking a walk in nature, doing something helpful for someone else and expressing gratitude. Sounds like a recommendation from the ascended masters, doesn't it?

Jesus gives us a similar blueprint for finding joy.

> *Joy, then, must come by an appreciation of small things and great, an appreciation of life as it is before you in a moment.*
> *Is it a glistening dewdrop?*
> *Is it the face of a child or a smile?*
> *Is it something precious that is without price, for it comes*

directly from the heart?

If you will, make a list of all those things that bring joy to you and affirm them.[15]

Making such a list also reminds us that we *do* have joy! I started to think about my own list and the top would be the opportunity we've been given in this lifetime, especially knowing the teachings of the ascended masters. How long have we been waiting for this? Ten thousand, thirty thousand, a million years to be at the right place at the right time, for the right opportunity, for the knowledge of who we really are?

I didn't know who I really was before I found these teachings. They gave me the understanding that there is a path to be walked and that the ascension is within our grasp. We have the violet flame that can transmute lifetimes of karma in *one life*, and we only have to balance fifty-one percent of that karma to make our ascension. Isn't that cause to shout for joy? Think of it! It's incredible!

In her book *Breaking the Age Code* Dr. Becca Levy wrote that results of a study on aging and retirement showed that, on average, people with the most positive views on aging were outliving those with the most negative views by seven and a half years.[16] Isn't that amazing? Think how much violet flame we can do in seven and a half years!

The aches and pains or financial problems or other concerns we may have are not fun. But let's hold onto the ultimate understanding deep within our being that we have arrived at the point where we have the tools to do what we need to do, where we have dispensations given to us as never before, where we can finally *be* who we really are. We had an embodied guru to lead the way. Everything's ready; the table is set. All we have to do is to partake of the feast of graces laid before us as we engage in the Path. Is that not a cause for joy? Whatever else is going on in our worlds, let's rejoice in that.

A Bubbling Stream of Joy

And let's not forget the unparalleled joy of loving God—putting aside the world and our karma and simply loving our Father-Mother God.

Lanello reminds us:

> Your Mighty I AM Presence with you, shining in all the splendor of the Father-Mother God, does continually radiate to you joy. And the descending crystal cord is a bubbling stream of joy. It is a bubbling stream of joy, beloved, as the light cascades into your heart.[17]

Joy is pouring through us 24 hours a day! So what happens to it? Well, we qualify a portion of this bubbling stream with our human creation. We sometimes put our thoughts, our doubts, our pride, whatever misqualified energy is in our being into that stream of joy, so it cannot fully manifest in our outer consciousness. Joy is there if we will avail ourselves of it.

Creating a figure-eight flow between you and your mighty I AM Presence brings you great light, love, comfort and most certainly joy. To help us with the process of experiencing joy, Lanello admonishes us to "*abandon a sense of martyrdom! Abandon a sense of self-condemnation! Abandon a sense of nonjoy!*"[18]

Before I started researching this sermon, it never occurred to me that I might have nonjoy. I never even thought about it. But after reading Lanello's words, I determined to add any nonjoy to my dweller calls. If I have it, I want it gone!

Most of us are familiar with Saint Germain's statement that

"Joy is indeed the motor of life!"[19] But have we really considered what that might mean for us personally? He continues:

> *This, when properly understood and harnessed, will cause the regenerative processes within the forcefield of individuals to amplify the light energy within the cells. Thus a renewal of the power of eternal youth occurs within the dimension and forcefield of the individual because God is there and pours out his limitless light, even as the sun gives forth her energy.*[20]

Eternal youth! That's certainly an inspiration for those of us who have labored long in the vineyard of the Lord. If we weren't sold on joy before, we should be now.

The Joy of Forgiveness

In their dictation titled "The Joy of Forgiveness," the Angels of the Cosmic Cross of White Fire and the Ruby Ray spoke about forgiveness.

> *Know this, beloved, for it is your liberation. It will liberate you whether you are harboring sin, disease and death or the evils of the underworld. Harbor the light and the greater light, until you ascend on that light and you say to yourself, "What a waste of time it was to dislike this one and to dislike that one when our God is the indwelling God who lives within all!"*[21]

It can be good to ask ourselves, "Is non-forgiveness of someone blocking my joy?"

Reviewing the dictation in preparation for this sermon reminded me of a week when God taught me two lessons on forgiveness. The first occurred as I was waking one morning.

I had a sudden revelation and hurried to tell my wife, "I have to forgive myself for the karma I have in this life!" Seems like an obvious thing to do, doesn't it, since we know the teaching about forgiveness. But it was quite clear to me, and I felt it so strongly that I knew I had not completely done it—I had not forgiven myself for my karma!

As lightbearers we are often burdened with a sense of shame about our mistakes, our unworthiness, our karma. Yet it can be a point of pride not to forgive oneself! So affirming that I forgave myself was liberating. It was a joy to forgive myself while acknowledging, "Yes, I may have karma but by the grace of God and the light of God and the joy of God, I'm going to move forward and balance it."

My second lesson on forgiveness needs some background. In one place where we lived, we had a neighbor that for some reason didn't seem to like me. He tended to avoid me, and I respected that. Interestingly, after a few years of living there, our dog started to bark at him and his wife whenever they drove into their driveway. Well, nobody likes to have a dog bark at them, so I should have been more sensitive to its effect on them. The neighbor used to honk his horn at the barking dog in what I thought was a playful way. It took me a long time to catch on to how much it actually bothered him; when I did, I stopped our dog from doing it anymore. Still, the neighbor continued to ignore me and would walk the other way whenever he saw me.

Besides my recent mistakes, I wondered if I had some unresolved karma with him from another life. So, one day I saw him working and I asked if I could speak with him. I apologized profusely for the barking and anything else he felt was unneighborly. It was clear he was harboring a lot of feelings about this, as he lit into me with a stream of vitriolic language and energy

I have seldom encountered. I decided to just take it and let him run out of steam. I apologized again, and that unleashed some more of his anger. Eventually, he had no more to say, and after another apology and recognition of his concerns we parted company. Afterwards, I was hopeful that we could move on and start afresh, but it was not to be. Even after my apology his behavior towards me did not change.

Sometime later, I was walking down our driveway to get the mail and he was walking to get his. When he saw me, he turned to walk the other way. That bothered me more than I liked, and I asked myself why I still felt unresolved. Then it hit me in a flash—I had not forgiven him for not forgiving me! I immediately did so, and I felt a freedom and joy that was absent before. Forgiveness had liberated me!

Sorrow Prepares You for Joy

In John 16:20-22 Jesus teaches us about sorrow and joy: "*Verily, verily, I say unto you, That ye shall weep and lament, but the world shall rejoice: and ye shall be sorrowful, but your sorrow shall be turned into joy. A woman when she is in travail hath sorrow, because her hour is come: but as soon as she is delivered of the child, she remembereth no more the anguish, for joy that a man is born into the world. And ye now therefore have sorrow: but I will see you again, and your heart shall rejoice, and your joy no man taketh from you.*"

Sorrow is clearly part of the Path. There is the sorrow of our karma and the pain it causes ourselves and others. Sorrow teaches us *compassion* for life in pain. I love the teaching that offers a way to help others through our own physical pain or illness. We know how hard pain can be sometimes and we naturally seek to be free from it. But as long as we have pain, we can offer it up and ask God to use it to help others.

We are admonished by the ascended master Phylos the Tibetan, "May you see yourself in every life who suffers."[22] He advises us to self-empty, to help others and to build a reservoir of good karma to pass through adversity and the dark night of the soul. But he does not portray the Path as only one of sorrow. He also stresses having joy:

> The spiritual devotees on the Path have their work cut out for them, but I stress the joy. If any man or woman think that this is a path of martyrdom, let him depart hence; for martyrdom is not the way to the kingdom of God but a true compassionate self-givingness.[23]

Rumi, the 13th-century Persian poet and Sufi mystic, spoke of how sorrow is the precursor of joy.

> Sorrow prepares you for joy. It violently sweeps everything out of your house, so that new joy can find space to enter. It shakes the yellow leaves from the bough of your heart, so that fresh, green leaves can grow in their place. It pulls up the rotten roots, so that new roots hidden beneath have room to grow. Whatever sorrow shakes from your heart, far better things will take their place.[24]

Sorrow prepares us for joy! In her lecture "Your Sorrow Shall Be Turned into Joy," Mother explains how sorrow can do that.

> It's a process of integration with God, the process of becoming the Christ because one has experienced the sorrow, dealt with it, lived through it, worked through it. And the sorrow is turned to joy by an act of free will, not by suppressing

the experience and walking away from it and saying, "There's nothing to it." ...

It's natural to cry at your mother's funeral. It's natural to be sorrowful when you lose a loved one. And if you don't allow yourself to experience the loss and the sense of loss, you can't transmute it into joy.[25]

You can't have that joy unless you experience the sorrow and rise above it. It is a process to go through. Mother reminds us, *"Just as you do not jump full blown into the mantle of Christ, you do not jump full blown into joy."*[26] It's not like waking up, flipping a switch and saying, "I'm going to have a positive attitude today." You put on the true joy of God through the experiences that he brings to you.

We honor joy. We cultivate joy. We make it a focus in our life and we focus on giving it to others. We also know there is sorrow, there is karma, there are hard things in our lives, but that doesn't mean we can't experience joy. It is our choice.

Most of us are familiar with the biblical reference concerning the Truth being *"sweet in the mouth, but bitter in the belly."*[27] Many leave the path of their ascension when the challenges become too great. Others continue, but with a certain bitterness. Mother talked about this:

Some people blame and accuse God for the injustice of the painful process of getting to the joy. And they're so caught up in the agony of the climb or the agony of the trek that when they get to the end of it, they're so disgruntled, so irritated and so critical of either the helpers on the way or fellow chelas or the organization or whatever seemed to make the whole event unpleasant that they miss the prize. They miss the prize of the birth of the Manchild in their hearts because they are so caught up in the sense of the inconvenience and the injustice that was part of the birth process.[28]

We put on joy gradually. It's a birthing process. We have tools to use that help us experience joy and see joy in things around us. But experiencing the fullness of joy is a process, and it comes to us in increments. It's not just about a positive attitude. It's about allowing the true joy of God to fully blossom within us.

The path Home is worth every sorrow and every joy that we encounter. Jesus says, *"The Holy Spirit comes with an unmitigated joy, a joy that is the acceptance of things as they are, of things that cannot be changed and therefore will be dealt with in joy."*[29]

Think about that. There are some things we cannot change; it's just not going to happen. When Paul asked about the thorn in his flesh, Jesus said, *"My grace is sufficient unto thee."*[30] When we see something that can't be changed, we shouldn't feel depressed or discouraged or hopeless. We just have to turn it into joy by accepting it as a necessary step on our homeward path. While we sometimes see the most beautiful souls with the most difficult karma, we can acknowledge that it's necessary for them to go through it to have their victory. So if God gives us something to bear (it could even be from a hundred thousand years ago), when we are truly on the Path, we recognize it is necessary for us to pass through it.

When we balance 100% of our karma, we will leave behind the sorrows that it caused. At the same time, we have been told that the ascended masters continue to know sorrow, perhaps through seeing the pain of others and the wrong choices they make. Even so, it does not take away from their joy!

Uriel and Aurora explain: *"Yes, we bear our sorrows. Yes, we are acquainted with our burdens. But the joy of God that is perpetually* with us and in us through the unfed flame is beyond all of this."[31]

On a similar note, Lady Master Magda explains why some noble souls may not outwardly appear joyful, though deep within joy is the very motor of their life.

> *Therefore, if you are not in the sunshine of joy, beloved, it may be because in your sensitivity to world pain you are carrying a certain weight of planetary karma. It is not that you are without joy but it is that you brace yourself moment by moment in order to continue to bear that karma. And you bear infirmities in the flesh that others know not of because you are so concerned about the rising tide of world karma and you recognize that your bearing a share of it can make the difference between night and day for millions of souls whose karmic load precludes their carrying even so much as an additional ounce of the world weight.*
>
> *At times, then, this lawful concern you carry for the karmic state of the world and her population begets a face of solemnity such as you would see on anyone who would strain at lifting a great and heavy weight. The serious mien is no sign that the joy flame has gone out; on the contrary, it is a sign that the joy flame is the very motor of your life. And that joy flame is truly great in the heart of my Lord, for he rejoices that you are willing to take on the burdens of others, even to carry some of their karma that they might yet live to know the joy of the rising Sun of Righteousness in their own beings.[32]*

The Challenge of Anti-Joy

For Kuan Yin to become the Goddess of Mercy, she had to overcome the entire force of non-mercy in cosmos. So as we strive to embody joy, let us be aware that the force of anti-joy will not be far behind. Think of how livid the fallen ones must feel in the presence of joy! It is something they can never experience unless they bend their knee. Joy has the potential to unleash anti-joy in others who may be jealous or angry because you have joy and they don't. They may believe that you don't have the weight of karma or the problems they do. The irony of this is that the opposite is often true—those with the greatest true spiritual joy gained it by overcoming pain and sorrow, not because hardships were absent from their lives.

When you are joyful, you may even be accused of being a "Pollyanna"— a person characterized by irrepressible optimism and a tendency to find good in everything.[33] Perhaps a Pollyanna sees what is real in the world and not the unreal. Yes, we have to be practical and realistic, but that does not mean being without joy.

Jesus teaches us how joy can help in time of great travail and pain:

> *Beloved ones, moments after some seeming tragedy has come upon you, you can [by the joy flame] see through it to the other side and experience joy because God has shown you that this is something that you must pass through.*[34]

A superficial joy, a pretend joy is never going to survive tragedy and pain and loss. Even when you have the joy of knowing that God wants you to go through something, it can still hurt. You can have sorrow, but you don't have to deny yourself inner joy. Yes, grief needs to be healed; pain needs to be healed. But you can do that while still having joy. This is accomplished by a childlike trust in God and the confidence, as Paul wrote in Romans 8:28, "*that all things work together for good to them that love God, to them who are the called according to his purpose.*" Joy is an affirmation of life, and the force of anti-joy cannot touch it if we do not allow it.

At the same time, we have to be watchful of the spoiler energy. The dark forces don't like it when we're happy, when we have joy. So Mark Prophet taught us to make calls on the spoiler energy when we're having a celebration or honoring a victory. It's important to make that call because the forces of darkness will try to spoil things for us, and we don't want to allow the joy of our victories to be tarnished by that energy.

Where the Joy Bells Ring

Some months ago I was reflecting on my nighttime prayer rituals. I always included asking for forgiveness for my errors during the day. I would also bring my petitions to God for adjudication and give thanks for my many blessings and the opportunity to balance karma. But I felt something was missing.

Then I remembered Mother's teaching on praying at the altar of our threefold flame in the secret chamber of our heart. Jesus says:

> And that threefold flame is more powerful, more wonderful, more wisdom-filled, more love-inspired and infired than anything else one could ever acquire in many universes and many, many millennia into the future or the past.
>
> Your threefold flame is it, beloved! It is your treasure. It is surely the white stone and the white cube. It is surely the fountain of eternal youth.[35]

It is our treasure, our fountain of eternal youth! Pretty strong declaration, isn't it? Makes one wonder if we have neglected our threefold flame. We know we need to balance, blaze and expand it. But have we really given honor to that wondrous flame within us? Jesus reminds us that the fallen ones will try to tempt us away from the *"cathedral of the heart, where the joy bells ring!"*[36] Just imagine that wonderful sound!

Truly this light of God within us is worthy of our praise, our love and devotions, and honoring the joy it embodies. Jesus tells us:

> So walk with that sense: "My threefold flame is the fount of eternal Life in all universes, in all being I could ever contemplate. Right here in me is all that I AM, all that I need—the joy-filled abundant life."[37]

So I began adding the visualization of kneeling at the altar of my heart and giving my praise, my love and my gratitude for my threefold flame. Such an easy thing to do! Well, I won't tell you what I experienced, but I will encourage you to try it for yourself.

That magnificent threefold flame is the gift of God within our hearts. It is the very presence of God within us.

The Serious Business of Heaven

C.S. Lewis wrote that *"Joy is the serious business of heaven."*[38] Isn't that an interesting concept? Joy is also the serious business of our chelaship. We can ask ourselves, "Can I win my victory without joy?" Maybe we have denied ourselves greater joy because we have not fully understood how important it is and how we can choose to have it.

We can *choose* to have joy. We can ask Jesus to teach us about joy, to teach us how to expand joy within our hearts, to teach us how to put on joy as we're putting on our Christhood.

Now, we all want to be happy, right? Of course we do! But not just the superficial happiness where all the bills are paid, and we're healthy and the sun is shining. While all of those things are nice, we want to experience the true joy that is deep within us.

Jesus challenges us:

> *There must be a moment in your life when you say: "I will let no man take my crown of joy! I will stand and still stand. I will find the joy in every happening, in every occurrence I see. And where I see nonjoy, I shall have within myself such a momentum of joy that I may fill the vacuum!"* [39]

He gave us a fiat: "I will let no man take my crown of joy!" You know, we've been under such condemnation these past two thousand years from orthodox Christianity that even though we know the Truth, maybe there is some part of us that swallowed the lie of unworthiness. Maybe we are so used to being subservient to the Church or the priest or whatever that we have failed to take that stand: "I will let no man take my crown of joy!"

That fiat is a declaration of *war* against the force of non-joy, not only in ourselves but in the world. We don't tackle this force alone; we have help and support from the masters and angels. But if *we* don't take that stand, no one else is going to do it for us. It's as simple as that. The path of joy is a path of action not of passivity, so we have to determine to experience it.

As we approach the serious business of joy in our lives, let us remember that our striving for joy will not necessarily be easy. It does not mean the end of sorrow or grief or the challenges of karma. What it does mean is that joy is a choice. If we go out of here today determined to have joy, it probably won't be long before we encounter anti-joy in someone or something that wants to burst our bubble of joy. So we have to *choose* not to allow that to happen.

The ultimate core of joy in our being does not depend on outer conditions. But experiencing that joy is a choice. No matter what may come our way, we can choose to find joy because joy is the nature of God, and we are created in His image. Joy comes from our I AM Presence. It's in the threefold flame within our heart. It surrounds us. Only by absenting ourselves from that flow of Spirit can we exclude joy from our hearts and our being.

If we sometimes struggle with finding this joy, let us remind ourselves that we put on joy much as we put on our Christhood—in increments. Allow yourself time to experience and increase joy within your heart. Don't get discouraged if it doesn't suddenly wipe the blackboard of your life clean because it won't. But it will give you a different perspective, a different energy, and it will offer you a choice regarding how to qualify energy. Joy is coming through us 24 hours a day. We can grumble or feel that this is a life or path of pain, and sometimes it is. But we can make the determination to remember that joy is within us and joy is flowing through us. We can choose to have greater joy, and it will build as we put it on increment by increment.

Jesus was joyful to go to the cross because he knew it was his mission, his divine plan to fulfill. He also knew what grace it would bring to the world. Similarly, we can find joy in going through aspects of our karma to fulfill our dharma. God is returning our karma to us because we *want* it. Can we be joyous about our karma? Yes! Because balancing our karma is a necessary part of preparing for the *ultimate* joy—union with God.

The Ultimate Joy

In the spring of 1971, I was about to graduate from the University of Colorado in Boulder. On April 9th my spiritual search led me to the Easter conference of the Summit Lighthouse in Colorado Springs. I knew very little about the ascended masters before then, and I heard my first dictation that day. It was by Mother Mary titled "The Chalice of My Heart" and it is the dictation we will be hearing today. It's not in a *Pearl of Wisdom*, but it is published in *My Soul Doth Magnify the Lord*.

I didn't remember much from the dictation at the time; I was just trying to experience it. But I remembered the ending very clearly. Mary said it is our time and our place to do as Jesus did. It is our time and our place to stand in the presence of God within us and go through the resurrection and ascension. She said:

> *But none will ever do it for you, beloved ones; for the joy is so great to do this oneself that no angel or Cosmic Being would be so selfish as to deprive you of that opportunity and that joy. Therefore in rejoicing we cheer you on as though in a grandstand, a cosmic amphitheater. And so it is your time; it is your place.*[40]

The joy of victory is before us. We don't want to be like the person Mother described who grumbles all the way to their victory, irritated that the Path is hard, angry about this or that or their treatment by so-and-so, or the chastisement they received, or their health or finances or whatever. We want to maintain Buddhic peace and joy, while dealing with these various things in our life.

The ultimate joy awaits us—the joy of becoming all that God has intended for us. Can we even imagine the joy of that day when we stand on the dais at Luxor and have the ascension flame seal our victory? Doesn't it give you the chills to even think about that? It's a real possibility. It's what we've been working for and striving for, not just in this lifetime, but in other lives too. It is *there* if we will work to achieve it. Aren't we willing to do anything God asks of us to prepare for that day of destiny?

Meanwhile, we do not have to wait to experience joy. As Gabriel asks, *"How can the Path that leads to perfect joy be without that joy?"* [41] There is a line in the Christian hymn "Blessed Assurance" that says, "Oh, what a foretaste of glory divine." That makes me think of a foretaste of joy divine, for the joy that we can experience today is but a foretaste of that ultimate joy. As Jesus told us, having joy on the Path (even though we may not do everything perfectly) will help us get Home.

I felt a little chagrined in researching this topic, wondering why I had not understood the alchemy of joy, why it had not been obvious to me. God even put it in front of me in the name of my wife (Joye). But what was blocking greater joy in my world? What might be blocking greater joy in your world? It's simply *not* choosing it! It's simply not understanding it and not going after it in the same way we go after our Christhood.

We can get depressed about what's going on in the world, and though it's obviously a matter of great concern, it doesn't have to take away our joy. When we have joy in our hearts it can be contagious. Other people can feel it in our auras, and it can give them hope and strength to keep on keeping on. Besides our calls and prayers and rosaries, being joyful is another thing we can do for souls in need.

You can carry joy in your aura when you go places, and

people who are downtrodden or burdened will feel that joy of God, even though they may never know that it came from you. Isn't that a wonderful thought? It's like Johnny Appleseed scattering his apple seeds. He didn't stay around to see the fruit, but the fruit came. The day of our ultimate joy will come, but until then we can have a foretaste of that joy.

It is our birthright and our destiny to have this joy. But we have to *choose* it.

HEAVEN'S PERSPECTIVE

When you want to be like God, you shall be!

—SAINT GERMAIN

TWO

Heaven's Perspective

Today we will be taking a journey with the Cosmic Being Maximus. As we listen to the dictation, he will take our hand and ask us to ascend a ladder of light that the angels have lowered, in order for us to gain *"a vision of the Promised Land"* [42] and a *"perspective of life."* [43]

As we climb this ladder with Maximus, the earth begins to recede, and we see just how small not only the earth is, but also the portion of ourselves that is *"vested in that life."* [44] He teaches us that on earth *"all things loom large, even gnats and flies and little petty problems."* [45] I think we can all attest to that happening in our lives. And while our life is our coordinate in time and space, Maximus reminds us that it is *"but an inch in a cosmic inch of measurement."* [46]

Many years ago, I got a foretaste of this. I was walking to work along the skyway system in the downtown area of Minneapolis. As I was walking, it suddenly felt like I was lifted up and was looking down at myself from quite a height. It was strange to see myself wearing a suit, walking along, carrying a briefcase. It seemed unreal, almost as if I were wondering,

"Who is that person down there? What is he doing? Where is he going?" The feeling passed, but I have never forgotten the experience.

It's good to sometimes ponder, "Who am I really?" Morya comments about this:

You may come to the realization, beloved, that I would give you in this moment—that you are not mortals! But because you think you are, you have become mortals. It is like a dog who thinks that he is a rabbit or a skunk or a this or a that.[47]

When I got up that morning in Minneapolis, I believed I was a banker. And in some ways, perhaps that was good, since I don't think the bank would have paid me to be a chela on the Path! Yet, in our various roles, have we forgotten who we really are?

It might be tempting to simply say, "Well, I am an ascending one, with a magnificent causal body who is just stopping over in this 'inch' of cosmic time and space, and none of it is real anyway." While that may be true, this "stopping over" has become millions of years for some of us. So it would seem obvious that somewhere along the way we actually *did* forget who we really are.

The fact that our world in its present state is ultimately unreal does not mean that it is unimportant. It is very important to the masters and all of cosmos. And what we do in our life matters not only for ourselves but also for billions of other souls who call earth home. We are on the stage of life, and we must pass our tests and demonstrate a certain mastery so that we can free ourselves and others from the Gordian knots of karma.

The God and Goddess Meru remind us:

Your inheritance is to be a king, a queen, a priest, a priest-ess at the altar of the Most High God. Why, then, does one lifestream attain and another fall back? Is it perspective? [48]

That is precisely the reason Maximus takes us on this journey—to gain perspective. So let us take advantage of the lofty heights that Maximus has brought us to, and, for a change, see through the eyes of heaven. Let's take a glimpse at what the angels and masters see and perceive in the world at large, as well as in the lives of their devotees.

The following thoughts and teachings are meant to enlighten and encourage us to keep on keeping on and are not intended to burden us in any way. Think of how blessed we are to know the teachings! Imagine how many souls stand before the Karmic Board for their life review and think, "If only I had known more! If only I had understood!"

I remember the Goddess of Liberty said that before we came into embodiment we begged her to help us find the teachings so that we would not be in that very predicament. Yet most of us need reminders and a respite from the "gnats and flies and little petty problems" of our lives in order to regain or expand our perspective on the world and our own path.

It's very easy to be busy. There are many important things and little details that take up our time every day until, before we know it, nightfall comes and we're tired and need to unwind and go to bed. We can get into a regular routine day after day, week after week and unknowingly slip into a rote consciousness and lose perspective. That is when we need heaven's perspective to help us refocus our lives.

At this crucial time in earth's history the door of opportunity for spiritual acceleration is open wider than it has been for thousands of years. So it's good to periodically step back from our daily routine and remind ourselves how important our striving, our service and our path of Christhood is to ourselves and the planet.

America's Values Are Changing

America, the hope of the world, is changing. When I grew up, we were a Christian nation ascribing to Judeo-Christian values and honoring life and freedom. Without knowing Saint Germain's name, we were a people that honored him and the flame he endowed America with.

It is no news that society has changed. While there are still many who ascribe to those values, American culture is quite different today. A recent poll reported in The Wall Street Journal revealed that "The values that Americans say define the national character are changing, as younger generations rate patriotism, religion and having children as less important to them than young people two decades ago."[49]

When the baby boomers are compared to Gen X and then to Gen Z and the millennials, the importance of these qualities or feelings drops almost in half. For the youngest generation, religion and having children are important to only about 30 percent of them, and these are the very people who will be shaping the future of America.[50]

There is another trend among young people called "moralistic therapeutic deism." That's a mouthful so I will repeat it: "moralistic therapeutic deism." A Catholic archbishop succinctly described what this is:

This term was famously coined by two sociologists to describe the amorphous set of religious beliefs to which many American young people subscribe. This belief system is moralistic in that it emphasizes moral behavior, vaguely defined as being nice, kind, pleasant, respectful, responsible, and so on. It is therapeutic in that it envisions God as on call to take care of problems that arise in our lives, but not otherwise interested in us nor holding us accountable for our choices. It is deistic in that it views God as having created the world but not personally involved in it. Such views fall short of the Christian understanding of God, who does hold us accountable, who gave his Son for us to save us from the devastating consequences of sin, [or as we say, "karma"] *and who desires to be deeply involved in our lives. The Church of Nice is not the Church of Jesus Christ, who came "to cast fire upon the earth"* [51] *and longed to see it blaze up.* [52]

What a powerful perspective on today's world. When we were all searching for the Path, I don't think we were looking for the "Church of Nice." Yet people have swallowed this philosophical lie in part because they have never been told the truth. When you think of the things that continuously bombard souls on this planet and the myriad plots against our true identity—wrong diet, distorted media, pollution, humanism, political correctness, perverted sex, easy access to drugs, and so on—we can understand how the psyche of the people gets worn down. So people go for the pablum instead of the meat of the Word. They go for something weak and watered down because they think that's the way to safely navigate the world, to not be thought of as strange or different from the new norms of society. Perhaps they are thinking, "I'll just go along with things, and, oh yes, I'll be a good person and love everybody."

But the Church of Nice is not for the sons and daughters of God! And the Church of Nice and those who follow it do not have the fire of God needed to save this planet.

The Cause of Mother Mary's Tears

Unfortunately, this trend is not only happening in America. For the most part, the people of the entire earth have not answered the call to return to their true identity in God.

Some time ago a friend said to me, "You've got to read this dictation," and so I did. It was a dictation by El Morya delivered on August 8, 1988. I will be referring to it a lot today, as it gives us many glimpses into heaven's perspective. In the dictation El Morya shared with us what happened when Mother made a pre-ordained call.

> Do you know, beloved—and you do not, therefore I shall tell you—that while you invoked the light here yesterday the Call was made as it was destined to be made by the Messenger in that very hour. [Yes,] a million years ago it was destined that that Call be made in that hour yesterday. And therefore the Messenger did [make the] call in the person and mantle of the Divine Mother that she does bear at inner levels, Kuan Yin and Mother Mary with her, [and she] did cry out to all Lightbearers of the world (all of whom recognize her [as the Mother]) [and] did implore every one of those Lightbearers to let go of their cups of materialism, to let go of the money beast, to let go of this civilization and to come apart—imploring and giving call after call after call for all legions of the Divine Mother to cut them free.
>
> And with all of this and these centuries of service of our bands, beloved hearts, at this crucial hour of the handwriting on the wall, how many (apart from the Body of God already separated out) of those Lightbearers on the entire planet do you think responded? I tell you, 5 percent [of the Lightbearers on planet earth] left their hold upon the money beast and heeded the Call of the one whose face they have known forever![53]

What El Morya told us is stunning, not only to us, but it seems to the masters as well. Most of us have seen pictures of statues of Mother Mary with tears coming down. But do you know why she is weeping? El Morya explained it's not for what's coming on the earth; it is for the failure of the lightbearers to respond to the truth and the Word already spoken.[54]

Let this be an inspiration and goad for each of us to come up higher, and let it also inform our perspective on what the future could hold for life in America and on the earth.

Lord, I AM Worthy

Then what about our future? We may all be at different places on the Path, but we will all face similar challenges on our journey Home. The masters and the messengers have often mused about why more souls do not respond to the light when it is so apparent, or why they do not truly understand who they are in God. The God and Goddess Meru ask:

Why do they remain outside the law of being? Why do they not claim the God consciousness of their own, in their own, and as their own being?

It is a question of identity and of identification, and it is a question of ignorance. It is a lack of determination, a lack of will.[55]

I'll repeat that last part again: "*It is a question of identity and of identification, and it is a question of ignorance. It is a lack of determination, a lack of will.*"

I looked up the definition of identity and found something to ponder: "The fact of being who or what a person or thing is."[56] The fact of being who a person is. Well, if we still think we're mortals—human beings in a human world—then, as Morya said, we have become mortals. And we will remain mortals if we think that somehow our mental body is the solution to life's problems or if we identify success in worldly terms. Oh, yes, we may acknowledge that God is within us and that we have a destiny, but do we always live that way?

Even when someone is living the right way, there is a tremendous amount of condemnation heaped upon the lightbearers on this planet. The Christian church has long condemned them by saying, "You are a worthless sinner." Social media and cyberbullying are modern ways the fallen ones can use to attack and condemn God's people. And for thousands and tens of thousands of years, the Nephilim and fallen angels have gotten lightbearers to identify with them instead of with God. They have programmed lightbearers to accept the blame for what they themselves have done. It's a plot that's been quite successful, hasn't it? And on top of all this, most lightbearers are sensitive souls who condemn themselves for real or imagined errors. Sadly, when we accept any condemnation, we are identifying with the mortal and not the divine.

Lightbearers are under a serious burden due to the constant pounding of this aggressive mental suggestion. Even those within our organization who know the truth are bombarded by thoughts levied against them, "Oh, you're not a very good chela. You should have been up at 5:00 a.m. this morning, and you slept till 5:30." Some of the criticisms that are projected against us are ridiculous. Yet even though we know the truth, sometimes we are vulnerable because of fatigue or lack of attendance at the altar or any number of things, and we can fall prey to the onslaught.

We need to beware of all these things because they can add up to an intense projection of worthlessness. And we need to counteract that feeling with the fiat we've been given: "Lord, I AM worthy, make me worthier still!"

Becoming One-Hundred Percent God

It helps to receive encouragement along the way and be reminded of our worth and who we are in God. I love this quote from El Morya, and even though I've used it before, it's worth revisiting.

> *You are not the 'hewn' man. You are made in the image and likeness of God.*
>
> *Cease your strutting about to be good humans doing good works, always busying yourself to reinforce your self-image as a good human being. Cease all of this. Become zero that God may become the one-hundred percent of Being where you are.*[57]

Accepting Morya's teaching is one thing. Following it and becoming the fullness of Being is another. We cannot keep trying to be human and divine at the same time, straddling the fence between the human world and the divine. We need to learn to become zero that God may work through us, unhindered by anything human. That is heaven's perspective.

When we surrender to the will of God, when we become zero in the sense of losing our human consciousness, we don't lose our unique identity. There's no soul that I know of more devoted to the will of God than El Morya. Well, he hasn't lost his identity, has he? God doesn't tell him how to run the Darjeeling Council, but he's so aligned with the will of God that he chooses to do it according to that perfect will.

We can have a certain fear or reluctance to letting go of our humanness. Acting like a "regular human" can feel like an escape valve for us when we don't feel like being a chela on the Path. However, escape is different from balance, and it's understandable to need balance. Sometimes Mark Prophet or Godfre would watch movies. Sometimes we need to read a book, go for a walk, share with friends or do something to keep that balance. But we cannot allow our humanness to define who we are. We need to let go of the thought that we are simply mortals.

We are not mortal unless we choose to be. We have a divine identity that the masters have come to remind us of, but they cannot do the work of becoming that identity for us. Our knowledge of the Law or the mysteries of God or even our friendship with the masters will not do it. We ourselves must take the responsibility for becoming the Christ.[58]

Last summer when we heard the replay of Saint Germain's landmark dictation "May You Pass Every Test," I was stuck by his parting words: *"When you want to be like God, you shall be!"*[59] What a loving admonishment: When you want to be like God, you shall be!

Well, we might say, "Of course, I want to be like God—that is why I have spent years, decades, or most of my adult life following the path of the masters." Yet, after all this time and effort, are we really where we want to be? Do we desire to be like God enough, or is part of us afraid of being like God? The saints endured much to be like God, yet they all seemed almost eager to go through it. "Whoa," you might say, "this is uncharted territory for me."

There comes a time on our path when love impels us higher, when nothing else matters as much to us. We're willing to pay whatever the price and to be inconvenienced, as Morya said. We reach the point where we want to surrender in greater and greater increments. And when we reach the point where we are absolutely determined to let go of the human and embrace our God, then—as Saint Germain tells us—we *will be like God*. It doesn't happen by storming heaven or by just announcing to God and the universe one morning, "I will walk the earth as you in manifestation." It happens by humbly submitting ourselves to the God within us and by finally surrendering those things that have kept us from our victory.

To help with the process, we might ask ourselves some questions. "What are some things in my life that could be holding me back? Are there some very practical and realistic things I can do to refocus or revitalize my chelaship, not just for my path, but also to help hold the balance in the earth? Have I underestimated my karma and what it takes to not only make my ascension, but also to hold enough light that the many might be saved?"

These things might be easier to see from heaven's perspective. And even though we've been given some understanding, I don't know that we will be able to fully appreciate what the messengers' journey was like and what they have done for us and this planet until we get to the other side.

Constancy—the First Lesson

Meanwhile, we can take some easy, practical steps to move forward on our journey. For instance, it's good to remember the quality taught in the first Keepers of the Flame lesson—constancy. It is one thing to remain constant for a few weeks or months or even a few years, but to sustain that virtue over a lifetime is crucial for success on the Path.

When I lived in the Ashram of the World Mother, I witnessed how important this quality is and what could happen when it was absent. Some students felt the standards at the Ashram were too demanding, and they felt like they had to leave. They always thought they had a good reason—they needed to take a break for a while, earn some money, go to school, or any number of reasons. The reasons were not all wrong, but they took people away from focusing on their path and from steady attendance at the altar. And after they left, many of these people never returned to the Path.

In the same 1988 dictation I mentioned earlier, El Morya reinforces just how crucial constancy is:

> *My love falls on the just and the unjust. I may not love you less for your indiscretions, for your absence from the fiery altar of change, but, blessed ones, and I speak to those throughout the field, when you leave off your devotions for periods, you are weakened, the distance grows between thyself and the Flame of the ark of the covenant, between thyself and my heart. It is imperceptible [to you]. The adjustment to lesser vibrations is easy [for you]. It is the broad way that leadeth to destruction. And that which is lost, not being capable of being perceived, is no longer missed....*
>
> *And so, beloved, by and by even the memory does grow dim in the mist, and as though looking through dense fog, one can no longer see the heights one has left. Blessed ones, we have observed this happen in a single seven-day period of a lifestream.*[60]

The God-quality of constancy. All of you wouldn't be here in the snowstorm today if you didn't have it. And for those who need to reconnect and get back on track, there is still time and space to get right with God and move forward on the Path.

Pay as You Go

Some decades ago Jesus asked us to take back our personal karma. It was our time to bear it, and by our assuming our own karmic burden, Jesus could then help others as he had helped us. That was a very tangible event. A definite shift took place when that happened.

El Morya's dictation also gave us a key to navigating this new territory:

> Blessed ones, I stand at a moment when I desire to give you all of my causal body for your victory, all of my experience and all of my counsel. The Karmic Board has sent me to tell you that for the blessings received from my heart in these thirty years, from this day forward if you desire intercession it must be upon the principle of "pay as you go."[61] For each day's intercession there must be abundant action on the calls to my flame, as you know, the [decree] number 10.03. This call, beloved, is the key to my causal body and to my Diamond Heart and to the more that we can give to you through the Messengers.
>
> Blessed ones, I shall return to you many, manyfold, as the Law will allow it, your offering of the calls to the will of God. And then, beloved, what is not used up in the given day may accrue as a reservoir, as a sphere of light, therefore, that you will have in reserve that portion [which is] so needed [—when you need it].[62]

Simply put, we need to build reserves of light. We know our karma is going to return, and it's the grace of God that is does. But we never know when it's going to be a little parcel, a big parcel, or a dump truck at our door. So by giving calls to the will of God, we build up a reservoir that allows El Morya to intercede for us when he could not do so otherwise.

He gave us something clear and tangible we can do to help our path. Of course we want Morya's intervention in our lives! Therefore it is enlightened self-interest to give the decree to the will of God daily. If you are not doing that, now is a good time to start. You can start with one or three or whatever you can do but it's good to do it every day to build a momentum. Then perhaps later you will find a way in your schedule to increase that number. Personally, I have found it helpful to use the CD "Decrees and Songs of the First Ray" that has eighteen 10.03 decrees given at a moderate pace that allows you to focus on the words.

The Power of Confession

There are many components to aligning with God's will and getting "right with God," including confession and repentance. In the same dictation, Morya shares:

> I say to you, beloved, if you are outside of the Law, whether human or divine, you must quickly confess your sins to the appropriate persons, make rectitude, correct such states and come into alignment. For the sin not confessed, the illegal posture not acknowledged, though none may know about it, does prevent the karma from descending and therefore [does prevent] the expiation of that karma—even if you give the violet flame decrees daily.
>
> The making right of all things with all persons in embodiment or elsewhere is most necessary...[63]

Isn't that enlightening? You can't receive the karma for your mistake or your out of alignment condition unless you confess it. The precision of the Law is a great comfort. While some may think, "Well, I don't want that karma," our soul actually *does* want the karma because how else will we get right with God? Morya said that even if we give the violet flame decrees daily, it will not work for us without confession. We can give the violet flame ad infinitum, but unless we have confessed and repented and worked to balance the karma, it cannot free us.

Morya continues:

> *Thus, if there be not the confession and then the repentance and then the willingness to balance the karma, there is not the tight coil of [our] oneness—a coil so tight between us that I desire to have with you, that there be no separation heart to heart, breath to breath, soul to soul, chakra to chakra. I desire your chakras to be one with my own and my chakras to be yours when you have need of them.*[64]

Are we willing to do the very best we can to have El Morya's chakras congruent with our chakras? His breath with our breath? We still have accountability for what we have confessed and a responsibility to make it right, but he is offering all that he is to help us get Home. What an amazing grace!

"Seventy Times Seven"

Forgiveness comes following confession and repentance, and forgiveness is a healing balm for our soul and the souls of all those whom we have wronged.

Last week I was out doing an errand when I noticed a car in front of me with a mystery message on its license plate. It was one of those vanity plates that have cryptic messages that you can't help trying to figure out. Well, this one had the number 70 and then an X and then a 7. Anybody guess what that is? Forgiveness, of course! Seventy times seven. Matthew 18:21-22 tells us: "*Then came Peter to him, and said, Lord, how oft shall my brother sin against me, and I forgive him? till seven times? Jesus saith unto him, I say not unto thee, Until seven times: but, Until seventy times seven.*"

Perhaps some of us consider our sins so great that they cannot be forgiven. El Morya has a comforting message regarding that:

> *Beloved, the law of forgiveness will serve you well. Think of the most heinous crime for which you sense guilt or do not. All can be forgiven if the heart be contrite and be willing to pay the price of penance in service to the Lord, in service to the Brotherhood, in service to the little ones of God.*[65]

Isn't that precious? For our own path and for the victory of earth, let us resolve that nothing—including our "sins"—will come between ourselves and dear Morya!

As we bring ourselves into greater alignment with the Path, are we better human beings? We may be, but that is not the point. What happens is that we become clearer windowpanes for God to do his work through us. God is the doer of all good things and the more we bring ourselves into alignment with his will and the Path, the more we can be of greater service to him and the fulfillment of his purposes.

I was speaking to someone recently who told me they like to use what they call the "three Hs" to govern their day-to-day lives: honor, humility, and holiness. Those are virtues that will help us grow closer to God, and I think we can all benefit by practicing them. And since we are each unique, what this person did is something we can all do in our own way. We can decide which virtues we would like to amplify in our lives in order to draw closer to God and to his perfect will for us.

The Bended Knee

Along with practicing virtues, we might ask ourselves, "How do I position myself in order to be more of God and less of the human?" Well, when we're standing upright and, as Morya says, *"strutting around trying to be good human beings,"*[66] isn't it harder to let God work through us and to know God is the doer?

We all have responsibilities, problems to solve, chores to complete. But even as we fulfill our obligations, how can we position ourselves so that God can work through us in a greater way? A simple way to begin is with our physical posture.

As I have shared before, one of the most profound changes in my path came when I began to pray on my knees daily. I found a beautiful teaching on a Catholic website about praying on our knees.

> When we pray on our knees, the body prostrates itself and the heart surrenders itself. This attitude of prayer ... expresses submission to God, obedience to his will, adoration, humility and penance. It reflects an attitude of faith, par excellence. How much the saints have been taught on their knees before the Blessed Sacrament!
>
> To pray on our knees is to communicate an attitude. As with any bodily gesture or posture, the act of kneeling before God says something. The body communicates a message.
>
> To place ourselves on our knees is to "speak" adoration and penance, which requires a certain humility.
>
> ...This attitude makes us more free, because it situates us in

the truth of our human finiteness.

We recognize that God is everything for us and that without his merciful love, we are, literally, nothing.

To be on our knees, near the floor, somehow nourishes this attitude of humility (humus) and of interior stillness, so essential for adoration.

Adoration, in Greek, calls for a posture of kneeling and prostrating oneself. To bend our knees before God is to recognize humbly that everything comes from him.[67]

As we kneel before God, we can start by praying, "God, deliver me from whatever in me is blocking my being a greater instrument of light for you." We can offer our personal confessions, our prayers for forgiveness, and our petitions for the needs of the day. We can pray for God's solutions to the many problems in our communities, in America and the world. Along those lines, we've been asked to pray on our knees (along with Saint Germain and Godfre) for the Mighty Blue Eagle from Sirius to come for the salvation of America.[68]

As I have shared before, it is so important to take time to kneel at the altar in the secret chamber of our heart where the blessed threefold flame resides, where our Holy Christ Self and Jesus tend the altar. We go there not to petition or ask for problems to be solved but to honor the light, to embrace the light, to vow to defend the light, and ultimately to unite with the light. As we give adoration and praise to our mighty I AM Presence, our Christ Self and threefold flame, we will *become* that light. And when we become that light, we will be human no more! Praise God!

Holy Christ Self, Work Through Me!

As we move farther along the Path, we have to adjust to the increased light, be able to hold the balance for that light, and deal with the opposition to that light. That is why God will increase it incrementally, one step at a time, so we can adjust, so we can grow, so we can come up higher to hold greater light in harmony. Daily progress is essential. It gives us co-measurement to remember that even Mother did not become a messenger overnight.

God will teach us how to make progress. Every day we can ask him, "God, teach me how to hold a greater increment of light in harmony and how to defend that light. Teach me to be a greater vessel for your light this day." And if we make a mistake, we confess it, we call upon the law of forgiveness, and we move on. We do make mistakes; that's the nature of living. But we will make fewer mistakes as our determination grows.

It is up to us to take the initiative if we want to move from our current baseline. The masters are watching us, and they will do anything the Great Law will allow to help us. But we need to use the tools, the techniques, and everything the masters have taught us to secure our victory. And while the decrees are key, it takes much more to put on our Christhood. So we must continually submit and surrender to God even as we pray, "Holy Christ Self, work through me."

Nevermore to be Separated

In closing, I would like to leave you with some precious words from our dear El Morya. He has said that in the Eastern tradition of the guru-chela relationship, a chela may go one or five lifetimes with *"scarcely a look of encouragement or praise"*[69] lest they let down their guard. Well, fortunately, Morya knows we in the West need it a little more often. And if you ever feel you need some comfort or encouragement right away, just pick up a *Pearl of Wisdom*. Virtually every *Pearl* reminds us of how much we are loved by God.

Morya is considered a stern master by some, yet he is completely devoted to his true chelas and their victory. He knows our burdens and reassures us:

> *Therefore do not feel downhearted or condemned by what has been your lot, for you were "chelas mine"*[70] *from the beginning and you shall be, by God's grace if you will it so, chelas mine unto the end....*
>
> *Laugh with me, beloved, for you are here and I am here and none shall stand between us forever. I pledge it to you from my heart, beloved, that all that I am and all that I am to be and all that I can give I shall give to you determinedly as the Great Law will allow it. O beloved, so also invoke Kuan Yin and Mercy's flame that there might be even that bridge between us [of scientific mantra] when I have no more dispensation....*
>
> *I desire nevermore to be separated from thee, O my beloved....*
>
> *Now, beloved, I commend you to the high road and the rugged road of Victory. The future is golden. It is white light before you. If you have the nerve and the stomach, the will and the astuteness and the contact with Hierarchy and the thread is not broken, you will be there on a golden shore when the Light is all-effusive.*[71]

"I desire nevermore to be separated from thee, O my beloved." Doesn't such love demand that we honor it, that we honor the preciousness of Morya's heart, knowing that the sternness and the rebukes that we have received are because he loves us so dearly? His way is not easy because he knows what it is going to take for us to have our victory. We have done many good things on this path. We have made tremendous progress. But we're not Home yet, and as Morya said, some have failed in as little as seven days.

How are we going to gain our ascension and get out of this revolving door of incarnation on earth? Who wants to live again and again and not be getting anywhere? We now have the time, the space, the opportunity and (thanks to Maximus) the perspective to see who we are and what we need to become.

Why would we ever want the human when we can have God? Why would we ever want the paltry playthings of this earth when we can have God? And as you'll hear in the dictation we're listening to today, Maximus gives a perspective of not just the planet, but also beyond: *"Eye hath not seen, nor ear heard, neither have entered into the heart of man, the things which God hath prepared for them that love him."*[72]

The universe awaits us!

Before we return to our place in time and space, let us pause at the top of the ladder we climbed for a new perspective on our lives and the world. Let us vow in deepest love before our God that—whatever the price, whatever the karmic pain, whatever the "inconvenience" (as Morya would say)—by his grace, we will fulfill our cosmic destiny.

Let us remember this vision from the heights. Let us remember our bond of love with El Morya. Let us remember who we are and who we will be.

Just when will we put aside the human? When we *want* to put aside the human! It's as simple as that. It's not going to happen before then. It is the law of God.

As we return to our inch in the universe, let us also remember, the choice to put the human aside and become Godlike is ours—and ours alone.

TRUST AND THE CHELA

The basis of the guru-chela relationship is trust. You trust El Morya and he trusts you—that's the name of the game.

—MOTHER

※

Trust is not merely a word; it is a way of life.

—MOTHER

THREE

Trust and the Chela

The face of the guru is often inscrutable. The Merriam Webster dictionary defines inscrutable as "not readily investigated, interpreted, or understood: mysterious."[73] Do you remember the first time you saw a picture of our beloved El Morya? Did it seem inscrutable, as if you weren't quite sure what to make of the guru's countenance and expression? Perhaps Morya's visage seemed mysterious because you didn't fully understand his consciousness or you wondered what he might think of you.

Those who have the privilege of receiving chastening fire directly from their guru can sometimes tell what the guru is thinking at the time. But for the most part a chela doesn't really know exactly where he stands on the Path save what he or she can glean from experience or by sincerely reflecting upon their personal striving and questioning their progress: "Is my habit pattern that was acceptable yesterday still acceptable today? Did I pass that test? Is the guru happy with me?"

The chela learns to treasure the words of the guru, whether blessing or chastisement, realizing that both will lead him to his victory. In *Autobiography of a Yogi* Paramahansa Yogananda tells us that his guru told him that he loved him when he first embarked on that path. It was *decades* before his guru told him that again, yet during the intervening years, Yogananda never wavered in following the guidance of his guru. A true chela!

On the Path, becoming a Chela with a capital "C" is the highest honor anyone can receive. Did you know that Saint Germain does not initially accept everyone who asks to be his chela? He first sends the would-be chelas to El Morya for training. Then once a year Saint Germain (and I suspect other masters as well) are invited to Darjeeling for a special ceremony that I know each one of us would be thrilled to be included in.

Saint Germain explains:

> Beloved ones, I do not accept all. I send them first to the Royal Teton Retreat and then to the Chief of the Darjeeling Council of the Great White Brotherhood, beloved El Morya. And when they become chelas of whom Morya can be proud, whom Morya can trust, the Chohan of the First Ray will say, "Saint Germain, may I present to you my chela who is my trusted friend." I tell you, it is a moment in Darjeeling when I am invited to that occasion each year, when a few chelas can be presented to me and I may say, "Come now. Come to the Cave of Symbols."[74]

Imagine the scene! After all our striving, all our pain, all our tests and initiations, El Morya pronounces us to be his chela and his trusted friend. Don't you get the chills when you think about finally being accepted by the master we have been seeking as our guru? It is a moment we will cherish forever.

Having the Chohan of the First Ray trust you is like a spiritual rite of passage. Being Morya's "trusted friend" is a credential that opens many doors in heaven. Mother teaches, *"The basis of the guru-chela relationship is trust. You trust El Morya and he trusts you—that's the name of the game.*[75]

When I was searching the *Pearls of Wisdom* online, this concept of trust showed up time and time again. In the dictation we will hear today, Prince Oromasis and Diana teach us that trust is a two-way street between the masters and their chelas.

What does having two-way trust look like? As we review the dictionary definition of trust, let's consider it in that context.

1. "reliance on the integrity, strength, ability, surety, etc., of a person or thing; confidence." We rely on the masters, and they rely on us.

2. "confident expectation of something; hope." Isn't trust tied to hope? If we had no hope, how could we have trust?

3. "a person on whom or thing on which one relies." Interestingly, *"God is my trust"* is the exact example the dictionary gives for this definition!

4. "the obligation or responsibility imposed on a person in whom confidence or authority is placed: *a position of trust."* And that, of course, applies to the responsibility of leadership of this organization or any other—it's a position of trust.

5. And the final definition we will consider, "charge, custody, or care: to leave valuables in someone's trust."[76] Well, we know what the valuables are, don't we—the teachings, the land, the light? And since our messengers have gone on, God has now entrusted them to us.

Job and Abraham

We can certainly see that trust is a virtue, but what exactly does it look like on the Path? The Bible contains so many references to trust that we could spend hours reviewing them, but here are just a couple to contemplate.

Take the story of Job. As hard as our path may sometimes seem, I think we would agree that Job had it even harder. Yet after all he had been through, he made the definitive statement recorded in Job 13:15, *"Though he slay me, yet will I trust in him."*

I think we can assume that Job was at the end of his rope and did not know what else he could humanly do. He was ready to die. But he didn't say, "I give up." He didn't complain, "God, this is unfair." He affirmed, "I will continue to trust him." What a powerful testimony!

When things are looking very bleak in our lives (and every one of us sometimes faces problems that seem to have no solution), let us strive to be like Job and affirm our trust in God—come what may.

And what of Abraham? God called upon him to sacrifice his beloved son Isaac. It's hard to even imagine that, isn't it? Nonetheless, Abraham was obedient and traveled a long distance to fulfill God's request. We might wonder what he could have been thinking along the way. I suspect he would have preferred sacrificing himself. But he trusted God, even telling Isaac that God would provide the sacrifice.

In Genesis 22:12, an angel spoke to Abraham: *"And he said, Lay not thine hand upon the lad, neither do anything unto him: for now I know that thou fearest God, seeing thou hast not withheld thy son, thine only son from me."* The New Century translation of the Bible replaces the word fearest with trust. In other words, Abraham so trusted God that he was obedient even when he was asked to do the unthinkable.

Bricks of Trust

These two examples reflect the ultimate test of life and death. But what about the daily challenges we face, the uncertainty of our karma and the world in turmoil? Where does trust come from within us, especially if our trust in others has been violated? What can we expect when we trust the guru? And how do we develop trust?

Well, when I was doing my research, I learned that faith and trust are basic building blocks of the Path. Apollo and Lumina teach us:

This path...begins with faith in yourself and trust in your Guru.

I would speak to you, then, of the requirement for faith in yourself and your ability to be a chela on the Path. For this you need a goodly portion of self-confidence, which must needs be built first and foremost on spiritual foundations— self-knowledge that you have come from God, that you will return to God and that because your soul is deeply rooted in Reality you can weather any storm, from the worst to the best of your karma, from the crucifixion to the descent into Death and Hell and back again. This is the track of your inner life. It is a path of soul initiation that you walk by faith.

...The faith you accumulate by your own consistent faithfulness becomes bricks of trust cemented in the deep foundations of being. Because you are faithful to yourself, made in the image of God, you have solid, unswerving trust in El Morya, faith in your I AM Presence and Holy Christ Self, and faith in God.[77]

What striking imagery: "bricks of trust cemented in the deep foundation of being." Don't you feel like you could weather any storm if the foundation of your entire being were the bricks of faith and trust that you had laid? That firm foundation is not only what allows us to meet the challenges of daily living but also to pass the ultimate tests of life and death.

Trust is the Code of Hierarchy

When I first learned about the path of the ascended masters, I didn't have trouble trusting Jesus, but I didn't know the other masters as well—especially those like Shiva and Kali who had more than two arms! The guru-chela relationship itself can also seem foreign and somewhat challenging for those of us raised in the West. I confess that when I first heard that the origins of the word chela related to being a slave, I wasn't quite ready to jump in!

As beginners on the path of the ascended masters, we don't fully understand the requirements and nuances of the Path, and many masters are totally unknown to us. Therefore, we don't necessarily have an immediate trust of either the path that lies ahead of us or of all the masters.

To help us, Lanello succinctly explains just how important trust is: "*Trust is the code of hierarchy and of unascended chelas.*"[78] He further elucidates:

> *Therefore I say, invoke the flame of trust, which is the beginning and the end of the cross of Alpha. The trust of God is the necessary crucifixion of the lesser self that nobility and honor might rule the Divine Us....*
>
> *Let trust be the motto of those who trust in God and those in whom God may place his trust. Let trust be, then, the point of mediation between our octave and yours. For where there is trust, you see, there the handshake will be when you place*

*your hand in my own and in the hand of Christ and in the hand
of Saint Germain and El Morya and in the hand of the Elohim.
And the shaking of the hand will provide the crisscrossing of
the pattern of the figure eight so that the hand of man clasp-
ing the hand of God will show the nexus where that energy is
received.*

*That handshake is the symbol of the covenant betwixt God
and man, which is fulfilled in you this day.*[79]

Don't you love the visualization of shaking the hand of
El Morya or Saint Germain? It is a reminder of the covenant
God offered to the Israelites in ancient times. What a comfort.

We have been taught that the universe functions smoothly
because every master, elemental and cosmic being does their
part to ensure that all goes according to the laws of God. They
all trust each other to do their respective jobs, and if just one
were to violate that trust, all would fail.

Can you imagine if, God forbid, Cuzco were to stop his constant monitoring of the earth and making the adjustments
needed to keep it intact? We would not have the platform we
need to balance our karma and win our victory. But he is faithful, and that demonstrates why trust is the code of hierarchy.

We want to do our part too. But what if we struggle with
having trust in God and the guru? It can happen to any of us.
Sometimes we may not trust God and maybe we're not even
sure why. Archangel Chamuel and the Covering Cherubim
offer the following explanation for a lack of trust in God.

*So, beloved, know, then, that all absence of trust at var-
ious levels of your being can be traced back to the moment
not when God forsook his trust in you but when you forsook
your trust in your Father-Mother God. Then fear and doubt*

crept in. And inasmuch as you could not trust yourself to fasten yourself to God come what may, you inverted this psychology, if you would call it that, and began to mistrust your Father-Mother God.

Well, you see, beloved, there is [in reality] no mistrust in God, there is only mistrust in oneself.[80]

It always seems to come back to us, doesn't it? Our mistrust of God actually comes from our forsaking our trust in God, leading to fear and doubt and mistrust of ourselves.

Just consider the impact that leaving the Mystery School and the guru's presence had on our psyche. Perhaps initially we pretended it wasn't a big deal and we were going to do all these great things. Then over time what we had really done eventually began to sink in: We had forsaken the Path. We had walked away from the guru and the sponsorship of the Great White Brotherhood. And I suspect for many of us it was a very long time before we finally chose to return to the Path and do whatever it took to get back Home.

Lanello adds to our understanding of why we have trouble trusting God and the ascended masters. He says:

Let, then, those who cannot trust their God or the ascended masters look to see whether or not God or the ascended masters can trust them. If you have been untrustworthy toward your God, then why do you wonder that you have not the trust in your being directed toward the God of love?[81]

So if we don't trust God, it can, indeed, be that we have not been trustworthy ourselves. But instead of condemning ourselves, we should consider ways we can regain trust.

One way to restore trust in ourselves is to forgive ourselves for leaving the Mystery School or for whatever we may have done—known or unknown. When we forgive ourselves and accept God's forgiveness, then we can reach a new level of soul integration and integrity that leads to trusting God.

We should also be cautious not to overpromise or underdeliver to God, which many of us have probably done at one time or another. As we fulfill our obligations and promises to God and the guru, they can then place their trust in us.

Some years ago I was in a community meeting discussing an important topic for the organization. Mother knew that we were meeting and had a secretary phone and give us instructions to do a rather long series of decrees. We were very surprised, but we immediately began to do them. One of the leaders of the meeting got up and left. I thought how unfortunate it was that he didn't seem to understand how important obedience and trust in the guru were.

Being faithful in big and small things alike will help us develop trust in ourselves as chelas as well as trust in God.

Trust Is a Way of Life

As with any God-quality, we need the *seed* of trust within us in order for it to grow and expand. It's the same with faith or hope or any virtue—the seed has to be there first before the virtue can expand.

Lanello also states that trust is a flame. We think of the violet flame, the cosmic honor flame and other flames, but I never thought of trust that way before. So trust is a flame, and we can fan that flame. We can visualize that flame expanding in our auras, just as we can envision a seed growing. We can use mantras such as "In the immaculate heart of Mary, I trust" and "In the sacred heart of Jesus, I trust." Those are affirmations that not only link us to their hearts but also fan the flame of trust.

Mother has good advice for those who want a *"greater trust if they slip into moments of doubt and lose faith,"*[82] which I think includes us all. She says:

> *"Trust in the LORD with all thine heart and lean not unto thine own understanding."*[83] *As soon as you try to understand, it's as if the trust crumbles. It's the same with faith. We don't see faith, but we have faith. So you have the Lord, your Holy Christ Self, and you have your I AM Presence. Trust in the Lord with all your heart and never try to resolve a situation otherwise.*
>
> *Lean not unto thine own understanding. As long as we're in duality, our own understanding is always incomplete. So we can't listen to that. We always go back to God. You see, trust always takes us back to God. And then we trust him to know if there are evildoers or fallen ones or calamities about to happen, and so forth. It's that trust.*
>
> *So, trust: it all comes down to this. Do you trust the guru? If you don't, you might as well not be here. Trust is not merely a word; it is a way of life.*[84]

We need to affirm that way of life!

We've been told to call for trust and pray for it if we don't have it. And after watching or reading the news these days it's easy to feel overwhelmed and not know what we can do. So we turn in trust to God and the masters. We know to make our calls, and we pray, "Lord, give me trust in thee and thy divine purposes." As we do our part, we *know* that God will do his.

"Lean not unto thine own understanding" is important advice to keep in mind as we walk the Path. I remember one of the masters saying that our karma is so complex that we cannot begin to fully understand it. Although we may sometimes know where our karma is coming from, most of the time we do not. There may be things in this embodiment that cause it, but it often goes back much, much farther.

Trust is a Prerequisite for Mercy

What about mercy? Is there a single one of us who has not cried out to God for mercy—for ourselves, our family, our nation and the planet? I often speak quietly under my breath, "May God have mercy." What I didn't realize before I read the teaching was that *trust is a prerequisite for mercy*! I had always equated mercy with grace, something unearned, but that's not always the case.

Mother Mary explains:

As a Cosmic Mother, it becomes my natural concern to in-spire all the dear souls on earth, reminding them also of the precious gifts which the Father has prepared and holds in store for all who trust him enough to believe in and invoke his mercy!

At first the idea of trust as a prerequisite to receive the grace of mercy may seem a little farfetched to some, yet I guarantee to all that the greater trust one has, the more easily the mercy of God is obtained and can act in one's world. ...on earth today it is sorely needed wherever the karma is gross and wherever the sense of trust is either slight or wavering. The fact is that wavering feelings (or lack of trust) act so as to prevent the full aspect of God's mercy from springing into action to assist the one requiring it!

... We therefore lovingly advocate that all our chelas obtain now and daily "by request" (by asking their own God Presence

for it) a very real sense of divine trust. In times of personal and world peril such as presently face all mankind—poised as they are on the brink of world evolution (of the spirit), or world revolution of the so-called godless forces of materialism—this quality of mercy is needed more than ever!...

Childlike trust is never wrong! No degree of sophistication can ever replace the spiritual values of life or the great power of trust to release mercy's balm to individuals or the world.[85]

Aha, childlike trust! Perhaps we spend too much time in our mental bodies. God obviously expects us to do what we can do to resolve our challenges and problems, and that requires some thinking and planning. But we're not going to find the solution to everything in our mental body. Many problems may seem unsolvable, but childlike trust in God can lead to the mercy of God that will resolve even the knottiest problem.

Trust No Man

And what of those who have put their trust in others or in institutions and had that trust violated? Hercules and Amazonia remind us of what Lanello taught regarding that:

Yes, beloved, remember, then, the charge Mark Prophet gave to you: "Trust no man." Now, adhering to this could make life very sad if you did not know the teaching behind the axiom. You see, it is wise not to trust the human consciousness that wavers from hour to hour, but to trust the Christ in each one. And so you speak to the Christ in each one. You speak to that Oversoul, you speak to that guardian angel, and you go to the very heart of that which is real in all whom you meet. And you support the soul who has not quite made it to the altar to be made the wife of her Spouse.

Yes, beloved, you can be everyone's friend and you can maintain a relationship of trust as long as it is God whom you trust in the individual.[86]

In our life, there are times when we are so divided with others on an issue that it's hard to even talk about it. There is a teaching that in such instances we can write a letter to the Holy Christ Self of the soul(s) involved and then burn it. That bypasses the human consciousness to help resolve the most difficult issues. We don't know what pain the soul(s) of the other person(s) may be in, and this is a way to bring resolution by bypassing their outer mind. I have found that this usually results in things taking care of themselves or in being able to have a harmonious discussion with the people involved that brings resolution.

Now, resolving issues of the loss of trust in others requires effort on our part—including forgiveness. As always, the masters have encouraged us to earnestly work on our psychology for issues that are repetitive and may require the aid of a trained therapist. Mother outlined an additional approach to help resolve these issues that clearly incorporates the path of the Ruby Ray.

When you trust the path of the Lord Sanat Kumara and the mighty lineage that sponsors us, you rejoice in the chastening fire. If you cannot trust that path and that lineage, then work with the ruby ray and bind your dweller. Bind that dweller daily or hourly. Trounce your dweller.

Implore the intercession of God until you have purged yourself of the cause, effect, record and memory of times in this life and many lifetimes where people have failed you.

Humans will fail you, but God will never fail you. So get past that point of pride that says "I cannot trust, I cannot trust" just because someone once deceived you. Trust leads to the chela's surrender to the chastening fire.[87]

It's not our soul that strongly resists the chastening fire. It's our dweller! Don't you love the intensity of Mother's teaching? She doesn't just say, *"Bind your dweller."* She says, *"Trounce your dweller."* Makes me wonder what progress we could make if we gave dweller calls hourly? Maybe we should try it!

Karma and Duty

As I was preparing this sermon, I could not help but think of times in my life when I would have truly benefited by a greater trust in God and the Path. I'm not condemning myself for those times, but I realize I could have passed some of my tests much more quickly, probably not failed as many, and experienced less pain along the way.

What are some circumstances when our trust is tested the most? Well, karma is an obvious one, but so is initiation, when nothing may seem to make sense and the unexpected lands on our doorstep. To help us pass these tests, Serapis Bey admonishes us:

...I kid you not! It does take all of your striving and your love and your trust. It is a trust that says, "I know my God will do the very best for me if I have the courage to face my karma and do my duty."[88]

We certainly need courage to face our karma. When we embark on the path of our ascension, on the path of chelaship seeking to become a Chela with a capital "C", a couple things happen. First, the masters pay attention—at long last, we are taking a stand for the Path and for our ascension. We're told that the second thing that happens is our karma accelerates. Did we all sign up for that? Yes, we did, because that is how we are going to make it!

Maybe we think that because we trust God and the masters, we will be spared some karma or somehow have our psychology magically resolved. That expectation can lead to a lot of distress, discouragement, and even anger at the masters.

In his Easter 1993 dictation Jesus makes it very clear who is responsible for our situation in life:

> *We remind you once again that we are not your human parents. We are not your human siblings. We are not the cause of your fractured and fragmented psychology. You are the cause of it yourself! And the longer you hang on to it, the longer it will stick to you like taffy, and as you lick your fingers and eat some more, it will stick some more.*
>
> *Yes, beloved ones, it is time to say, "I trust God," and to reinforce that trust daily no matter what you see coming your way that would lead you to believe to the contrary.*[89]

So on the path of trust with the ascended masters, we trust that God and the masters will know exactly what we need at exactly the right time to balance our karma and to pass our tests. If we try to plan it out for ourselves, we might wander aimlessly in the world, going from karmic bounce to karmic bounce. But when we affix ourselves to the star of the ascended masters and the path of our ascension, we are serious about our commitment and our daily disciplines and our observance of the Word.

There can also be times when we make calls for something again and again and yet it doesn't happen. In such cases, we must trust that God wants us to face a particular situation or adversity in order to pass a test or even to gain some humility.

Trusting God and the masters to bring us exactly what we need at exactly the right time does not necessarily mean it will be what we want. Our human desire may be for something entirely different, or we may not want to face a particular test, saying, "Oh, Lord, let this test pass from me if it be thy will." Well, it wasn't God's will for Jesus to forgo the test on the cross, was it? So we can pray, "If it be your will, O God, take this from me," but if he doesn't take it, we must trust in him and know that it is his will for us to go through it.

Trust is not a "get out of jail free" card. Trust is the equation that allows us to know that the master, the guru, God is in charge, and that if we do our part nothing will come our way that is not the will of God.

Lessons of the Apostle Paul

For my last birthday, I received a biography of the Apostle Paul by an English theologian, N.T. Wright. It's simply titled *Paul, A Biography*. Wright helped me understand the context of Paul's life in a new way because I did not previously know what was going on with the Corinthians when Paul wrote his letters to them.

We know Paul initially persecuted the Christians because he was such a dedicated Pharisee and a zealot. We also know he stood by and watched as Stephen was stoned to death. Yet on the road to Damascus Jesus appeared to him, converted him and suddenly Paul was an apostle!

Was that the beginning of good times for him? I can assure you it wasn't! In fact, I didn't even know how bad things got for him after that. In 2nd Corinthians Chapter 11, verses 23-28, Paul tells us:

> *I have worked much harder, been in prison more frequent-*
> *ly, been flogged more severely, and been exposed to death*
> *again and again. Five times I received from the Jews the forty*
> *lashes minus one. Three times I was beaten with rods, once I*
> *was pelted with stones, three times I was shipwrecked, I spent*
> *a night and a day in the open sea, I have been constantly on the*
> *move. I have been in danger from rivers, in danger from ban-*
> *dits, in danger from my fellow Jews, in danger from Gentiles;*
> *in danger in the city, in danger in the country, in danger at sea;*
> *and in danger from false believers. I have labored and toiled*
> *and have often gone without sleep; I have known hunger and*
> *thirst and have often gone without food; I have been cold and*
> *naked. Besides everything else, I face daily the pressure of my*
> *concern for all the churches.*[90]

Despite all this Paul trusted God. He definitely had his diffi-cult periods, but he never gave up, never lost trust.

As we know, fear and doubt are the enemies of trust. Lord Maitreya teaches:

> *Therefore it is true and learn the lesson well: the individual*
> *must have enough balance within himself, within his psyche*
> *to hold friendship with the Guru, not to fear the Guru! And*
> *therefore, fear having been cast out, doubt will also disap-*
> *pear. But out of doubt, beloved, [which is] the [willful] with-*
> *holding of trust [in the Guru], there does come hatred of the*
> *Guru. You may have covered it over many times and sugar-*
> *coated it again, but yet it remains [in both the subconscious*
> *and the unconscious].*[91]

It's quite sobering to know that we have hatred of the guru within us. It may be there from fifty thousand years ago or a hundred thousand years ago when we were angry at the guru. It may even be from something in this life. "Guru, why did you do this to me?" "Why did you take my loved one?" Whatever its origin might have been—though we've hopefully moved beyond that point in our lives and our evolution—that hatred may still be somewhere in our consciousness.

It's embarrassing to consider, isn't it? That hiding in our subconscious or unconscious may be resentment or anger against the guru or any aspect of God, perhaps anti-Father, anti-Mother, anti-Son, anti-Holy Spirit energies. As devotees of our Father-Mother God, the fact that there could be hatred of God or the guru lurking in our being is quite distressing! However, as mature chelas, we must be willing to look at this part of ourselves. We do not deny our accountability, but we realize it is no part of who we want to be. Whatever the hatred—of ourselves or God or the Path or anything else—we know it is not who we truly are, and it has got to go!

The good news is that we were given a simple call to add to our dweller-on-the-threshold calls that can help free us from this substance. "I cast out the dweller-on-the-threshold of: The anti-guru, anti-chela, anti-Holy Spirit, and all hatred and anger towards the guru."

We are ready for this test because we love the guru and do not want to be a burden on them. And so it's another case of taking the necessary action and not being afraid to make this call. We want that negativity removed from our consciousness as quickly as possible. That's why we do our dweller calls every day and trust the Lord will take that substance drop by drop, whether it is ours or was implanted in us by the fallen ones during a vulnerable moment. Let's have the courage to make the calls and clear this negativity!

We know that trust is the cornerstone of the guru-chela relationship and because we want to be chelas with a capital "C", we want to trust. We walk this path because we love God, we understand that our karma must return to us and that we must pass the tests and initiations that come to us.

Pain Along the Way

There is pain on the path of our karma and testing—something to be endured, something to be mastered. But pain is also the key to getting to bliss because the pain itself can liberate us from past momentums and resistance to trust.

We also know that trust is a prerequisite for mercy. We know that trust is a two-way street. It is a question of honor. The masters trust us to fulfill those things which they have asked us to do. It's good to consider what we are holding back from the guru, what part of ourselves we are not surrendering. We want to be able to say to God, like Job did, "Do whatever you want to me, but I will not lose my trust in you."

When we embark on this path, we know that God will bring us tests and initiations, perhaps not as physical as Paul's, but demanding, nonetheless. We continually affirm our trust in God, and we work to cast out doubt and fear.

Our desire and goal is to balance our karma and make our ascension. We don't let go of that vision, but we know that between here and there we can expect more than a few bumps in the road. There will be dryness. There will be loneliness. There will be pain. Why? Because we need it. We need to learn specific lessons. We need to gain mastery. And we need to demonstrate that we love God more than human comforts, more than an easy life, more than doing those things that we see others do. We need to reach the point where we say, "God, I want you more than anything. I am willing to pay the price, and I trust in you and your mercy." That becomes our stance and our identity. We know that the fire of trust—and it is a fire—will consume any doubt and fear and will lead us through the greatest trials.

Not everything in our lives will end up the way we want it to be. Paul had a thorn in his flesh and Jesus did not heal it; instead he said, *"My grace is sufficient for thee."*[92] Everything will not be perfect in our lives. Some things will not be fixed; some pains may not be healed. But we know that God is in charge, and because we know that, we can trust.

Trust is freedom. We do our part. We live the life of a chela. We do everything we know to do, and we trust in the outcome.

In the Immaculate Heart of Mary, I Trust

In the dictation we're hearing today, Oromasis and Diana give us another way to increase trust. They counsel us that when doubt and fear creep in we can challenge them by immediately reciting, *"In the Immaculate Heart of Mary, I trust."*[93] What a powerful mantra that is! This is what Mother Mary says about it:

I have come to give you peace. So you may say, "In the Immaculate Heart of Mary, I trust." And this, too, may be your mantra—In the Immaculate Heart of Mary, I trust. It is the Ma-ray that I AM incarnate. That ray does not begin or end with the "I" who does speak. It is a giant loop through the Central Sun and back again. Thus, In the Immaculate Heart of Mary, I trust—this does give you, therefore, oneness with me always. Through my Immaculate Heart you may say, "In the

Sacred Heart of Jesus, I trust." Doors beyond doors leading to the Holy of Holies—thus understand hierarchy as a chain of the cosmic rosary.[94]

Just imagine! Our words spoken into the air become part of a giant loop that goes through the Great Central Sun and comes back again. And in the process, our doubts and fears are replaced by trust.

Mistakes and Victories

Ah, what about mistakes? Well, as we all know, making mistakes is part of being human, yet we cannot allow them to dissuade us from the Path. Oromasis and Diana tell us that all is not lost when we make a mistake—it can be remedied.

We are in good company when we err as even the ascended masters make mistakes. Did you ever think about that? Saint Germain says:

Have you considered that ascended masters make mistakes?...

How do you think we feel when we release the science of nuclear fission to mankind and then they take that knowledge to destroy one another?...

How do you think we feel when through our hands knowledge is given because we trust mankind and the life flame in the heart to use that knowledge for life and the preservation of life, [and then that knowledge is misused]? [95]

Saint Germain tells us what the masters do when they make a mistake:

We go before the LORD God. We call upon the law of for-
giveness and we say, "Father, I have erred. I have placed thy
sacred trust in one unworthy."[96]

We all make mistakes; we do our very best to correct them.
We call upon the law of forgiveness and we keep on going. We
know that when we strive, good things happen. We also know
that when we're slack unfortunate things can happen.

As we learn to trust God and the masters and have proven
"without a shadow of doubt" that we are trustworthy, there is
a precious mantle waiting for us. Mother shares this vision:

Remember the phrase in the Book of Revelation "king and
priests unto God."[97] *The mantle and the office of that king-*
ship and that priesthood unto God are the bestowal that God
would make upon all Lightbearers of the world. Such are the
crowns and scepters that are there to be bestowed. It is as
though your mantle and your royal or priestly robes (or both)
were hanging on a hanger in a retreat, waiting to drop upon
you when you fulfill your reason for being.

So know, O my beloved children, that it is the Divine Mother
who will carefully take your robes from the hanger and put
them on your shoulders when you will have proven without a
shadow of a doubt that you are a trusted servant of the
Light—trustworthy to the end.[98]

Can we even comprehend what God has in store for those
who love him and trust him? Whatever the pain, whatever the
sacrifice, whatever the challenges—learning to trust God and
our guru will lead us to our mantle of kingship in God.

Do you think of yourself in that sense, as having kingship
in God? Well, we should expand our horizons to include that

vision because it is God's divine plan for us.

Our stay on planet earth has perhaps been much longer than we intended, but by God's grace our victory is nigh. Let us trust him to take us all the way to the finish line and our ascension.

Our robes await us!

THE LARGESSE
OF YOUR HEART

Not long before his death, Saladin advised his son: "If I have become great it is because I have won men's hearts by kindness and gentleness."

—MOTHER
quoting from Saladin: Prince of Chivalry

The Largesse of Your Heart

Kahlil Gibran wrote, "*Beauty is not in the face; Beauty is a light in the heart.*"[99] The beauty of the light in the heart of the ascended masters is often described by an outstanding quality they developed over lifetimes. We even refer to them by this quality of their heart: the sacred heart of Jesus; the immaculate heart of Mary; El Morya's diamond heart; Saint Germain's purple, fiery heart; Kuan Yin's merciful heart; and Lanello's magnanimous heart.

Pondering the qualities of their hearts should give us a clue as to just how crucial developing our own heart is to our soul's path and her victory in the ascension. It should also encourage us to consider what heart quality (or qualities) we would like to embody on our journey Home.

Lanello is a wonderful example for us to emulate, especially since he was so recently embodied. He experienced many of the trials of modern life, overcame all obstacles and ascended from our midst. A brief review of some of his lifetimes will show us how he became known for his magnanimous heart. The following is a series of short excerpts from a lecture entitled "The Magnanimous Lives of Mark L. Prophet," given by Mrs. Prophet at the dedication of St. Mark's Church in Livingston, Montana.[100]

> *Looking at Mark Prophet's past lives, we see that they span the many cultures and religions of the world. Think about it. He was Noah, Lot, Ikhnaton, Aesop, the disciple Mark, Origen, Lancelot, Bodhidharma, Clovis, Saladin, Bonaventure, Louis XIV, Longfellow and the Russian czarevitch Alexis Nikolayevich.*
>
> *His soul was at home in the East and in the West, in the Christian and the non-Christian world. His soul knew no boundaries of race or creed or culture. His soul knew only the transcendent language of love and magnanimity.*
>
> *... Let's consider the definition of the word "magnanimous."*
>
> *"Magnanimous" means literally "great spirit" or "great soul." It is taken from the noun "magnanimity." Magnanimity is loftiness of spirit that enables one to bear trouble calmly; to disdain meanness, pettiness, resentment, jealousy and revenge; to generously disregard injuries; to make sacrifices for worthy ends. It is noble generosity.*
>
> *Thus the definition of "magnanimous" is: showing or suggesting a lofty and courageous spirit; nobly brave or valiant; proceeding from or manifesting high courage; showing or suggesting generosity of mind and nobility of feeling and conduct; nobly ambitious; lofty of purpose; high-souled; forgiving.*

The Magnanimity of Ikhnaton
(Pharaoh of Egypt circa 1300 B.C.)

> *James Breasted, the eminent Egyptologist, says: "There died with Ikhnaton such a spirit as the world had never seen before.*

He was a brave soul, undauntedly facing the momentum of immemorial tradition that he might disseminate ideas far beyond and above the capacity of his age to understand. In an age so remote and under conditions so adverse, he became the world's first idealist and the world's first individual, the most remarkable of all pharaohs, the first prophet of history."[101]

Beloved members of the community, take Ikhnaton as your role model of love and magnanimity.

The Magnanimity of Origen
(Third-century Greek theologian)

Origen's student describes how his master's love of the Word sparked a bond of love between himself and all his students. "Like some spark lighting upon our inmost soul, love was kindled and burst into flame within us—a love at once of the Holy Word and of this man, God's friend and advocate."[102]

Beloved members of the community, take Origen of Alexandria as your role model of love and magnanimity.

The Magnanimity of Saladin
(Twelfth-century Muslim leader who conquered and unified the Muslim world)

[Historian Will] Durant says: "Usually Saladin was gentle to the weak, merciful to the vanquished and so superior to his enemies in faithfulness to his word that Christian chroniclers wondered how so wrong a theology could produce so fine a man."[103]

[Another historian, Charles] Rosebault writes, as an interesting testimony to Saladin's generosity, that "this conqueror of vast wealth died so poor that there was not enough left to pay for his funeral. He had given away whole provinces, yet, wrote his secretary, 'he left neither goods, nor houses nor real estate; neither garden, nor village nor cultivated land nor any species of property.' In his treasury there remained only one Tyrian gold piece and forty-seven pieces of silver."[104]

Not long before his death, Saladin advised his son: "If I have become great it is because I have won men's hearts by kindness and gentleness."[105]

Beloved members of the community, take Saladin as your role model of love and magnanimity.

The Magnanimity of Bonaventure (Thirteenth-century Seraphic Doctor of the Church, known as the "prince of mystics")

Bonaventure taught that true magnanimity comes in the execution of small, daily duties. In The Lives of the Fathers, Martyrs and Other Principle Saints, Reverend Alban Butler writes: "Saint Bonaventure places not the perfection of Christian virtue so much in the more heroic exercises of a religious state as in the performing well our ordinary actions." Bonaventure says: "The best perfection of a religious man is to do common things in a perfect manner." A constant fidelity in small things is a "great and heroic virtue."[106]

Beloved members of the community, take Bonaventure as your role model of love and magnanimity.

The Magnanimity of Longfellow (Nineteenth-century American poet)

Perhaps the most remarkable traits in Longfellow's character were his accessibility and his charity. Though a great worker, he seemed always to have time for anything he was asked to do. He was never too busy to see a caller, to answer a letter, or to assist by word or deed anyone that needed assistance.

[When someone] proposed to the president of Harvard

University Visiting Committee that Longfellow should be placed on that committee, the president replied: 'What would be the use? Longfellow could never be brought to find fault with anybody or anything.'[107]

Beloved members of the community, take Longfellow as your role model of love and magnanimity.

What a diverse set of lifetimes—and those are just a few! Mother asks us to take Lanello in his many embodiments as our role model and encourages us to develop the same virtues he demonstrated. The virtue that is unmistakably clear is the magnanimity of heart that he embodied over and over. And that same quality of *our* heart can be the key to our ascension.

The Ascension Process is for Everyone

The dictation by Lanello that we're going to hear today is entitled "The Ascension Process is for Everyone."[108] What a bold statement! It is a challenge to anyone who thinks they are unworthy to ascend or that they are not ready to undertake the path of their ultimate victory. It basically challenges *any* excuse that we might come up with to not strive toward that goal.

Lanello warns us to not believe the lie that we will win our ascension by intellect or pride or this or that. To have a highly developed intellect can be a great help to the aspiring chela, but it can also be a trap that leads to pride. Being highly intelligent without developing the heart can be a great disadvantage because we lean upon our mental body to do the things that our heart should do. Some people have an almost encyclopedic knowledge of the teachings, and others often have idolatry of such individuals because they wrongly equate intellect with attainment. The path of intellect alone is the path of the

Nephilim who have no light and, in their pride, reject God and condemn his children.

Lanello states very simply that we will win our ascension by *"the largesse of your heart."*[109] I was intrigued by the use of the word largesse when I read that. I thought I knew what it meant, but since we know the masters choose their words carefully, I decided to consult the dictionary to make sure I didn't miss any of the word's nuances.

Largesse is a noun defined as "generosity in bestowing money or gifts upon others; an example of how it might be used is 'dispensing his money with such largesse.'" The synonyms are: generosity, liberality, bounty, bountifulness, beneficence, altruism, charity, philanthropy, magnanimity, benevolence, charitableness, openhandedness, kindness, big-heartedness.

Doesn't that sound like we're describing Lanello?

We might wonder to what extent we embody those qualities. Whatever our level of attainment, I am sure each of us would like to embody more of them. So perhaps we should consider what we need to do to have more largesse of heart.

One suggestion is to listen again (or for the first time) to Mother's lectures on Lanello's various embodiments. The quotes I read today gave just a small glimpse at those lifetimes, and we can learn much by imitating the Christ that he embodied. While the manifestation of such love of the heart is a lifetime pursuit, we need to start somewhere. And imitating the virtues of his various lifetimes is the perfect place.

Another thing that is helpful is to call for Lanello's mantle. He says:

> *Blessed ones, I am grateful to be with you on this day of the celebration of my ascension. I give to you my mantle as you are able to receive it. I ask you to claim my mantle daily.*[110]

The grace of his mantle upon us daily will surely assist us in developing and expanding our heart and extending it to others as he did!

Non-Condemnation

Remember that Longfellow never found fault with anyone. So one quality of the heart that we can focus on developing is non-condemnation. The Bible relates that Jesus demonstrated this same quality toward the woman caught in adultery, *"And Jesus said unto her, Neither do I condemn thee."* [111]

I studied a number of near-death experiences and found that people who have gone through them have shared an almost universal observation: Along with the feeling of being surrounded by tremendous love, there was also a feeling of total acceptance and non-condemnation. This brought them great peace, joy and happiness.

Even with the teachings we have been given, it is sometimes hard not to enter into a vibration of condemnation. Many who do this characterize what they say as "constructive criticism," but that can very easily be a rationalization. At the same time, non-condemnation does not mean that we fail to exercise discrimination in dealing with others. We must call on the Holy Spirit for discernment and be careful of the razor's edge between discerning someone's error and condemning them for it.

The lightbearers on this planet are under a constant weight of condemnation. Lanello explains:

> *That condemnation comes from one source: it comes from out of the pit itself. It comes out of the fallen angels. It comes out of those who wish to destroy you, to put you down. Let us be done with it.* [112]

It is interesting to note that we don't even realize this weight is upon us because we experience it twenty-four hours a day. It's like a constant grating that wears on us. Sometimes it's greater than at other times.

Years ago I learned an unforgettable lesson about this weight. One night when I was attending a Saint Germain service at Camelot, I felt sharp pain in my abdomen and eventually had to leave the service. Fortunately, there was a doctor in the service who could help me. After he examined me, he sent me to the hospital with a possible intestinal blockage. Mother was informed, and she had some staff make calls for me.

The hospital confirmed the diagnosis and decided to wait until the next day to determine if surgery was needed. Notwithstanding the pain, I was truly surprised at how good I felt. In fact, one of the doctors who was treating me asked me to stop being so cheerful! Then it hit me—the energy of condemnation was off me because of the calls being made by the messenger and staff! That gave me a co-measurement of just how heavy a weight we all carry every single day. I can honestly say I have not felt so free of that weight since then! And the other good news is that I didn't have to have surgery.

As you'll hear in Lanello's dictation being played today, we have to challenge that weight of condemnation because sometimes, in the most subtle ways, we start to believe it. A part of this condemnation can manifest as "aggressive mental suggestion." Archangel Chamuel describes this as *the aggressive voices of the night that hammer the brain with their lies!... Aggressive mental suggestion is the germ warfare of the fallen ones."* [113]

Chamuel explains how we can know when we are being subjected to this energy:

You can identify this energy. You can know it well. ...at any moment of the day or night when you feel waves of irritation

*and mild dislike and a separation from brothers and sisters on
the Path through barbs of criticism and waves of anxiety and
nervous tension and you feel your energies seized with a certain dislike for this or that individual or an action of intense
condemnation or judgment of a co-servant...* [114]

We need to recognize this energy as a projection from the
fallen ones seeking to tear us from the Path or to entice us to
make negative karma by tying into it. The shield of Archangel
Michael and an awareness of this plot will help free us from
condemnation, whether within or without.

Sadly, it all too often comes from within as self-condemnation. This can come from our revolving of past errors or believing the lie that we are worthless sinners. When we condemn
ourselves, we condemn God because He is in us. We exclude
ourselves from the circle of oneness with our God Presence
when we do this. If we are burdened by our shortcomings,
we should call upon the law of forgiveness, work to correct
our mistakes or patterns, and stand in the dignity of our own
Christ Selves as we earnestly walk the Path. Self-condemnation achieves nothing and separates us from God. Let us be
done with it!

Whether from within or without, it is up to us to recognize
condemnation for what it is.

Meeting People Where They Are

I know of two unfortunate instances that happened in different teaching centers during the past year where the energy
of condemnation was put upon souls who were new to the
teachings. On both occasions it was a new seeker's first time
coming to a Sunday service. And each situation could have
been handled with more grace, kindness and understanding.

During the visit of one of these seekers, a community member engaged them in a full-blown political discussion. It was definitely not what the person had come for, and the political views were quite different from what he believed at the time. As far as I know he never came back.

On the other occasion, a person showed up brimming with enthusiasm. Despite his excitement about the teachings, it was evident that his current lifestyle was not in keeping with the standards of the Brotherhood. A community member felt the need to point this out to him right away, rather than meeting him where he was and extending compassion. He never came back again either.

When greeting a new seeker, it is always good to remember how much effort the angels and masters put forth to get someone to one of our lectures or centers and just how important it is for that soul to be introduced to the teachings of the ascended masters. It could be one of the most important days for them in many lifetimes.

The messengers met all of us where we were and gently lifted us up. Perhaps some of you remember the story about Florence Miller (now the Ascended Lady Master Kristine) knocking on the door at La Tourelle, the Summit Lighthouse headquarters at that time in Colorado Springs. When Mark Prophet opened the door and met Florence, she was wearing a bright red outfit with red boots. Now, we know that ascended master students avoid the color red because it is associated with a perversion of the pure energies of the seven rays. Nonetheless, Florence was welcomed with open arms, and the rest is history.

This is not about compromising the standards of the masters. It is about having a compassionate heart and extending that heart by meeting people where they are. Mother has taught us that every soul deserves a gentle introduction to the ascended masters' teachings.

Often in our enthusiasm, we give too much teaching to someone too soon, which does not allow them to take little bites until they are ready for a full meal. At some point after learning the masters' teachings, individuals will need to make decisions about how they want to live. But let us not force that decision upon them before they are ready.

I can witness to the fact that Mother and the masters extended great grace to those who came to their organization. Many years ago I worked in the marketing department at Camelot. We conducted a survey of our membership regarding how they found the teachings and how it had changed their lives, and it was my job to read and compile all the surveys. I can assure you that the past of many stalwart Keepers and staff members was not the way of the ascending ones. It didn't matter. Everyone was welcomed in a spirit of non-condemnation. And when they were taught the truth, they turned their lives around to follow it.

Expanding Our Heart with Compassion

In contemplating compassion and largesse of heart, it is helpful, even necessary, to consider our own soul. Jesus taught, *"Thou shalt love the Lord thy God with all thy heart, and with all thy soul, and with all thy mind. This is the first and great commandment. And the second is like unto it, Thou shalt love thy neighbour as thyself."* [115]

We are to love our neighbor *as we love ourself.* If we have self-condemnation or believe the lie of the fallen ones that we are sinners or that we are unacceptable to God, we have not followed the commandment of God.

We might say, "Well, of course I love myself." Perhaps we do. However, I think all too often we confuse loving the human self that we identify with, with loving our true self—our I AM Presence and Holy Christ Self. The world strongly reinforces identification with the human self, totally disregarding the concept that we are made in the image and likeness of God. That divinity within us has nothing to do with outer appearances or, for that matter, the negative karma we have made during our many lifetimes. We love the Presence of God with us and our precious soul ascending the steps to her heart chakra and her Christhood.

On the anniversary of his Ascension Day in 1984, Lanello gave a dictation titled "The Covenant of Compassion." While it is one that many of us are familiar with, his teaching on compassion is paramount to our work in expanding the largesse of our heart. As you ponder his words, it can also be helpful to think of extending comfort and compassion to your own soul and inner child. For when we truly love God and the God Presence within ourselves, we can more fully extend that love to others.

Therefore, in the bonds of love and service and for the exercise of your own heart, it is well to deal with each one as a tender flower. And remember that those who appear on the surface as having the toughest skin may often have the most sensitive hearts.

Thus, into this community of love and understanding shall many be drawn who truly do need understanding. There are many who are sick who need healing, but I have not sent them; for I desire a professional stance from the career son and daughter of God—a point not only of non-condemnation, but the point of positive warmth and giving and welcome.

I would like to dedicate this year of my victory to my own Guru, El Morya, who heads the Order of the Good Samaritans. I would like you to think of Camelot and the Inner Retreat as a hospice—a place where the weary traveler may come and find a welcome and food and warmth and shelter, where the needs of the man, and the human, might be seen as paramount, as all know how the human problem can weigh so heavy that it must find surcease before the spiritual teaching can begin. But it already has begun the moment you extend love, for this is the essence of your heart and your path.

You will always find that the ascending ones nearer and nearer the goal seem to enter into a life of doing for others often little things seemingly insignificant. And even the recipients of such gifts and graces sometimes wonder, but in each such gesture there is a transmission of love. This increases the capacity of the heart of the giver but also brings great solace and comfort to those who receive, even though they may not perceive it.

For I tell you, beloved hearts, in many the hungers, the pain and the crying is so great that the hurt of all of this is sealed away in some dark corner of the subconscious. And the individual who is striving and determined puts all that aside and goes forth to battle, seeking what he, too, may give to life.

Thus, when the healer comes with the great comfort flame and with love as a mother's heart, when these individuals who have set aside their self-concerns and burdens begin to feel that comfort and they begin to feel the ability to rest and be at ease, for a time perhaps the entire record of the hurt may surface. And then it is that the healing love is most efficacious in transmutation.

In the presence of love, those most self-sufficient may let go and release the burdens, not fearing the opinions of their peers, not fearing to be judged or to be thought any less than the model role that they are pursuing and determining to externalize merely because they, too, may have had some difficulty, some problem, some experience that seems to be less than what the model chela or disciple would have.

Therefore, as the strength of each individual is pursued and builded upon, and as that one becomes strong in service, there are cycles also when all that is beneath will pass through the violet flame because of the presence of the Comforter in any one of you and in all of you.

Once you are determined to be [to fulfill the office of] that loving Comforter to each and every one, you will begin to be amazed as to how much you can help, how many problems you can heal, how much of a past record can go into the flame—a knot of some past lifetime, a situation that has created almost scar tissue. Your presence, your voice, your comfort, your love, your companionship can dissolve it in a moment. And you will watch how that one will take flight and soar, barely realizing that such a record has been taken and perhaps not even knowing just how much the ruby-ray love of your heart has been a part of the alchemy of release.[116]

Isn't that a profound and motivating teaching from our role model Lanello?

One skill that will help us expand our heart's love is the ability to listen. My wife has an old decree book that she used at Camelot. When you open it up, there is a quote from Mother at the top of the first page that she wrote there during a service so she wouldn't forget it. The quote is, "True love is a listening heart."

Quite often people don't want you to fix things for them, they just want you to listen to them. They need someone to understand what they are going through. As you allow them to talk, you can always ask their permission to share a teaching or a perspective that might be helpful for them. But be careful not to give them more than they can use or assimilate.

One thing I've learned in my ministerial work is that you can only help people to the extent they want to be helped. That may seem like a funny thing to say because you might think everyone would want to be helped as much as possible. But that's not necessarily the case as they might not be ready for that next step. We need to have attunement and recognize when someone doesn't want more, even though we could offer more. We need to allow them to process what they have received.

Compassion versus Sympathy

In other words, as we develop and practice largesse of heart, we must also know when the best thing for a particular soul is to *not* help them. This takes great discernment. One key is understanding the difference between compassion and sympathy. I did a search in *Pearls of Wisdom* for dictations that talk about both emotions and fifty-five dictations came up! It is easy to see the importance of understanding the difference between them, both for the progress of our own souls and for those we would help.

Gautama Buddha said:

> ...the bond of human sympathy is a shadowed, false counterpart of divine compassion. For sympathy always reinforces human bondage, while compassion seeks by the expression of truth to bring mankind speedily to his ultimate freedom.[117]

Kuan Yin, who is the embodiment of mercy, has this to say about sympathy:

> At this point I desire to remind you that the human tendency toward sympathy can become a maelstrom of destructivity which the powers of darkness use to draw men's energies downward....
>
> Those who are sympathetic to others often prevent them from learning the lessons that life intends to teach. Then again, sympathy pulls the sympathizer into the same vibratory action, the same human mess, as you would say, that the one with whom he is in sympathy is in—without ever raising the unfortunate soul out of his misery! Oh, there are moments of temporary assuagement of grief; there is comfort in having other people agree with you, even when you are wrong. But how much better it would be if individuals would learn to face themselves, to face life, and to live with reality rather than illusion.[118]

We know that there are those who would take advantage of a compassionate heart, so we must discern when it is better for a soul that we say or do nothing. There is a time to extend compassion and mercy in the form of comfort and help, and there is a time when it is compassionate and merciful to allow the soul, as Kuan Yin says, to personally face those things that they must overcome for their victory.

Along those lines, I remember Mother relating how she would make calls for Keepers of the Flame who had passed on and were caught in the astral plane. She said on some occasions El Morya would do nothing in response to her call. The clear implication was that the soul needed to experience a season in the astral plane to hopefully learn from the consequences of her choices.

An Openness, A Givingness

By now I think we can all see that a major key to balancing our karma and making our ascension is the same largesse of heart that Longfellow had—an openness, a givingness, never being too busy to help someone in need. This same quality is also reflected in the life of the soul described in the book *Messages from Heaven.* He reported that his willingness to help anyone who came to him was his passport into the etheric octave. Though he did not practice our teachings to the extent that many of us do, he was always ready to jump in and lend a helping hand, and *that* was his entrée into heaven.

In Lanello's 1997 dictation that we're hearing today, he mentions that he balanced 100 percent of his karma that year. So consider this. He ascended in 1973, and it took him *twenty-four years* to balance the rest of his karma, which he said was an ancient karma like a noose around his neck.[119] It took twenty-four years, even with all the books that had been released, all the dictations and teachings he had given being continually played, and his twin flame, Mother, still actively working in the earth. That amazed me. As I recall, he had balanced seventy-some-odd percent of his karma when he left embodiment. Yet it took twenty-four more years for a soul of such great attainment and light to balance the rest of his karma.

As my years on the Path have gone by, I have developed a much greater respect for the demands of karma, what it takes to balance it, and how the quality of our heart is paramount to our victory. Though we may know this, perhaps we have resisted taking the next step of going one level deeper into opening our heart, into increasing the largesse of our heart.

No matter where we are on the Path, no matter how long we have followed the Path, whether measured in months or decades or lifetimes, Lanello has a powerful message for us in his dictation. He shatters the notion that the ascension process is only for the few and says the ascension is for everyone. However, he makes it clear that it is going to take great effort to make it happen. And for those who have already passed the fifty-one percent mark in balancing their karma, great effort is needed to face the difficult challenges and tests of the emotional and physical quadrants on our path Home. Lanello urges us to implore the Maha Chohan for one or all of the gifts of the Holy Spirit to assist us along the way.

Listen, Love and Encourage

Many of us have pondered the future of our community and what it will take to attract lightbearers to the path of the ascended masters. Have you wondered what will magnetize the souls who can ascend in this life to the teachings now that there is no embodied messenger? Well, besides the books and recorded teachings of the messengers and masters, we also play an essential role. New students need to see the teachings alive in us, just as we saw them in Mark and Mother.

I think we can all agree that it is the magnet of our heart, the largesse of our heart individually and collectively, that will help draw the lightbearers to this community and these teachings. Yes, we need marketing; yes, we need books; yes, we need lectures. We need all these things. But people are going to read the vibration of our hearts, and that will help them know if this is the path for them.

I remember when Pastor Richard Wurmbrand, the author of *Tortured for Christ*, did a Summit University Forum with Mother. He told her that people come to church because they want to be loved. Don't we all want that? And don't we want to extend love to others?

Do we have the quality of heart, the non-condemnation, the willingness to listen that so many need? We can learn so much about what's happening in people's lives by simply asking, "How are you doing?" and then truly listening. Even though we're all busy people, we can't be insensitive to that little prompting that someone has a burden they would like to share with us. You can be the listening heart that simply listens and extends love and support.

Everyone needs encouragement at one time or another, and simple words can be quite effective. "You can do it! I know you can do it!" We can always find something in a person to encourage and reinforce. "You have a tremendous heart of love and have been serving for many years. I know you have it within you to face this initiation and pass it!" That's compassion. That's extending love. That's reinforcing the strength of the soul that may be temporarily overcome by a weight of condemnation or a karmic burden. We all have days when that happens, and we all appreciate kind words to help us.

Expanding Our Threefold Flame Through Action

To have greater compassion, to develop our hearts, we need to expand our threefold flame. We know that a balanced threefold flame is a requirement for our ascension, but we also need to grow that flame. Expanding our flame from the 1/16th of an inch height that many lightbearers currently have requires action. For co-measurement, Jesus' threefold flame was bigger than his body!

In her landmark address "Out of the Heart are the Issues of Life," Mother explained:

...beloved, the threefold flame will not expand except by

deeds. It is action that does expand each of these plumes. Action, right action nullifies wrong action of the past karma....
The flame of the heart of divine love does grow and intensify in great strength as you serve to set life free, to rescue life, to love life until those you love are made whole...

...the wisdom plume...expands only by taking wise dominion over karmic circumstance, over every opportunity, neglecting not responsibility, duty, helpfulness toward life.... Wisdom, then, is truly illumined action...

The blue plume of the will of God that is divine power must be the will of God in action....

Thus, the will of God that is good is a free will that is exercised to confirm and affirm God's will in action, not God's will contemplated but God's will in action. The flame of Christhood developed, these three together in all of one's daily life is the sharpening of the sword for the defense of God on earth, for the defense of God in his lightbearers, in his little ones, always serving for the betterment of life, for the protection of the innocent, for the binding of those who interfere with the cosmic and global plan for peace and for freedom.[120]

Mother makes it quite clear that the only way to expand the three plumes of our heart flame is by action, by deeds. The three acting together can not only help individuals but also the whole earth and cosmos!

While contemplating a heart full of love is wonderful, we must do more. To have largesse of heart, as Lanello admonishes us, we must be love in action! And that ties back to Mother encouraging us to follow Lanello in his various lives as our role model of love and magnanimity.

Greater Love Hath No Man....

We've barely touched the hem of the garment of Lanello's heart in today's service, but it is a beginning. Let us not hesitate to share the largesse of our hearts. As we give our love, we *become* that love. Let's not be afraid to take the next step. We're all loving people. But there's a deeper love—a love and magnanimity that becomes the magnet in our heart that will attract people who need to find these teachings and make their ascension in this life.

People are so inundated with the lie of the Nephilim culture and the culture of death that they have trouble seeing the truth. They often can't see the light, and it can be a turning point for them to see it in one of us. It takes tremendous fire and love to reach a soul that is so burdened. Lanello did it. Mother did it. God can do it, of course. But it's good to remember that God also works through us and through our heart that contains his love. How is the legacy of Lanello's magnanimous heart going to be passed to people around the world if not through the largesse of our hearts as a reflection of his heart?

Nurture life. Nurture life wherever you find it. The world is in pain. Lanello tells us that we will experience pain and sorrow as he did so that we can know the meaning of pain and can bring surcease to others who have it.

Our soul's opportunity has been bought with a price. Let the sacrifice made for us not be in vain. Let us honor Lanello by *being* Lanello. Let us call for his magnanimous heart to be placed over our hearts so that we might know the joy of giving, as he knows it.

Let our legacy be of one who truly demonstrated the largesse of our heart.

THE PATH TO
UNCONDITIONAL
SURRENDER

Surrender is an act of pure love for me. I say this that you might remember that, as you surrender, I am able to come down from the cross and walk with you the path of the resurrection and the life.

—JESUS

FIVE

The Path to Unconditional Surrender

Towards the end of World War II there was a movement in England to stop the war with a negotiated settlement. The logic was that millions of lives would possibly be saved if the war ended sooner than later. Though that might have been true in the short term, it is not hard to imagine what Hitler might have done if he had gotten a way out of his defeat. Winston Churchill and the Allies were adamant about what they wanted: unconditional surrender. That is how it had to be and that is how it played out.

Similarly, there is no halfway with our surrender to God. We cannot remain half human and half divine because, as Jesus said, a *"house divided against itself will not stand."*[121] How could we put on our Christhood if the dweller-on-the-threshold remains?

God has given us time and space to work out our destiny. And, ultimately, it is our decision whether we want to surrender to God or not. Yet the truth is that there is a freedom and a peace in accepting that absolute and unconditional surrender is our divine destiny and the key to our individual Christhood.

Jesus Showed Us How to Surrender

So how do we get to unconditional surrender from where we are now? We need look no further than the example our Lord demonstrated, not only on Good Friday but also in the Garden of Gethsemane. While most of us are familiar with the story of what happened in the garden, a careful reading of the Bible verses shows the depth of the sorrow and pain Jesus was feeling.

We read in the book of Mathew, chapter 26: "*Then cometh Jesus with them unto a place called Gethsemane, and saith unto the disciples, Sit ye here, while I go and pray yonder. And he took with him Peter and the two sons of Zebedee, and began to be sorrowful and very heavy. Then saith he unto them, My soul is exceeding sorrowful, even unto death: tarry ye here, and watch with me. And he went a little farther, and fell on his face, and prayed, saying, O my Father, if it be possible, let this cup pass from me: nevertheless not as I will, but as thou wilt....*

He went away again the second time, and prayed, saying, O my Father, if this cup may not pass away from me, except I drink it, thy will be done....

And he left them, and went away again, and prayed the third time, saying the same words." [122]

More detail is given in Luke, chapter 22, verse 44: "*And being in an agony he prayed more earnestly: and his sweat was as it were great drops of blood falling down to the ground.*"

Sorrowful unto death, sweating drops of blood, he asked *three times* to let this cup pass from him. Knowing what was coming, we can understand the depth of his anguish. But let us also remember the key to his victory— "*Not as I will, but as thou wilt.*" The test he passed was one of unconditional surrender to God and his will.

Not only is this an example of our Lord's devotion and love for God but it is also an example that is helpful to remember when we are striving to surrender things in our own lives. If we are struggling with surrender, it is an inspiration to know that our Lord struggled as well.

As we follow our Lord on our path to the ascension, we too must reach the point of complete surrender if we are to fulfill our Christhood and have our victory. Hopefully, our test will not be as physical as Jesus', but it is ultimately the same test: to surrender to God's will.

We might wonder if it was so difficult for Jesus, how can we, in our lesser estate, meet this challenge? How can we reach the point of absolute surrender to God and his will?

Motivation to Surrender

Even though we are all different souls with different karma, perhaps there are some keys that apply to all of us.

Let us be honest with ourselves and with God about our true desires. Do we want to become zero, as El Morya teaches, so God can become the All where we are?[123] Desiring that does not mean you have no other desires. Jesus was conflicted, so it is no surprise that we may be.

We might ask, "What keeps us going? What gets us up in the morning to say our prayers? What helps us go about our business, trying to apply the ascended masters' teachings in our lives while thinking about God and fulfilling his purposes? What motivates us?" We wouldn't be here if there wasn't a very strong motivation, and aside from wanting to save our own soul, I think that motivation for most of us is our love for God and God in others. We also have the vision and understanding that there is more to being successful in life than just our day-to-day human activities, much more.

Some of you may remember the old days of Greyhound dog racing. What got the dogs to run was a rabbit held on a stick in front of them so it was always slightly ahead of them. And guess what? No surprise. They never caught the rabbit!

What I have discovered in my life is that as we pursue the spiritual path, God gives us a glimpse of the "rabbit" of victory but he doesn't fully give it to us until we're ready. So there is always an incentive to keep going and keep striving to reach our goal. Ultimately, by God's grace and our striving we will all get there. In the meantime, we just can't stop running!

What will motivate us to work to fulfill all the requirements of the path to our ascension? Few in the world seem to be interested in climbing this mountain. They're quite happy living the way they are or perhaps they don't want to make the effort because if Jesus can save them just by them confessing him as their Saviour, why all the bother? Unfortunately, many people have sincerely believed the lie that he has totally saved them and that they aren't responsible for their own karma. So they miss the joy and satisfaction that working and striving towards their soul's victory provides us.

Just wanting to ascend is not enough. As I mentioned earlier, I believe a core requirement on this journey to unconditional surrender and victory is love of God. True love for God will see us through balancing our karma, defeating our dweller, and becoming zero so God becomes the All in us.

Jesus put it so sweetly:

Surrender is an act of pure love for me. I say this that you might remember that, as you surrender, I am able to come down from the cross and walk with you the path of the resurrection and the life.[124]

Surrendering is an act of pure love and Jesus will come down from the cross and walk with us on our path! Do we need any other motivation to surrender than that? Don't fall prey to the aggressive mental suggestions that the Path is too hard and surrender is too hard. How can anything be too hard if Jesus comes down from the cross and walks with us?

Jesus demonstrated his love for God by his total surrender to the will of God. Even with the many conflicting desires we may have, our love of God will keep us going, no matter what the challenge. As Morya has taught, to make our ascension we only have to get up one more time than we fall down.

If this seems a bit overwhelming, I have some good news for you. We don't have to—and it's not possible to—surrender all at once, even though our final surrender must be complete. El Morya put it this way, *"Thus, even if you would surrender all of your human creation in one night, it could not be so."*[125]

We have been surrendering incrementally all along. Think of all the things you have surrendered since you started on the Path. The easy things may have gone first. Some things may have been harder, but many just dropped away as your understanding grew. You probably don't even think about them anymore. Now we are hopefully much better prepared to tackle the tough things that we have consciously or unconsciously avoided so far. I believe many of us are ready to face some of the issues that have burdened us ever since our fall from Maitreya's original Mystery School.

Many of the deeper unresolved issues within our being only surface when we are ready. And now is the hour when we have the tools and the willingness to tackle them, knowing that by taking the hand of the guru, taking the hand of the master, we can get through them. By God's grace, we will not let this opportunity be wasted!

Keys for Overcoming Challenges to Surrendering

Surrender is a journey. The well-known cliché is that the journey of a thousand miles begins with a single step. But to take that step—and all the ones that follow—there are teachings and actions that can help us at each level of surrender.

It's good to affirm within your being, with the fire of your heart, that you can do this, not only because of your love for God, but also because you know there are angels and masters who can guide your journey and bring you exactly what you are ready for, at exactly the right time.

Let's consider a few keys found in their teachings and how they can help us overcome the challenges to our surrendering.

1. Embracing the Will of God

There is comfort in the will of God. We see so little in the band of our awareness, but God sees it all. We also know that God has a divine plan for us and following his will is the way that plan will manifest. God may sometimes take us on what we consider a detour, but if we embrace his will then it will surely get us to the point where we can achieve our goal of total surrender.

Accepting the supremacy of God's will is a surrender in itself and a must for this journey. Embracing the will of God is aligning ourselves with the divine plan for us that has been in place for eons. What else in this universe could we possibly want in its place?

Archangel Jophiel and Archeia Christine admonish us:

> *Apply yourselves to the heart of the will of God and see how you have gotten out of alignment and why for no good reason you no longer embrace that will.*

Surrender to the will of God is just that. It is not surrender to a human person or to an Archangel. It is surrender to the Great God Self and to your own real being.[126]

Several years ago, I decided that I needed to affirm God's will in my life daily. So every morning and evening I ask God to take my free will which he has given me and return onto me his will. I do it twice a day not because I think God isn't listening, but because I want to affirm with every part of my being that I desire his will. I have found that doing this has brought me a deeper peace.

We must not shy away from the will of God but embrace it. It's not a small choice to surrender our free will. It takes a powerful love and a trust in God, knowing that he will bring us those things we need. There is safety in the will of God. There is protection in the will of God. There is comfort in the will of God. We *cannot* get these things through our own human will.

Jophiel and Christine say it so clearly: "... *surrender to the will of God is the key to your destiny.*"[127]

2. Conflicting Desires

If you have conflicting desires, welcome to the club! However, let us not be like Esau, who sold his birthright to Jacob for a single meal.[128] There is one lawful desire—to be one with God. Yet we are in human bodies, with human needs, and a very long history of conflicting desires.

A good way to deal with unwanted desires is to work to replace them with God-desire. We must consciously engage in doing this. Using our dweller-on-the-threshold calls to root out unlawful and unwanted desires and using affirmations, such as "I AM one with God-desire" can help. Such simple affirmations are extremely powerful in displacing darkness within us.

I used to give "I AM one with God-desire" when I walked from where I parked my car in Minneapolis to where I worked, which was about a mile away. I gave it every morning, over and over again, and it changed my life. Conflicting desires got resolved, and I even forgot about them!

But even before we make such calls, we have to be sure we want to be free from certain desires. We might think some of them are not really that bad. It can be pretty easy to rationalize, right? Again, let us be honest with ourselves about our desires.

Along with making your calls, it is helpful to tackle desires one at a time. Each time you overcome one, your momentum of victory will help with all the encounters that follow. Also, don't let one or two mistakes take you into self-condemnation or dissuade you from keeping on.

3. Trusting God and the Guru

Some years ago I ran out of excuses to not do the inner child work that Mother Mary and the messenger recommended we do to help resolve our psychology. I was more than a little nervous when I sat down with the therapist for my first appointment. Being a banker by vocation, I wanted everything in black and white. I asked her, "How long will this take? How many appointments before I can make peace with my inner child and resolve my psychology?" I could see a sweet, knowing smile form on her face as she gave her wise response, "Trust in the process." I never forgot that. Trust in the process.

As we are working toward absolute surrender, let us trust in the process that God has for us. After all, the core of the guru-chela relationship is trust. We must trust the guru to lead us where we need to go, even as he or she must trust us to do our part in fulfilling the purposes of our chelaship and maintaining the figure-eight flow between us.

For example, if we borrow money from somebody and don't pay it back, how can they trust us? If we borrow light from the ascended masters and make no effort to pay it back or return it to them, how can they trust us? Trust, integrity, and honor: these are all different words for the same thing, and they're key to our path.

We trust the guru to lead us on this journey of overcoming, a journey we are incapable of taking on our own. We may feel very much alone as we go through the surrender process, but we also know there is a mathematical precision to every initiation.

Some of us have been very good at insulating ourselves from challenges along the Path. To truly surrender we need to let go of the defenses that we have grown quite adept at using to avoid the initiatic encounter. When we see Lord Maitreya coming down the road towards us, we must not run or hide, but rather gird up our loins and joyously welcome his tests.

Trusting in the guru will overcome a multitude of fears.

4. Obedience to Our Higher Self and the Guru

I can so clearly recall Mother's frequent admonition to "Obey immediately" when prompted from within. Or the prophet Samuel's chastisement of Saul when he told him, *"Behold, to obey is better than sacrifice."*[129]

When we are working on surrender, we don't always know where the guru will take us. Archangel Chamuel and Archeia Charity remind us: *"The act of surrender to God is a sign of humility and obedience."*[130]

Along with trusting the guru we need to be obedient to the promptings from within about what we need to do and when to do it. We do need to *"try the spirits"*[131] to ensure the prompting is from God, but after we do that we need to act.

I faced a test like that quite recently. I was in a big store and saw a person working there that I knew, so I went up to say "hi" and we visited briefly. I made what I thought was a good-natured attempt at humor and was on my way. I hadn't gotten too far away when I got the strong feeling that what I had said was not only not particularly funny, but also not appropriate in the circumstances. I knew I should go back and apologize to him, but I wasn't really keen on it. I tried to rationalize not doing it, but soon gave in to the compelling call to act.

Have you ever had that happen, where you are compelled by your Higher Self, your voice of conscience, to do something? And, of course, we want to be obedient to the voice of conscience because if we don't listen, it won't speak to us anymore.

So I went back to him and told him I was just trying to be funny and hoped he was okay. He didn't seem concerned and said he was fine. Going on my way again, I continued shopping. It wasn't long before the feeling returned that I wasn't done. What I heard was, "You didn't actually apologize." "Well, yes, not in so many words," I admitted to myself. But I thought I had done enough. I thought, "If I go back there again a third time and apologize, he's going to think I'm out of my mind!" But soon the charge became so strong that I knew I had to do it. So back I went and formally apologized. I think he was somewhat bemused at my actions, while at the same time he was gracious about the apology.

I was finally at peace because at last I was totally obedient. It was far more important to me to obey than to avoid looking foolish.

5. Willingness to Take the Next Initiation
The path to becoming the bride of Christ is not an easy one. It is hard, but not *too* hard. Do not believe the lie that this path

cannot be walked. It *can* be walked. And, yes, it's demanding because the reward is the greatest reward in this world. To be a chela of the ascended masters with a capital "C" on planet earth is the highest honor anyone can receive.

We have every piece in place, every tool we need, including the violet flame, sponsorship, and freedom of religion. Then what can prevent us from our victory? An unwillingness to take the next initiation.

Some chelas will go so far on the Path and say, "I've had enough. This is just too hard. No more!" And with those tragic words, initiation will stop. It will stop because we stopped it. We decide our destiny.

During the 1993 Easter conference beloved Hercules soberly addressed this situation, describing why some people leave the Path:

> *They leave it early on because they see the handwriting on the wall after they have been around a few years. They see that if they don't have a mind to pass their tests daily, they aren't going to get anywhere, so they might as well leave. Or they leave the Path later because they have come to their twelfth year or their fifteenth year or their eighteenth year with the Ascended Masters and they finally say, "Hey, wait a minute! This isn't for me. I'm not prepared to make the sacrifices that are required at this level—or the surrender." What's more, they haven't defined the word surrender vis à vis their relationship to God.*[132]

Hercules further tells us why this is such dangerous behavior:

> *Let those who depart the Path recognize that it is almost like playing Russian roulette, because you never know when it*

is the last time that you will have the opportunity to pass that same test.

If I were to put before you now the record of the Keeper of the Scrolls and read to you the names of lifestreams you have known and some whom you have not known, and if I were to tell you when and where they began to decide that they would not take a certain initiation, you would see that the record goes back to Lemuria and to past ages that predate Lemuria that have not even been mentioned in the texts that have been written regarding earth's early history.[133]

We know the teaching that we will face the same test over and over again until we pass it. If any of us fall into the category of stopping at a certain point and refusing to take any more tests, then we need to challenge that momentum in ourselves. This time, things *can* be different. We are prepared to break that self-imposed limitation and take the tests we have refused to take in the past. By the grace of God, we will *not* fail this time.

For those who are the ones Hercules is referring to, surrender becomes critical if the soul is to make it on the Path and continue to have opportunity. For those who may think the Path is too hard, look at life in the world. Many people have a much more difficult life than we do just dealing with their own karma and situations in the world—and to what purpose? Whereas the life of the chela has the greatest goal and reward possible—the ascension!

The process of absolute surrender can free us from those issues that keep holding us back. Be willing to embrace the next initiation and the next and you will eventually get where you want to be—one with God. Saint Germain has told us that some of us are closer to our Christhood than we think. By taking the tests that come to us, we can not only overcome past momentums of failure, but also work to achieve the long-sought goal of our Christhood and oneness with our Lord.

It's time to be strong in the Lord, to take comfort in his words, to take comfort in the examples of the ascended masters and what they went through and the victories they won.

6. Honor What Comes to You

When we have embraced the will of God, when we have surrendered what we can, when we have striven to be trusting and obedient, we might still be very surprised by what lands on our doorstep. However, we cannot let it dissuade us from our victory.

God has the right to test us and we have the right to be tested. We shouldn't be surprised when we get "re-tested" on things we thought we had mastered. We have been taught that God either causes things to happen or allows them to happen. So grumbling is not part of the Path!

Early on in my chelaship, I wanted a very predicable path with no surprises, but I soon learned that is *not* the path of chelaship. God makes the rules, and we need to follow them.

For a Chela with a capital "C" everything comes for a reason. Gautama Buddha comments about this in the life of Job:

Therefore remember, beloved, how Satan did tempt Job and how God freely allowed Satan to tempt Job. Why was that, beloved? Because the Lord God trusted in his servant, knew he would not succumb to these fallen ones and these tempters continually going after him. Therefore Job did surrender his pride. Therefore in humility Job did pass his tests.[134]

Expect the unexpected and honor whatever God brings to you or allows to happen to you because it is always for a purpose. Again, it goes back to trusting the guru. Though we might squirm a little at things that come our way, when we have implicit trust in the guru, we can accept them as necessary to our path.

Sounds Good, But...

All this sounds good, but you might be thinking, "What will it be like to surrender unconditionally? What will my life look like after that?" Let us remember that we are surrendering to Almighty God, the Creator of the universe *and* of us. Let us also remember the amazing exchange we are engaged in—we are surrendering *unreality* and receiving the *fullness of God.* Archeia Charity puts it very succinctly: "*God surrenders to you the universe as you surrender to him the minutest part of yourself.*"[135]

Isn't that incredible? God surrenders the whole universe to you as you surrender to him the minutest part of yourself. And Cyclopea says: "*The tiniest surrender will cause the angels to rush to your side.*"[136]

Isn't that sweet? Don't we want the angels by our side? So don't discount the good that can come even from your small surrenders. Don't discount the value of giving up some recreational activity to go pray for what's happening in the Middle East or anywhere on the planet, don't discount the grace that comes from taking time away from your projects to help a friend in need, and so forth. The littlest surrender can bring great light to our worlds!

Besides Jesus' surrender in Gethsemane there are numerous examples of surrender in the Bible. While hanging on the cross Jesus surrendered: "*Father, into thy hands I commend my spirit...*"[137] Paul surrendered his non-belief in Jesus and became the greatest exponent of his teaching. Abraham loved and trusted God so much that he was even prepared to surrender his only son.

I found myself asking, "What part of this don't I get?" Surrender is not just a good idea, it is *imperative* for progress on the Path. Beloved Mighty Victory in his indomitable way affirms this:

> *Unless men and women are ready to surrender, there is no hope for them save round after round of mortal consciousness. And the struggle and the straying go on. And I think, if you will pardon the expression, the braying goes on rather than the praying!*[138]

Surrender and Power

Besides our own personal path Home, there are additional compelling reasons for surrender to God. Along with striving to save ourselves, we are also striving to help save the world.

It is sometimes quite easy to choose a dictation for a Sunday service, while other times it can be difficult. In looking for a dictation to go with the path of unconditional surrender, I found hundreds of references in the *Pearls of Wisdom*, but most references were just a small part of a dictation that contained so much more. As I reflected and prayed about it, the dictation we're hearing today came to the fore, partly for its teaching on surrender and partly because of its overall message.

In 1977 El Morya delivered the dictation "The Gemini Mind"[139] that tells the story of the battle between the forces of light and darkness a long time ago on the planet Mercury.† No doubt some of us were with him. As you will hear, there is an amazing parallel between the war on Mercury and exactly what is unfolding on earth now—the challenge of artificial intelligence and the robot creation. When El Morya gave this dictation

---

† Like the civilization on Venus, life on Mercury functions at a different vibrational frequency than physical life on Earth.

almost fifty years ago, few on earth could have envisioned this particular challenge.

One of the key teachings Morya gives is the need for sufficient power to defeat the adversary. The question that automatically arises is, "How do we get that power?" Morya explains that we get power by totally surrendering every part of our being to God. That surrender allows God to give us the greater power we invoke without the danger of us misusing it.

In other words, God is willing to give us the power that can change what is happening on this planet, but he won't give it to us as long as there's a risk we will misuse it. That might involve losing our temper, being agitated, criticizing others, things like that. That's the challenge. So one of the reasons we work to surrender and resolve these things is so that God can give us a greater increment of light and the power needed to help turn things around.

It's become quite clear that the problems on this planet seem unsolvable save by the light and power of God. I believe that each one of us is dedicated to doing our part in saving America and the lightbearers on earth. We do that daily in our devotions and in our services. But is that enough?

We know we need to surrender to gain our Christhood, but have we really understood that surrender is key to playing our part in the planetary Armageddon? We can accomplish so much more with greater power from God which would make the battle much more winnable. God will not give us more power than we can handle, yet even a small increase could make a big difference.

A Greater Love

When we surrender, we are in essence saying to God, "I love your will and your plan for me more than I love what I am surrendering." Saint Germain said when we decide to become the Christ we shall be. It's as simple as that. When the love we have for God and for the Path and for our service is greater than all the other things in our world, then we are ready to take all that we are and lay it on the altar of God.

I was speaking to another minister recently and we started talking about the saints and how many of them offered themselves up as "victim souls," taking the karma of others upon themselves. I finally understand the consciousness that led these saints to voluntarily carry the karma of the world like they did. They reached the point where their love of God and for their fellowmen was so great that they could make no other choice. They didn't have the violet flame, so all they could do was offer themselves as a sacrifice.

That same love becomes the compelling force behind our actions. That same depth of love becomes the impetus that will help us work through every negative pattern in our world, every resistance to surrender, and will help us pass every initiation that God brings to us. It will allow us to sustain our souls on this path.

That love is what gets us up and going every day. It's not fear. It's not anxiety of what's coming on the planet. It's not thinking, "I should do this; I should do that." It's knowing, "I love God and I want to be a greater instrument of God and I'm going to do whatever it takes. I don't want this human consciousness anymore. It doesn't work. After eons I've finally learned that lesson. I want *you*, God." And God will be there for us. God's love for us is there; it's firm, it's strong, and it will see us through every single test. No matter what stands in our way, with God's grace we can overcome it.

We can't truly surrender until we reach that point in consciousness because, even when surrender is hard, it must be joyous. As El Morya says:

Note the sweetness of surrender. God does not care for a surrender that is halfhearted or sour. It must be a joyous surrender... Stepping into new shoes is the way of surrender—being willing to be a bit uncomfortable until the shoe fits, becomes one with you and you realize that really, by your surrender, you have become that which you always were.[140]

There is a sublime joy in surrender—let us not miss it!

Where Do I Start?

Godfre tells us: *"Total light must be applied for total victory; and total victory can be won only by total surrender—into the flame of all that is less than the Christ consciousness within you."*[141]

"Okay," you might say, "I am ready to give it a try. Where do I start?" You could very well start with something you know you need to surrender but haven't quite gotten around to doing it. If even that is too much, you can start with a simple affirmation Godfre gives to us:

In the name of Jesus the Christ, I surrender unto the flame of God all that is less than the Christ consciousness within me.[142]

I printed off a copy of that affirmation and taped it on an index card and put it in front of my computer screen so I would make the call at least twice a day.

Godfre explains what this affirmation will do for you:

And as you say this each day, day by day you realize more and more of what it means to be a God-free being, as you have less and less of that which encumbers you on the Path. And by

*and by as you repeat the exercise, you will come to know what
freedom in the soul truly is.*[143]

If we truly want to surrender, this is an easy and powerful
way to do it. So short, so simple, but so powerful! We can all
do this if we want to. There are also prayers and decrees that
help us surrender, such as the Surrender Prayer✝ and decree
10.18 by El Morya "Sweet Surrender to Our Holy Vow" which is
included on the following page.

Our closing quote from Archangel Raphael describes how
surrender leads to our oneness with the Bridegroom—our
Christ Self:

> When you surrender, you do not vacate the throne or the
> temple. When you surrender, it is into the arms of the Beloved
> whereby, by the sacred fire, your soul literally melts into the
> Christ Person that is the reality that is the plus polarity of your
> identity. This fusion is no loss, but gain—the gain of the crystal
> of the diamond-shining mind of God.[144]

Our soul literally *"melts into the Christ Person...This fusion is no
loss but gain!"* Isn't that beautiful?

Surrendering is not an option. It is an imperative!

Let us joyously surrender and anticipate what will unfold,
and let us be ready day or night when the Bridegroom cometh.

✝This prayer is taken from The *Fourteenth Rosary, The Mystery of Surrender* and can be
found on page 256 in Book One of *Practicing Sainthood.*

SWEET SURRENDER TO OUR HOLY VOW
by the Ascended Master El Morya

Meditation upon the God Flame:

Our will to Thee we sweetly surrender now,
Our will to God Flame we ever bow,
Our will passing into Thine
We sweetly vow.

Affirmation of the God Flame merging with the heart flame:

No pain in eternal surrender,
Thy Will, O God, be done.
From our hearts the veil now sunder,
Make our wills now one.

Beauty in Thy purpose,
Joy within Thy name,
Life's surrendered purpose
Breathes Thy holy Flame.

Grace within Thee flowing
Into mortal knowing,
On our souls bestowing
Is immortal sowing.

Thy Will be done, O God,
Within us every one.
Thy Will be done, O God—
It is a living sun.

Bestow Thy mantle on us,
Thy garment living flame.
Reveal creative essence,
Come Thou once again.

Thy Will is ever holy,
Thy Will is ever fair.
This is my very purpose,
This is my living prayer:

Come, come, come, O Will of God,
With dominion souls endow.
Come, come, come, O Will of God,
Restore abundant living now.

And in full Faith...

OVERCOMING SELF-IMPOSED LIMITATIONS ON THE PATH

Men shall see their limitations vanish in the unlimited sense of Christ awareness.

—EL MORYA

SIX

Overcoming Self-Imposed Limitations on the Path

How do you train an elephant not to move? In an article on self-imposed limitations, Davide Zaccariello tells us:

> *When they are very young the trainer ties them up with a ring on the foot chained to the ground. The little elephant tries everything he can to move and at a certain point he gives up. From that moment on, for the rest of his life, it will be enough to put a ring on his foot and the elephant will remain still. Once the elephant accepted the limitation, even if it will not be there anymore, he will behave as if it was there.*[145]

Are we like a trained elephant in some ways? Do we have self-imposed limitations that may have served a purpose at one time but are only holding us back now?

Oliver Wendell Holmes is credited with saying that all limitations are self-imposed.[146] As students of the ascended masters' teachings, I think we would agree with that statement. Ponder what is the greatest limitation on our spiritual growth.

Is it God? Obviously not. Is it opposition? That can clearly be a factor, but God is greater than any opposition. So, ultimately, *we* decide if there is any limitation.

When I was preparing to write my letter to the Karmic Board✝ this summer, I couldn't come up with anything new to request that would help me progress on my spiritual journey. What did I really need that I didn't already have?

Then I reflected back to November 1987 when Jesus told us it was time to put on our Christhood. Thirty-six years ago—a *long* time! So we don't necessarily need new dispensations, we need to be using the teachings we have already been given in order to fulfill Jesus' call to become the Christ. As I wondered what has taken us so long, what came to me was our need to deal with self-imposed limitations. It is a definite key to our victory.

We Need Help Overcoming Self-imposed Limitations

A major reason we have not put on our Christhood is that we have created self-imposed limitations that have denied us the complete action of grace in our being. Helios tells us:

> *Self-imposed limitation bars man from effectively grasping cosmic principles and thus denies him access to the consciousness of the ascended masters. Man...has also created a great deal of adversity by his self-erected barriers. These, being both mental and emotional, have prevented the great cosmic light from acting in his world.*[147]

✝ Traditionally, students of the ascended masters handwrite personal letters to the Karmic Board on New Year's Eve and the Fourth of July offering their service upon God's altar and asking for divine intercession in their personal lives, the Community of the Holy Spirit, the nation, and the world. Their sealed letters are consecrated at the altar and then burned. The Lords of Karma review the petitions and grant dispensations of sponsorship to worthy souls for constructive purposes.

I get the sense that God is ready to pour help and blessings and light into our worlds, but we have erected self-imposed barriers that they can't get past. And what makes it worse is that we often don't realize we have created these blocks or that they even exist!

As Paul said in Romans 7:15: *"For that which I do I allow not: for what I would, that do I not; but what I hate, that do I."* The meaning is a little clearer in the International Standard translation: *"I don't understand what I am doing. For I don't practice what I want to do, but instead do what I hate."* Perhaps the first limitation we need to purge from our consciousness is the belief that we cannot be freed from our entrenched self-limitations!

To move beyond these limitations we need to consider what they are, where they came from, and how we can get rid of them. Before we can overcome a self-limitation, we have to understand what it is, how it operates and how to deal with it.

If you search self-limitation online, you find an almost universal recognition of the problems it causes. However, many of the solutions presented fall into the category of simply programing the mind to overcome them. Thinking positively and having a can-do spirit are wonderful, but do they really work? Do they get to the root of the problem?

A friend who wants to remain anonymous allowed me to share his thoughts from a book he is writing on changing mindsets that are a form of self-imposed limitations:

> *If changing mindsets were easy, that would eliminate one of the key reasons for writing this book. I would instead send you to the local bookstore to pick up one of thousands of self-help books filled with "good advice." I would have you hang inspirational posters in your bedroom that told you: "Just Do It!" "Winners Never Quit and Quitters Never Win." "Don't Run*

Away from Challenges, Run Over Them." Unfortunately, human beings are not wired to automatically implement what they know is best.

Makes one wonder if we haven't overcome our self-limitations so far, then how are we going to do it now? The answer from a spiritual perspective is that we can't do it alone—and we don't have to! As Jesus tells us in the dictation we will be hearing today, our mortal form is inadequate to hold the light of God that is released to us. However, Jesus also tells us, *"My heart in thy heart is the adequate vessel."*[148] If we do our part, then Jesus can help us earn our freedom and our Christhood by his presence within us.

I know that I don't really understand the fullness of all that Jesus is and the potential for his presence in our lives. While we know of his Palestinian incarnation, Jesus is not the same as when he ascended two thousand years ago. Just imagine who he is now—his causal body, his attainment, the magnificence and glory of God that he is! I'm not sure we can really comprehend it in our current state.

The point we *do* need to understand is that *there are certain things we cannot overcome by ourselves—we need our Saviour!* All the positive thinking, all the forms of self-hypnosis, all the other things we may try are not going to give us our victory. When we understand this, the equation of overcoming these self-limitations changes from "I tried and it doesn't work" to "With Jesus, I can do it!"

What Is a Self-Imposed Limitation?

From a secular perspective, I like the definition of self-imposed limitation given by Mr. Zaccariello, whom I quoted earlier. "*A self-imposed limitation is a boundary produced by the person, a self-protective mechanism. This type of limitations are not objective breaking points, they are just what we choose to believe to be the limit.*"[149]

Bobby Maximus, a physical trainer, puts it this way: "*Self-imposed limitations are shackles that hold us down and prevent us from achieving our potential.*"[150] The image that came to mind when I read that was the character Marly from *The Christmas Carol* who appeared to Scrooge covered in chains so heavy that he could hardly move. I wonder if our self-imposed shackles are weighing us down like Marly's chains? Bobby Maximus continues: "*When a person sets a limit, he or she puts a limit on what is achievable. That person will never evolve beyond the arbitrary standard set for him or her. People never evolve beyond their self-imposed standards, even if they are fully capable.*"[151]

So what have we set as the limit to what we can do? For most people it is the limit of their "comfort zone." This has been described variously as:

> ...*a psychological state in which things feel familiar to a person and they are at ease and (perceive they are) in control of their environment, experiencing low levels of anxiety and stress. In this zone, a steady level of performance is possible. Bardwick defines the term as "a behavioral state where a person operates in an anxiety-neutral position." Brown describes it as "Where our uncertainty, scarcity and vulnerability are minimized.*"[152]

Perpetually living in our comfort zone does not sound like the way a chela of the ascended masters would live, does it? An anxiety-neutral position does not create the impetus for real growth on the Path. If there is no creative tension in our lives, how can we grow?

Moving Beyond Our Comfort Zone

Before we are tempted to criticize ourselves for both self-imposed limitations and affection for our comfort zone, let's consider why we set those limitations and whether or not we still need them.

First, not all self-imposed limitations are bad. For instance, it's good to set self-limitations on actions that put us in unnecessary danger or to impose a limitation on ourself so we don't eat too much. On the other hand, many self-imposed limitations may have outlived their original purpose, continuing to hold us back without our realizing it, just as they do for a trained elephant.

Many of these limitations have their basis in fear or in circumstances that caused us emotional or physical pain. When a child or any person experiences trauma, they naturally do things to protect themselves. That's not only understandable, but it's also often necessary. An example is when someone close to us violates our trust and we subsequently set up barriers to automatically trusting others. Jesus tells us that if we want to receive him, it involves *"the letting go of all other persons, considerations and experiences that have led to disappointment and sorrow and vacancy, disillusionment, cynicism, despair."* [153]

Imposing self-limitations may have been useful at one time, but unless we recognize that we still have them when they are no longer needed, they will hold us back on our spiritual journey. A posting on the website peoplefirstps.com explains how we can fool ourselves into keeping limitations as a security blanket:

These self-imposed limitations cause us to give up or not to try at all. We convince ourselves that we shouldn't try because

we can't succeed. We insulate ourselves from failure by doing
only what we have already succeeded in doing before.

As a result, our possibilities become narrower, seemingly
affirming that we are, indeed, limited.

It's easy to let this happen because we are both creatures
of habit and seekers of comfort. But we are fooling ourselves
if we use our routines and self-imposed limitations as security
blankets.[154]

We know that in the teachings, as with anything else, it is
easy to get into a routine, a self-created comfort zone with limitations. So while we may be happy to live in that comfort zone,
it limits our spiritual journey. For example, though we may
have mastered giving our decrees and offering our service, we
are not always tackling the base elements blocking our spiritual growth.

That brings us back to working on our psychology. We've
heard about doing that for decades and we *know* it's important.
But it's not going to take care of itself. Our psychology won't
be resolved simply by our transition to higher realms. Mother
knew this and worked diligently on her own psychology. Can
we do any less?

Mother told the story of people who build a cave around
their heart chakra and are quite comfortable in that cave. They
are trying to prevent karma from coming upon them and are
isolating themselves from some tests and initiations. Until they
can break out of that cave, they limit their progress.

Being a chela of the ascended masters requires us to take
risks, to have faith when nothing seems to be working, to so totally trust in the will of God that we surrender our own will, to
be willing to leave our comfort zones and to do *whatever* it takes.

Are we afraid that carrying greater light will not only bring greater responsibilities but also greater opposition? Or that the cost of making mistakes will be much greater the more light we have in our being? Leaving our comfort zone requires a deep trust in the masters and the Path and a love for God that is greater than our fears. We know that *"fear hath torment."* [155] How can anyone be truly happy when they are fearful?

Can we reach the place where we can say, "You know what? I don't want to be afraid anymore. I just don't want to be afraid. I don't want that in my world, so I am going to trust you, God." It doesn't mean we'll never fear again but it strengthens us to go forward in complete trust. And that trust will allow God to do greater things in our world. That trust will open the door to our Lord and to our victory.

Recognizing Human Reasons

Mother told a story about a student that had just graduated from Summit University whom she had invited to join staff. The lady declined, saying she would miss her beautiful dishes at home! I don't know if she realized how ridiculous that reason appeared, but apparently it was enough to keep her from an opportunity her soul had perhaps been working towards for millennia!

In her article "Self-Limiting Beliefs: A Guide for Overcoming Limitations," Hannah Miller shares how these beliefs can be hard to recognize.

> *Limiting beliefs keep people from having an open mind about who they are, what they can accomplish, and how they can positively affect others. Any belief that hinders someone from growing and developing falls into this category.*
> *Sounds easy enough, right? Here's the issue, though: limiting beliefs aren't always easily recognizable. They often show*

up in disguise. Several of their favorite forms include excuses, negativity, complacency, steadfast opinions, and unconstructive self-talk.[156]

Besides excuses, negativity, complacency, steadfast opinions, and unconstructive self-talk, as chelas we also deal with aggressive mental suggestion. Whatever the reason, people in general seem to have an amazing ability to rationalize certain behaviors when it suits them. Any one of these self-limiting beliefs can be called upon when we want to find a reason for not moving out of our comfort zone.

Thinking we are unworthy or incapable of doing something can be a cop-out too. It gives us an excuse for not trying. This can manifest with self-talk that might go something like: "Well, putting on my Christhood may be too much of a stretch for me. After all, if I haven't made it by now, will I really make it in this life?" Or "With all that is going on in the world, I need to focus on my decrees and just surviving day to day." Or "I am not sure I could handle the changes in my life or the persecution that it might bring." On and on and on, ad infinitum, until we *choose* to stop indulging in this pattern of thinking.

We Will Not Like What We See

One of the challenges in facing our self-imposed limitations is that we will not like what we see. As we consider what these beliefs and defenses may be, we will discover just how much they have limited us and held us back. We may ask ourself, "Oh, what might have been if I had only recognized and overcome these limitations years ago?"

Moving forward, rule number one is: Don't get into any kind of self-condemnation! Some of these limitations served a purpose at the time we set them up, and now God is giving us the opportunity to be cut free from them. And guess what? Regardless of whatever limitations we may have, they have not stopped us from pursuing the path of our ascension. Nevertheless, it is time to face them with God's help and to accept El Morya's promise that *"men shall see their limitations vanish in the unlimited sense of Christ awareness."*[157] Isn't that inspiring and beautiful?

Besides, there is no need for us to take this journey alone. Jesus has taught us the 90/10 rule—we do ninety percent of the work, and the masters do ten percent. He said:

> *Claim the dominion of the Father-Mother God given to you in the Beginning, and you will have that victory. But understand, beloved, 90 percent is up to you. Ten percent we will give and multiply as you show forth mighty fruits in your labor.*[158]

And the gift of that ten percent can make all the difference between success and failure!

Just as we cannot overcome many obstacles on the Path by ourselves, we need the intercession of the masters to help us release self-limitations. Mighty Cosmos in a dictation given in 1988 took a stand for our freedom from these limitations:

> *...I direct your attention toward the reality which I now reveal to you, that for many the difficulty to move beyond the first seven rays into the initiations of the Eighth Ray and [of] the Eighth Ray chakra, [which is] the secret chamber of the heart, has been and remains an insurmountable difficulty.*
>
> *I come, therefore, wielding this sword for the binding of those barriers self-imposed [as well as those] superimposed*

by fallen angels, all of whom are alien to the mansions of God. This stumbling block, therefore, between that [six o'clock] line and the entering in [by the sons and daughters of God] to the center of Being by means of the eightfold, eight-petaled chakra must be removed by Divine Intercession.

I AM that Intercessor by the grace of God.[159]

Note that he said he comes "*wielding this sword for the binding of those barriers self-imposed.*" Since divine intercession is required and he is the Intercessor, our journey of removing self-limitations should definitely include calls to Mighty Cosmos to help us. If we do nothing else, we can at least make one fiery fiat to Mighty Cosmos to free us of our self-limitations. And daily calls to him would flood us with his freeing power. What a wind in our sails!

Identifying Self-Limitations

Identifying some of our self-limitations begins with prayer and a willingness to be completely honest with ourselves. As Mother said, "*This is self-observation. This is the path of the Buddha. The Buddha is always observing himself so that he knows exactly where he is.*"[160] It takes courage to look at ourselves honestly, but we must be willing to take this step so we can be free of these limitations, these shackles.

I remember when I was eight or nine years old, October came around and it was time to choose a Halloween costume. For some long-forgotten reason, I wanted to go as a convict, and I looked to my mother to figure out the costume. She bought me a new pair of jeans and a navy sweatshirt and used white surgical tape to make horizontal bands around them every few inches. She got a little hat and put bands around it too, and even found me a plastic ball and chain at the store. No question that I looked like a convict on the chain gang! When I went around trick or treating, I had to forgo the ball and chain because I kept tripping over it! Looking back on this experience I think God was giving my soul a not too subtle message: We are prisoners of our karma and we will remain on the chain gang until we balance it. When it is balanced, we will be shackled no more!

Although there is no all-encompassing list of self-limitations, we can recognize many of the basic ones. You may want to compile your own list with the ones that seem most important in your life and decide to go after one or two of them, remembering you will not be doing it alone. Once you have chosen one to tackle, remember to call upon Jesus for his help and know that with his help you *can* overcome it. If you overcome one self-limiting behavior this year it will be a great victory!

Our personal psychology can be a good starting point. Consider if there are records of pain or trauma that you have not processed that are holding you back. Remember the abiding love of the masters and be willing to see yourself as a little child taking the hand of Jesus on this journey as he tells us to do in the dictation we will hear today.

I was taught the lesson about buried psychological records in a very direct way. In the early 1990s I was out of work and needed a job. I embraced novenas as a solution, including giving 144 decrees to Cyclopea almost daily during my job search. Even with all my decrees nothing seemed to be happening on the job front. What *did* happen is that one day in church God showed me the effect of a childhood trauma that had a much greater impact on me than I had previously realized. Instead of helping me find a job, he showed me something that was more important to my soul than my immediate needs were.

I did eventually get the job I sought. Then a few years later when I did inner child work with a therapist, this childhood incident was the first thing I worked on. I felt a great healing from that work, and I thanked God for giving me what I *needed*, not necessarily what I *wanted*.

Another limiting factor to consider is non-forgiveness. One person can keep us from our ascension if we do not forgive them! I was recently talking to a friend that I knew had strong feelings about a former staff member he had some difficult experiences with. Although this staff person had accomplished a great deal in his service, my friend felt that he was not upholding the Christ in how he interacted with others and how he had treated him. Knowing his feelings were deep, I asked him, "Would you be unhappy if this person made his ascension?" The question surprised him as he had not thought of it in that way. After reflecting on the question he replied, "Of course not!" He said seeing things from that higher perspective made it easier for him to forgive the person.

And what about surrender or the lack of it? If we are holding anything back from God in our quest to put on our Christhood, then we are limiting what God can do in our lives. We have even been given "The Mystery of Surrender" rosary to help us with this. We might not be able to surrender everything at once, but we can start somewhere.

It is also important to look at *why* we can't or won't surrender something. What is behind it? What needs to be healed? In truth, surrender brings a freedom, a happiness that replaces the fear of surrender. I love Mother Teresa's quote *"When I see someone sad, I always think, she is refusing something to Jesus."*[161]

I once had a humorous experience with non-surrender. In the early 1980s, the Church had a visionary plan for the development of Camelot (Church headquarters located near

Los Angeles) that was called "Victory in the Holy City." Staff members were asked to visit local Keepers of the Flame to explain the vision in more detail, in hopes of encouraging financial support for the project. One day I phoned a lady to simply make an appointment for a visit when in the middle of a sentence she blurted out, "I'm not going to sell my Cadillac!" So much for her concept of sacrificial giving! Her point of surrender stopped at her Cadillac, even though we were not asking anything of the kind.

Fear Can Be the Origin of Self-Limiting Behavior

As I shared earlier, fear is often the origin of self-limiting behavior. We know all that fear can encompass. There is also a unique fear that we who are striving to be Chelas with a capital "C" must face—the fear of what the path of our Christhood will require of us, what price we must pay in pursuit of that path.

Like many fears, this one is irrational for the true chela. We are here because we love God and want to fulfill his purpose for our lives and for the planet. By God's grace, we have recognized the opportunity that is before us. We have declared ourselves as candidates for the ascension. We have studied the experiences of many saints. Yet there is still the unknown for us individually.

We know that the human cannot inherit the Divine and that our human consciousness, our dweller-on-the-threshold must be bound so that we may walk the earth as a Christed one. The price of our Christhood is the demise of all within that prevents our soul from becoming one with our Holy Christ Self. It isn't really a price—it is our freedom!

Do we fear suffering? The saints suffered and yet some said they wouldn't give it up if they could. Padre Pio basically said, "I *only suffer when I am not suffering!"*[162] We have been told that pain is the portal to bliss, but are we afraid of experiencing pain?

Do we fear surrender, that perhaps we won't have our favorite dishes or our Cadillac anymore? Do we resist forgiving ourselves or others? Is there fear of accountability and all that it entails? Fear of losing the excuses for not doing better or making the extra effort? I remember a sign stenciled on my high school gym class wall: "Don't make excuses. Make good." Short and to the point.

One of my favorite bible verses is from the Apostle Paul in 1 Corinthians 13:11: "*When I was a child, I spake as a child, I understood as a child, I thought as a child: but when I became a man, I put away childish things.*" We are mature chelas of the ascended masters and we have the knowledge and the way to eliminate the things that block our path. With the sword of Mighty Cosmos and our walk with Jesus, nothing need hold us back!

We Have a Saviour

I recall a dictation that told us that earth is a special planet because it has a Saviour. Our Saviour is Jesus, our elder brother whom God chose to be that Saviour! Can't you just imagine the scene of Jesus before the throne of Alpha and Omega being anointed as the Saviour of the lightbearers of earth?

What does having a Saviour mean to us? Christian orthodoxy casts Jesus' role as a "get out of jail free" card—Jesus did it all, and all we have to do is accept him and we will be in heaven forever. However, as students of the masters, we understand the truth is that he held our karma in abeyance for the past two thousand years so that we could work toward our ascension.

Beyond being our Saviour, Jesus is the lover of our souls, and his love for us transcends our current human experience. I believe many of us were with him on Atlantis during the Golden Age there. And no doubt many of us were with him during his Palestinian incarnation as well. In reality, he knows us better than we know ourselves.

We can have an intimacy with Jesus if we accept it into our life. I think the hymn "In the Garden" is so popular because it reflects that personal intimacy—"a joy none other has ever known"—our unique and very personal walk with our Lord.

Jesus knows how to help us get Home if we will allow it. He can help us overcome self-limitation. He has even offered to be in our temple and fulfill the role of our Holy Christ Self until we have achieved our own Christhood. In Jesus' dictation we are hearing today he says, *"As I have said to you, 'Occupy till I come,'*[163] *so I say to you now, allow me to occupy."*[164] So until we unite with our Christ Self, we can ask him to "occupy till I come." This is not an idle request. We *know* we need help. We must become dependent before we can become independent. In humility we bend the knee, accepting the presence of our Lord and asking his intercession.

He tells us he comes *"quietly, softly, gently."*[165] Isn't that sweet? He promises us that he has *"come to repair both the house and its occupant."*[166] But he cannot help us unless we allow him in—into our hearts, into our temple, into *"compartments of shame or self-glory or self-deprecation."*[167] To that end, he teaches us this prayer that allows him to enter in and do his work:

> *Jesus, I bid you enter my whole temple now!*
> *By my free will, by my God-dominion, I welcome you!*
> *And I let go of everything, my Lord.*[168]

It is a simple prayer, but I suspect it is more powerful than we can imagine. It is easy to remember, easy to give, and giving it daily will have a profound effect on our lives and the acceleration of our path!

A Warrior and a Carefree Child

Overall, I think it is accurate to describe ourselves as warriors of the Spirit. We have been called upon to go to battle not only with our karma and our dwellers, but also with the forces of darkness that would destroy our path and that of every lightbearer on this planet. However, there is a time in our lives when we must put aside this battle and simply love God for the sake of loving Him.

Mother told us that when her day ended and at long last the demands upon her receded, it brought her great joy to lie in bed and send her profound love to God. As warriors, we must not deny ourselves the love and nourishment of God and our Saviour. It is what will sustain us and, more importantly, help us put on our own Christhood.

We must know when to be the warrior and go after our self-imposed limitations and when to become the little child as Jesus calls us to do. This is crucial because we cannot be victorious without the help of our Lord. We need him to do battle over the part of our human consciousness that is stronger than our ability to overcome it.

We do not want him to come to us but be unable to receive him because of self-condemnation, our sense of unworthiness or our refusal to surrender all to him and to God. Jesus tells us that the way to begin the battle over these things and all self-limitations is to become as a four-year-old child, to take his hand and be carefree.

Can we remember what it is like to be carefree? Are we so battle weary that we cannot close our eyes and be again as that little child, so full of hope, so full of joy at picking a flower or trying to catch a butterfly? Our Lord is asking us to be like that child as the starting point of our journey. Being childlike is quite different than being childish. And by our dependency we will learn to be independent.

You will hear today of the deep and profound love that Jesus has for us. Knowing that our God loves us and will be with us is a comfort beyond words. Do we not long for the presence of our Lord? He tells us it *"is the springtime of love, when I receive you as my own, my very own disciple, and when you can receive me as your very own Master."* [169]

Can we integrate into our consciousness the love of our Saviour and all he has pledged to do to help us? Yes, if we begin as a little child holding his hand in absolute trust. Does a child have a sense of unworthiness before our Lord? Of course not! So we shouldn't either. We can simply pray, "Lord, I AM worthy, make me worthier still." We can walk our path with integrity, with daily striving, even with the remnants of our karma still unbalanced, even with work not completed on our psychology, even with any self-limitation that tries to hold us back.

Must putting on our Christhood in this embodiment be only a dream? We know the answer. And we know that to overcome our defenses, our self-limitations or anything else, we will do our part, and we will take the hand of our Lord to see the victory while we yet walk the earth. What a gift to give to God! What a gift to give to our Saviour!

"Here is my outstretched hand, my Lord. Please take it because I trust you, I love you and I surrender my all.

Jesus, I bid you enter my whole temple—now and forevermore! Amen."

THE ALCHEMY OF MERCY

*Therefore be thou not troubled, neither dread;
but trust strongly in Me, and in My mercy
have perfect hope...*

—THE IMITATION OF CHRIST

The Alchemy of Mercy

Today's reading is from *The Imitation of Christ:*

> *Wherein then may I trust, or in whom may I have any confidence, but only in the great grace and endless mercy of God? For neither the company of good men, nor the fellowship of devout brethren and faithful friends: neither the having of holy books or devout treatises, nor the hearing of sweet songs or of devout hymns, may little avail, and bring forth but little comfort to the soul, when we are left to our own frailty and poverty.*[170]

Considering that those words were written in the 15th century, it's obvious that the soul's plea for mercy is not a new one. The Book of Psalms, written long ages ago, is replete with the cries of one burdened by his sins and mistakes while simultaneously affirming the mercy of God. Take Psalm 25:7 for instance: *"Remember not the sins of my youth, nor my transgressions: according to thy mercy remember thou me for thy goodness' sake, O Lord."* I think most of us could say that prayer—"Remember not the sins of my youth!" Or consider Psalm 31:9: "*Have mercy upon me, O LORD, for I am in trouble: mine eye is consumed with grief, yea, my soul and my belly.*" By the choice of words, you can almost feel the author's despair and anguish. He doesn't know what to do. He cries out to God for mercy with his whole being.

Can't we identify with the pain of a soul in trouble, filled with remorse? And while we have the ascended masters' teachings to help us, many others do not. Mother Mary and the Seven Archangels said, "*We ask you to remember that many have far greater pain than you do. They are hopeless, and that hopelessness has been with them perhaps for thousands of years.*"[171] That's pretty stunning, isn't it? Hopeless for thousands of years!

Not much has changed since the writing of the Psalms or *The Imitation of Christ*. It's as if by praising God's mercy, we are affirming that very mercy in our lives. Mercy gives us hope as we face both personal and planetary karma. Again, from *The Imitation of Christ*, "*Therefore be thou not troubled, neither dread; but trust strongly in Me, and in My mercy have perfect hope...*"[172]

What wonderful, encouraging words—"in My mercy have perfect hope"!

Kuan Yin, the Goddess of Mercy, described mercy as "*the love that allows the brokenhearted to pick up the pieces of shattered, battered lives and to begin again.*"[173] Even if our lives are not shattered, unless we have hope, unless there be the mercy of God, how could we begin again after we wittingly or unwittingly continue to make karma.

Worthiness Before God

One of my favorite Bible verses is Hebrews 8:12: "*For I will be merciful to their unrighteousness, and their sins and their iniquities will I remember no more.*"

We can have a hard time forgetting our sins. We may be burdened that we have committed them. And then there are the little demons that continually whisper in our ears, reminding us of *all* our mistakes, not just from this embodiment, but our other embodiments as well. And that can weigh heavily upon us. Yet the truth is that once we balance the karma, which we're doing by God's grace, God will remember our sins "*no more!*" What a comfort to our soul!

Our sins and negative karma are *not* who we are. They are mistakes we have made and energy we have misqualified, but that is *not* who we are. We are *not* worthless sinners, as the orthodox Christian churches so often tell us. We are sons and daughters of God who have made karma. And by God's grace, we are going to balance that karma. We *are* worthy to balance that karma!

But is mercy for all? Is it freely given when requested? Is it given, as many Christians believe, without limit to those who are "saved" or perhaps even to those who are not? As students of the ascended masters, we are taught to understand mercy not as the end of our salvation, but as the beginning.

The book *The Masters and their Retreats* says that the ascended lady master Kuan Yin "*represents the qualities of mercy and compassion to the evolutions of earth. The mercy flame is the means whereby the Christ intercedes on behalf of those who have erred, who cannot bear the full brunt of the Law that demands swift recompense for each violation. The quality of mercy tempers the return of mankind's karma, staying the hand of justice until that time when individuals are able to stand, face and conquer their human creation.*"[174]

Do you remember some of the stories in the Old Testament? If you worshiped the golden calf or touched the Ark of the Covenant—ZAP—you were dead! Returning karma was often instantaneous, and you'd have to wait until your next embodiment for another opportunity.

But the grace and mercy of God manifested in the coming of our Saviour, Jesus, who has borne our karma for the past two thousand years so that we could prepare to bear it ourselves in this age. Mercy has been of supreme help to us in getting ready for this hour of our karmic reckoning.

Renewed Opportunity

God is merciful to our unrighteousness because, as Kuan Yin explains, *"Mercy, then, is extended to all of the Lightbearers of the cosmos this day as renewed opportunity—renewed opportunity."*[175]

Renewed opportunity. The days go by, the months, the years. Whatever age we are now, we were younger at one time, some of us much younger. Time moves on. What have we done with that time? Have we taken advantage of the opportunity that God has given us? All of us could no doubt say, "I could have done better." So today we can ask ourselves, "What about right now? Am I taking advantage of the opportunity that mercy has afforded me this day?"

It is mercy beyond words that God has given us time and space and knowledge as renewed opportunity. Even as the rain falls on the just and the unjust,[176] so does the mercy of opportunity. Every day is an opportunity. Every day is a grace.

We also know that there is a limit to opportunity and mercy for those who do not embrace it. In other words, there is both a personal and an impersonal aspect of mercy and they manifest in different ways. We have been admonished: *"Work while ye have the light."*[177] We take that seriously, following the Path and doing what we know to do to gain our soul's victory. Conversely, for those who adopt the philosophy of "Eat, drink, and be merry for tomorrow we die," that attitude can unfortunately become a prophecy for their souls.

Mercy endows us with the power of complete soul liberation. And can you imagine a greater gift of mercy than the violet flame? How many of us could hope to make our ascension in this life without the violet flame? Few, perhaps, so let us make sure we take advantage of the opportunity to invoke it.

I would guess that most of us don't let a day go by without asking God for mercy. But let us not forget the abundance of mercy that we already have—opportunity, knowledge, the violet flame. Truly, we are blessed!

Some may think of mercy as the surcease of struggle and karma, praying, "Oh, God, take this burden from me. It's too heavy." But the accelerated return of our karma is also a mercy when we have the violet flame and the power to forgive and be forgiven. Whatever can help us to put on our Christhood and get home to God is a mercy if we avail ourselves of it.

God is not asking us to practice extreme penances or to wear hair shirts like many of the saints did in the past. Nevertheless, the apostle James reminds us that life "is even a vapour, that appeareth for a little time, and then vanisheth away."[178] So while we have life and opportunity, it is a mercy that our karma comes back to us. If our karma did not return so we could balance at least fifty-one percent of it, we could not ascend!

The Requirements for Mercy

Mercy is not passive. It is active. If we want to receive mercy, the law has requirements.

In *The Book of Enoch* the story is told of the group of fallen angels called the Watchers that left heaven to pursue the "daughters of men." It explains that they introduced great darkness on the earth, including war. Because of all this, God proclaimed a judgment upon them that denied them any mercy or peace. This grieved the Watchers. So because they could not address God directly since their fall, they beseeched Enoch to write a prayer for forgiveness for them and take it to God. Imagine what a scene that must have been! Enoch did as they asked, but God denied the request, confirming their judgment.[179]

So what was lacking in the Watchers' petition? Simple. What was missing were the requirements for mercy: repentance and a willingness to do penance. Therefore, in seeking mercy, we repent of our deeds and we are willing to do penance, which means balancing the negative karma through decrees, prayers, and service to life.

Did the Watchers want forgiveness because they truly repented of their deeds? Or did they want forgiveness so they could continue their evil ways and still get God's blessings? Today, there are some Christians who believe that once you accept Jesus and are "saved," no matter what you do, you still get to heaven. I wonder who came up with that theology!

No matter how many good deeds or how seemingly observant we are of the Path and the Law, we *cannot* receive mercy without repentance and penance. Those are the requirements for mercy.

Kuan Yin teaches that giving mercy without the fulfillment of these requirements is the "*abuse of mercy.*"[180] And there are those who abuse mercy. Many of you may remember or have read about the pardoning of Richard Nixon by President Ford soon after Nixon resigned from the presidency. Nixon didn't show any repentance and certainly no desire for penance, which makes it seem that his being pardoned could be an example of the abuse of mercy.

Compassion Not Sympathy

A key teaching for anyone on the spiritual path is that mercy equates with compassion, *not* sympathy. While I have highlighted this in other sermons, it is such a vital teaching for our path, and the testings can be so subtle. Sympathy takes us down to a person's human level. By contrast, compassion raises a soul upward! And sometimes compassion is taking a firm stand with a person and allowing the soul to learn the lesson it needs, even if it is painful.

Mrs. Prophet gave the following teaching about this:

You do not need to go out and have sympathy for the human ego that is suffering because it has failed to bend the knee and enter into the love, the true love of the guru-chela relationship. And that is where children of the light can be caught, to squander their light through sympathy. And that is where you know you do not have perfect love. And that is where you recognize that there is a very intense magnetism that is put forth from those who are engaged in self-pity, through an enlarged and inflamed ego. And that pulling puts upon you a sense of obligation, "You owe it to me to take care of me, to help me, to give me your light, your money, your support, your time, your prayers because I can't do it for myself." That is the message that the fallen ones are sending over the wireless of the entire planetary body, and they enlist the lightbearers of the nations in their support. This is a perversion of mercy's flame.[181]

When we have misused energy it is not enough to say, "Oh, let's just move on, let bygones be bygones and start afresh." El Morya teaches:

...if you are outside of the Law, whether human or divine, you must quickly confess your sins to the appropriate persons, make rectitude, correct such states and come into alignment. For the sin not confessed, the illegal posture not acknowledged, though none may know about it, does prevent the karma from descending and therefore [does prevent] the expiation of that karma—even if you give the violet flame decrees daily.[182]

In other words, we can do violet flame daily for years but unless we have fulfilled those requirements, we cannot move on because that particular karma is still unbalanced. Confession, repentance and the willingness to balance that karma are necessary. Simply put, mercy cannot fully act in one's world until the requirements of the law are met.

Kuan Yin admonishes us to consider the *"quality of heart of Mercy."*[183] To embody that quality we must work for the softening of the heart so that there is no spirit of condemnation within us. *"Mercy, then, is not a state of the human consciousness,"*[184] but of the divine mind. Just as Jesus did not condemn the adulterer, so we cannot condemn anyone. God is the judge, not us.

However, we need to understand mercy's discrimination and how it manifests. Though the mercy of the law will bring a soul up higher, mercy does not always look like a big hug.

The Mercy of Judgment

Kuan Yin said mercy comes to the children of God in the form of the judgment of their oppressors. She further states, *"And that Mercy is also Mercy to the oppressors and even to the seed of the Wicked One."*[185]

One might ask how does that work? When the judgment

of mercy descends on those making intense karma, they are stopped in their tracks and may no longer continue making karma. They are paused, and in some cases even jailed, so they can contemplate their actions of years or lifetimes of unchecked attacks against people.

I recently saw a movie about Bonnie and Clyde, a couple who went on a prolonged crime spree in the early 1930s, traveling with a gang, robbing banks and stores and even funeral homes, stealing cars, kidnapping and murdering people, and engaging in all kinds of criminal activities. It was a reign of terror covering several states, and the police couldn't catch them. It took an ambush and shootout in which they were both killed to finally stop them. They could do no more harm or make any more negative karma in that lifetime.

When people go on karma-making sprees, it is mercy that they be stopped. That often occurs through circumstances and in some instances by death. It was a mercy for Bonnie and Clyde that they were not allowed to continue making more negative karma, as well as a mercy for possible future victims.

Kuan Yin states very clearly: *"the judgment of God itself is a great mercy to evildoers."*[186] Most people have probably never thought about judgment being mercy. For example, consider the question of capital punishment. Many Christians say, "We shouldn't stoop to the level of the murderer and take someone's life. That's not what Jesus taught." But that is a misunderstanding of mercy based, of course, on not believing in karma and reincarnation. Which is better for the soul's progress: that a person sits in jail for twenty, thirty or forty years, or that they give up their life through capital punishment, balance their karma or a great portion of it, and then reembody and start anew? Capital punishment is mercy when looked at from the perspective of a soul's eternal victory.

Mercy and the Lessons of Life

Now, what is mercy and what is justice? C.S. Lewis wrote, *"Mercy, detached from Justice, grows unmerciful."*[187] Isn't that interesting? Let's consider how mercy detached from justice can become unmerciful.

The term "post-Christian" has been used to describe the current state of western civilization. That state is very easy to see in today's skewed perception of right and wrong. We've all heard the terms "mercy killing" and the "right to die." Since man is viewed as an evolved animal in the so-called post-Christian era, then why not practice euthanasia and mercy killing? The truth is that while it may end temporal suffering and pain when little hope remains, it denies the soul's need for balancing karma and learning lessons through that illness or circumstance. It also replaces God's will for a person's life with *human convenience* masquerading as mercy.

Regarding the current standards of western culture, Kuan Yin says, *"...the concept of right and wrong is that pain is wrong and pleasure is right. And this, beloved, is not the standard of our God!"*[188] She goes on to explain that sometimes pain is a crucial part of the spiritual path:

> *For the transmutation of pain in the enduring of pain is truly the passport to bliss, for those energies invested in conditions that are pain-causing are the very energies that must be withdrawn that the bliss of God might descend when the karma is balanced.*[189]

The elimination of pain and suffering is truly mercy when it mitigates the person's karma of the wrong use of God's light. On the other hand, Kuan Yin says, *"But to take away pain and suffering at the price of the soul's learning the lessons of her karma is not the wisdom of the Law."* [190]

Why aren't we in bliss right now? Karma. Why aren't we walking in the garden with Jesus? Karma. We need to balance that karma so we may enter into the bliss of God!

Burdens come to people for a reason. The wife of Peter Marshall, the Chaplin of the U.S. Senate in the 1950s, told the story about the time she got very ill and the medical treatments she received did not help. Not knowing what else to do, she wrote a letter to every person she knew asking for forgiveness for anything she had ever done that might have hurt them. She took accountability, though she didn't even necessarily know what she had done wrong. But after she had sent the letters, she recovered from the illness!

Be careful not to exclude yourself from mercy by thinking, "Well, I'm balancing karma. I guess there isn't going to be mercy for me." Mother told us the story of one of her embodiments where she was the daughter of a king. She got upset, set a village on fire and burned down all the houses. Obviously not a good thing to do, and something that would normally result in serious karma! The law is exacting.

But as a result of the mercy of the law, all the service Mother had rendered, all the prayers and calls and violet flame she had given, the karma was mitigated. One day when she was cooking, she got a small burn on her hand. Mark told her that this burn served as a token to balance that karma. I think we can all agree that that was a great mercy. She had learned the lesson, so she could receive a token karma and not have to experience the full karma.

We know that our karma will eventually return, that we must face it and that we will not be totally excused from it. But let us not forget that we can receive mercy and grace as we apply the Law and follow the requirements for mercy.

We recognize that the honor of God requires that we work to balance our karma, and that is accelerated by giving violet flame decrees and serving life. We don't want a free pass to heaven! In the integrity of our soul, we want to balance at least fifty-one percent of our karma and right the wrongs we have done so that we might enter heaven standing in the dignity and light of our Holy Christ Self and I AM Presence. This is the mighty work of the ages that we might return to God after the *"long ages of the karma of separation."* [191]

We feel that karma of separation in our souls because we have been separated from God for a very long time. We left our first estate because of our free will choice to embody in the physical plane. We chose to learn the lessons of life, but along the way we forgot who we really are. We made mistakes and fell from grace. We were expelled from the presence of the guru in the Garden of Eden, and we have been separated from God for so, so long. I think that's why the song's words "O Father, O my Mother, I AM coming Home!" deeply resonate with so many people.

This has been an intense journey for our souls—a journey to experience free will, to make karma, to balance karma, to learn of the darkness that the fallen ones have brought and how that must be overcome. But we have come together in this hour and, if we choose, that long separation can come to an end. We miss God. We miss our true home of light, and we are ready to return.

We don't have to keep reembodying for another five, ten, or fifty thousand years. It's not necessary, and it's not God's will for most of us. Therefore, we need to take this opportunity to work with the Law, to work with mercy. We know that we cannot walk the Path without mercy and grace. They are the balm that soothes us after confession and repentance.

Anti-Mercy

Ascended Lady Master Kuan Yin was the chohan of the seventh ray before Saint Germain. She has great attainment on the violet ray. It is interesting to note that to embody the God-quality of mercy and receive the office of the Goddess of Mercy, she had to overcome the entire force of *anti-mercy* in cosmos.

Just imagine the challenge of dealing with the immense energy of anti-mercy that the fallen ones hurled at her: "So, Kuan Yin, you want to embody mercy? Fine. How do you like this?"

It takes tremendous courage to face that level of darkness. It takes being totally determined and centered in your heart. In fact, it takes great love to embody any God-quality which we have all been asked to do. Kuan Yin paid the necessary price, passed all the initiations, and won her eternal victory. That is why she can be the instrument of so much mercy. We can barely imagine how many prayers for mercy come to her each day! It doesn't matter what religion people follow or if they are even on a spiritual path, the plea for mercy is universal.

Kuan Yin's Advice for Receiving Mercy

But what about the sincere devotee who is praying for mercy but has a certain karma that is blocking it? Kuan Yin has the answer:

> *I ask you to prove me, to make your demands upon me and to command my Light and to keep on so doing until you should sense you have reached the limitations of my office. For I tell you, beloved, there is no thing of the will of God that I will not alchemically precipitate if you are able to bear it, [if you are able] to hold the harmony for it, and if you [will] seek the*

internal integration of the soul in the Seventh Ray chakra with the fiery heart of the living Christ Bodhisattva.

What I am saying, beloved, [is] if that for which you call is given to you and in your receiving of it you can deal with its manifestation and all opposing forces to its manifestation [and if you can be counted upon to make every effort to do so], then I, Kuan Yin, in the name of the will of God and my commitment to all Lightbearers of this planet, will surely bring that manifestation into your life.[192]

What a dispensation!

Let's consider the keys Kuan Yin gave us for receiving mercy.

• **Command her light and keep on doing so.** Give your prayers, your invocations, your calls to the violet flame, the Kuan Yin mantras. Command the light. Draw forth the light. We know we pay as we go, and as we draw forth that light, we are giving the energy to Kuan Yin to help us.

• **What we call for must be the will of God.** That should be self-evident, and it plays an important part in receiving mercy.

• There is nothing she will not "alchemically precipitate if you are able to bear it, to hold the harmony for it and seek the internal integration of the soul in the Seventh Ray chakra." In other words, **we have to do our part.** We can't be passive if we expect to receive mercy. We must be active. That's why if we are sick or very ill, we don't just plead for mercy or healing. We find and use the healing tools God has provided in this age. Hopefully, by mercy's grace, Kuan Yin will lead us to the right treatment at the right time in the right place. We must do our part and hold the balance as we are able, so that Kuan Yin may give us her mercy.

- **Deal with the opposition.** Yes, there is opposition to mercy. Do you think the fallen angels want mercy for the children of God? Of course they don't. So we make the calls for the binding of the force of anti-mercy that prevents the deliverance of mercy to the sons and daughters of God, especially for those who do not know how to call for mercy.

- **Receive and Extend Mercy.** Our part in receiving mercy is just as important as Kuan Yin's part in extending mercy because without both parts it cannot happen.

Mercy adjudicates the harshness of the law as we strive to balance even a token of the karma through our heart's devotion. Kuan Yin is ready to intercede on our behalf. We must be ready to do our part.

Kuan Yin has described mercy as *"...the fire in winter that kindles the hearth of home and chases the morning chill."*[193] Isn't that a beautiful image? Haven't we all experienced a moment when, in distress or discouragement, someone has been the manifestation of mercy to us? It may be as simple as the right word that addresses a soul's need for kindness. Sometimes just being with a child or a friend is a mercy, a comfort.

God Needs Us

Life is difficult for the lightbearers on earth. It is good to remind ourselves that the little things we do can be very, very important for other people.

Mrs. Prophet taught:

Sometimes these little deeds seem so insignificant that we do not perform them. It's not important to say something kind to someone. It's not important to stop someone and convey a

*message of the teaching, or it's not important to do something
very basic, such as feeding someone, helping someone change
a tire—very physical daily needs that people have. When we
think, "It really doesn't matter whether I do this or not, it really
doesn't matter whether I say my decrees or not," it shows the
absence of self-worth.... You have not realized how God really
needs you.... God has a need for you! God is not self-sufficient
even as man is not self-sufficient.*[194]

I read that and I thought, "Wait a minute! What does that
mean, 'God is not self-sufficient?'" What I believe it means is
that God is not self-sufficient on earth because he has given
us the mantle for this planet, and he needs us to be his hands
and feet here. That's our responsibility. That's our calling.
The earth is the Lord's, but it's our responsibility to be him
in manifestation here. Doesn't that give you a sense of self-
worth in God?

Mother continued:

*...Then when you have that sense that your love is needed,
you live life with such a great zest of joy and happiness and
fulfillment that no thing can take from you your joy.*[195]

Twice Blessed

Remember what the author of the Shakespeare plays, our
beloved Saint Germain, wrote in *The Merchant of Venice:*

*The quality of mercy is not strain'd,
It droppeth as the gentle rain from heaven
Upon the place beneath: it is twice blest;
It blesseth him that gives and him that takes.*[196]

Twice blessed: the giving and receiving of mercy. And you can't give mercy without receiving it at the same time. Mercy and forgiveness go hand in hand on the seventh ray. There are times when we need mercy and forgiveness, and there are times when we need to forgive and give mercy.

Mercy is transforming. You can't give mercy without becoming mercy. You must have mercy to give it. Remember what Jesus taught in Matthew: "*For unto every one that hath shall be given, and he shall have abundance: but from him that hath not shall be taken away even that which he hath.*" [197] In other words, with regard to mercy, if you have no mercy, you're not going to get it; if you have mercy, you're going to get more of it.

Does mercy always look the same for the giver and the receiver? Obviously not. I remember a story my grandmother used to tell where she was the giver of mercy and a friend of hers was to be the receiver. But it turned out that my grandmother was also the receiver.

She was a devout Christian and always tried to live her faith. This incident happened during the Great Depression when she had no car. It was late one Sunday night, and a friend of hers was sick and needed some things. My grandmother embarked on foot through the cold and snow to deliver what was needed. She related that getting there was much harder than she thought it would be. She came to a steep hill and felt there was no way she could make it up. As she was thinking about it and saying a silent prayer, she suddenly realized she was standing on top of the hill! She had no recollection of how she got there. She always felt that Jesus carried her up. Maybe it was Jesus, or maybe the angels, or perhaps Kuan Yin!

That is a beautiful story of mercy, where a soul decided to be the instrument of mercy, and mercy came to her in a very physical way.

Retreat Into Your Secret Chamber

It's a rough world. The vibration of this planet is harsh and coarse—the language, the music, the situations and energies that we encounter so frequently. All of this harshness makes it hard to perceive the delicacy of the presence of God, of beloved Kuan Yin and her mercy.

To get away from the crass sounds and vibrations of the earth, we need to go within, into our heart's secret chamber. That's a wonderful way to attune to and develop the merciful heart.

Kuan Yin called for us to teach the children to enter into the secret chamber of their heart, to kneel before their threefold flame, and to honor the Christ and the Buddha within.[198] This ritual is important for all of us.

At any time and in any place—in the middle of a decree or song, when you're walking in nature or taking a break at your desk—you can close your eyes and see yourself praying in the secret chamber of your heart. Your threefold flame, as small as it may seem, appears very large when you enter into that chamber, that interior castle. We honor and adore that flame because it is the presence of God within us. We bend our knee and acknowledge that light and our desire to become one with that light.

Allow yourself to experience God. *Go there to experience God*, to bow at that altar where your Holy Christ Self is present, where our Lord Jesus and Gautama Buddha abide. Go there and just rejoice in the light. Rejoice in the love. Rejoice in the presence of God which is real! That presence is the reality of life. Everything else is unreal.

That is how to deal with the harshness of life on earth. That is how to get to the point where you have the delicate sensitivity to recognize a soul in need. It's easy to see when someone needs a flat tire changed. It's not always easy to see when someone's soul is burdened and they are in great pain.

The Alchemy of Mercy

There is an alchemy to love and there is an alchemy to mercy—both giving and receiving. If we are to be the hands and feet of Kuan Yin, of Mother Mary, of our Christ Self and God, then we need to open our hearts. We need to perfect our hearts, soften our hearts, and call upon the flame of mercy, not only for our own souls, but for all the souls of light on this planet.

As we extend mercy, we will become more sensitive to the need for mercy, whatever appearance that takes. If you ask God to show you opportunities to extend mercy, you will get those opportunities. Giving mercy will be self-reinforcing. The joy of helping someone, of sharing, of giving of yourself, is the joy of life. We don't think a lot about our problems, our aches and pains when we're doing things for other people. If we want to have joy, it's good to give of ourselves.

If we want to be like Kuan Yin, we have to practice being the embodiment of mercy, whether it's helping someone on a very personal level, or it's saying "No" when they're crying for mercy for all the wrong reasons.

Kuan Yin says, *"The merciful heart is the heart of God. This is a basic truth. The conclusion is that when you have the merciful heart, you are the heart of God in manifestation."*[199] Isn't that precious? Isn't that the deepest desire of our hearts—to be "the heart of God in manifestation?"

God is incomplete on this planet because he needs us. We can be the heart of God to other people if we confess, repent, and serve. When we invoke the violet flame early in the morning and accept its amazing grace of mercy into our life, we can be free of the burden of our daily karma and move on to fulfill the purposes of God.

This is the path of happiness! It is the path of returning Home. And let us, like Kuan Yin who paused before entering heaven, not turn away from a soul in need. As painful as it sometimes is to hear the cries of the unborn or those in need, the Buddha is willing to hear those cries. The ascended masters are willing to hear those cries. And they are willing to respond to those cries because of the merciful heart of God that is within them.

Let us also expand God's heart of mercy here on earth. Today and every day the choice is ours.

THE POWER
OF REGRET AND
THE TRAP OF GUILT
AND SHAME

*A mistake begets a joyous desire for excellence,
for self-overcoming, for reaching the star,
for being like El Morya.*

—OMRITAS

※

EIGHT

The Power of Regret and the Trap of Guilt and Shame

It was the day after the 1977 Easter conference at the Church headquarters in Pasadena, California. I had just moved to the Los Angeles area to be near the Church community. Even though I had been a Keeper of the Flame for a few years, I had never attended a major conference.

I was a decree novice at best, but decreeing during that conference was different. I was there at almost all the sessions, decreeing my heart out and absorbing the light from the dictations. I was exhilarated, and when the conference ended Sunday night I felt transformed.

Then Monday morning came, and I was back on my regular schedule and my lengthy commute to work. I was waiting patiently at a freeway exit that was considerably backed up with cars. As I slowly approached the head of the line, I noticed a red Porsche approaching very fast on my left side where there was no lane. The woman driver cut in line immediately in front of me.

I was caught off guard and a surge of anger swelled up in me at her recklessness and rudeness. As I felt the anger, I also felt something totally unexpected. I felt the light that I had garnered during the conference flow out of me just like air flows out of a burst balloon. I realized I had been had! The fallen ones had tricked me and stolen the light I had garnered at the conference.

After it happened, I knew I had failed a test, and I was very disheartened. As terrible as I felt, I was also determined never to be tricked in the same way again. I have never forgotten that incident, and to this day, I am still helped by the memory and the determination that my regret caused.

The Power of Regret

The Oxford Language dictionary defines having regret: to feel sad, repentant, or disappointed over (something that has happened or been done, especially a loss or a missed opportunity).[200]

Daniel Pink in his book *The Power of Regret* describes regret as *"the stomach-churning feeling that the present would be better and the future brighter if only you hadn't chosen so poorly, decided so wrongly, or acted so stupidly in the past."*[201] Pink reflects that *"Regret is not dangerous or abnormal, a deviation from the steady path to happiness. It is healthy and universal, an integral part of being human. Regret is also valuable. It clarifies. It instructs. Done right, it need not drag us down; it can lift us up."*[202]

Is there a person on this planet who doesn't have regrets? Some people say they have no regrets, but is that really true? The power of regret can freeze us where we are or motivate us to greater things.

If you want to know just how powerful regret can be, think of Judas and his betrayal of Jesus. Whatever his motivation might have been, he betrayed our Lord and he couldn't go back and change what he did. And though he is still universally condemned by the world, the masters said his regret was so great that he ascended in his very next embodiment. That means he balanced that karma in one lifetime, while most of the other apostles had still not ascended by the twentieth century. Regret can obviously be turned into positive motivation.

In his book about regret, author Robert Leahy states, "We either self-criticize or self-correct."[203] He describes the danger in regret: "You can get stuck in it, revolving on what you chose to do or not do, discounting the positives in your current life, criticizing yourself, and getting hijacked by a flood of negative feelings like anxiety, sadness, remorse, disappointment and despair...I could have, would have, should have, and we are off and running, being chased by regrets. Some of us never escape."[204]

Dealing with our mistakes and failures can be especially hard on the Path. It's easy to think: "I should have known better," or "I feel like a complete failure," or "Maybe I'm not cut out for the Path." How we handle regret is not only up to us, but it can also determine just how far we will progress on the Path. As chelas of the ascended masters, it's important that we do not allow ourselves to become stuck in our regrets. Beloved Oromasis and Diana make that very clear:

> All is not lost because you made a mistake. All is not lost because you have tripped, you have fallen, you have digressed, you have taken a backward step. These things are remediable when your heart is right. And when your heart is right, your regret will be great enough to assist you in not repeating the same mistakes again and again....
>
> So, you see, beloved, you must have enough regret to stop all human nonsense.[205]

Think about that: "You must have enough regret to stop all human nonsense." Regretting a mistake can help us recognize that we need to change, that we need to stop identifying with our human self and bond to our Christ Self. So don't be too hard on yourself when you feel regret. Instead use it to learn and grow.

Making Amends

As positive as regret can be in our lives, there can be situations where we regret something that we did, and although we may learn from it, we cannot completely correct it, as was the case with Judas. This can be especially true for us in how we treated a friend, a spouse or a child in the past that left them with emotional scars and unresolved pain.

Pink (the author of the book *The Power of Regret*) took a worldwide survey on regret. Thousands of people responded regarding what their greatest regrets were. Some involved family or relationship issues. Some concerned careers. Some of the most poignant ones were incidents that happened years earlier where the person had a chance to be kind and didn't take advantage of it or they said something on the spur of the moment that they knew hurt someone and they never apologized or did anything to correct it. Decades later they were still filled with remorse and regret for these seemingly minor things they had done.

We know the violet flame can balance such karma, but sometimes healing comes from doing something very physical. There is a powerful example of this in a scene from the movie *Gandhi*.

A Hindu man whose son had been killed by Muslims, bursts onto a terrace where Gandhi, weakened by weeks of fasting, is lying on a bed.

The man throws a chapati at Gandhi and shouts, "Eat! I'm going to hell but not with your death on my soul."

"Only God decides who goes to hell," the Mahatma responds quietly.

"I killed a child!" the man screams.

Gandhi winces and asks, "Why?"

The man's eyes well up with tears, "They killed my son, my boy. The Muslims killed my son."

"I know a way out of hell," Gandhi whispers. "Find a child. A child whose mother and father have been killed. A little boy about this high; raise him as your own. Only be sure that he is a Muslim and that you raise him as one."

The man backs away slowly, with a crazed look on his face, stops, and then turns around and falls at the Mahatma's feet, sobbing like a child.[206]

We can definitely learn from our regrets. And even when we can't fully correct the error on the outer, God can create a way for us to make amends and balance our karma. We do no service to God, ourselves or others by remaining frozen in regret when there is a way out. The first step is to *forgive ourselves* as we seek a way to balance the karma. We don't want to be caught in regret that prevents us from going forward. But having learned a valuable lesson we want regret to be an incentive to move on and do greater things.

Guilt and Shame

While we can find value in regret, it's hard to find value in guilt and shame. Saint Germain refers to them as a *"trap"*.[207]

From personal experience, from talking with others, and in

ministerial counseling, I have observed the enormous burden of guilt and shame on many lightbearers. It can be something that never leaves people—a weight around their necks that bows them down and colors all areas of their life. The fallen ones use it as a prime tool to hold back the spiritual progress of many lightbearers.

The masters have clear and profound teachings on guilt, shame, and their harbinger, unworthiness. If you are burdened by these things, please be gentle and kind with yourself as you gain a greater understanding and explore ways to overcome them.

Very few chelas are too easy on themselves. Rather it's just the opposite because we're striving and want to do our very best. We're working to balance our karma, put on our Christhood, and serve the ascended masters. We do not want to allow ourselves to be tormented or plagued by our past mistakes or let the burden of guilt and shame take us off the Path. Therefore we accept accountability for our mistakes, knowing that every karma can be balanced. In the dictation we're hearing today, El Morya says that no sin is so great that it cannot be forgiven or balanced.[208]

Five Pitfalls and Heaven's Perspective

Now we will look at five pitfalls on the Path, including self-condemnation, unworthiness, guilt and shame. And we'll look at some of the wonderful perspectives that the masters have given us to overcome them. As we cover these pitfalls, you can consider how they might be affecting you. You will also discover that they are tied to each other in such a way as to be almost inseparable. We might call them a whole ball of wax that needs to be cast into the sacred fire.

1. Negative Bias

We start out with a strike against us because human beings naturally have a bias toward negativity. This bias is our tendency to not only register negative stimuli more readily but also to dwell on any events involved. This negative bias means that we feel the sting of a rebuke more powerfully than we feel the joy of praise, or as a friend of mine said, "Our inner critic is often more powerful than our inner cheerleader!"

As humans, we tend to:

• Remember traumatic experiences better than positive ones.

• Recall insults better than praise.

• React more strongly to negative stimuli. Scientists have even found that there's more electrical activity in the brain from viewing an image of something bad than of something good.

• Think about negative things more frequently than positive ones.

• Respond more strongly to negative events than to equally positive ones.[209]

Some of this may be tied to our DNA because survival was key for early man. A person could make one mistake and his life would be over. So assuming a defensive posture in order to survive is not necessarily bad. We just have to be alert as to when we are falling into negativity.

2. Original Sin

Added to this bias, we also have the burden of original sin that the fallen angels have projected upon Christians for almost two thousand years. The diabolical message of original sin began with St. Augustine and is not biblical at all. The following quote from the 1530 "Augsburg Confession of Faith" is one example of how condemning this concept is. *". . . all men, born according to nature, are born with sin, that is, without the fear of God, without confidence towards God, and that this original disease or flaw is truly a sin, bringing condemnation and also eternal death to those who are not reborn through baptism and the Holy Spirit."*[210]

It doesn't get any worse than that—condemnation and eternal death! And that is what many are taught from the earliest age. I remember a Catholic children's book we got our daughter when she was little. We had to skip over the part where a baby is condemned to hell forever if it is not baptized! Imagine people believing this!

I grew up in a conservative Christian church and I remember some people almost reveling in pronouncing their worthlessness and their sins. That belief and declaration can be a convenient excuse for not working to improve ourselves or resolve issues in our psychology. "God will take me just as I am, a sinner saved by Jesus." Some Christians think they don't have to do anything to get to heaven except admit they're a sinner. No wonder they become angry when they pass on and find out that is just not true.

Today we have the masters' teachings that there is no such thing as original sin, that it is a figment of the human imagination.[211] But at the same time we also have the records of our embodiments in the Catholic Church when we were taught the doctrine of original sin. Since we were humble and didn't question our superiors, we absorbed that lie into our consciousness. Though we don't believe in original sin now, we should be on guard to notice when that deep and subtle sense of condemnation shows up as part of our psychology.

3. Aggressive Mental Suggestion

Along with these burdens, we have aggressive mental suggestion hammering on us almost continually, telling us how worthless we are.

The Sponsors of Youth address this issue for us. They say:

> *Understand, beloved, that all have made mistakes. All have departed from the straight and narrow path. Put it into the sacred fire. Call upon the law of forgiveness. And never, never, never believe what the fallen angels will whisper in your ear: "You are not worthy. What's the use? Don't even try. You won't make it." This they will tell you as long as you will listen to them. Take the fiats and let the fiats drown them out, beloved.*[212]

When I was new to the teachings, I had a real vulnerability to aggressive mental suggestion, even though I didn't know what it was. I was already prone to self-condemnation and burdened by unspecified guilt and shame. One day as I was getting ready for work, I had the idea that I'd really like to go to Summit University. Without realizing what was happening to me, I was immediately subjected to intense mental aggression regarding my unworthiness. The worst part is that I started to buy into it and to mentally agree with the projections as the demons listed my sins and shortcomings. I was thinking, "Yeah, that's true, isn't it?" Right at that moment the demons attacking me overplayed their hand. I heard a voice in my head proclaiming "You are the worst person in the world!" That broke the spell and I had to laugh—even I wasn't going to buy into that! Laughing at the attempts of the fallen ones, I remembered what Thomas More wrote: *"The devill that prowd spirite, cannot stand to be mokqued."*[213]

4. Unworthiness

Though we are striving to move forward on the Path, we have all felt a certain unworthiness as we looked upon our shortcomings. And as we get closer to our ascension what is left of our human substance and our karma becomes glaringly apparent. At the same time we must recognize that feelings of unworthiness open the door for guilt and shame and must be challenged.

The masters have some strong words regarding the sense of unworthiness. Astrea teaches *"that there is an element of human pride in entertaining the sense of not being worthy."*[214]

Sanat Kumara is even stronger is his assessment of unworthiness. He says:

> *And those who chasten themselves, fearing they are unworthy, let them understand that this concept [of unworthiness] is itself a biting indictment that has no validity in the eyes of God.*[215]

Only God can determine our worthiness. Jesus never condemned anyone. Did Jesus say to the adulterer caught in the act, "You are unworthy?" No. God will not condemn us and so we cannot condemn ourselves. God in us is worthy. Even so, a sense of unworthiness, resulting from guilt or shame, becomes a self-limiting and self-defeating energy. Mother Mary warns of the danger of this. She says:

> *When you entertain any sense of worthlessness whatsoever, or unworthiness, then that is the highest level of expression you reach. And you determine this each day.*
>
> *Because you have said to yourself, "I am not worthy to be that Christ, I am not worthy to be one with Mother Mary," you*

act the part and you have placed that ceiling above you. Well,
beloved ones, that ceiling does not stay put. Once it was twelve
feet high, then it was nine, then it was seven. And pretty soon,
if you are going to stay in that box of worthlessness, you will
find that the room will shrink and you will know the shrink-
ing-man, the shrinking-woman syndrome.[216]

Not only do these things hold us back on the Path but they
can be self-fulfilling. If we build a sense of unworthiness, we're
going to be constricted. And as long as we affirm that consciously or unconsciously we aren't growing in God, in fact
we're shrinking.

Entertaining a feeling of unworthiness can create a prison
for the soul that can stop our spiritual progress. It is an indulgence we cannot afford! We make a mistake or we remember a
past karma and we decide that we are unworthy and we have to
punish ourself for our sin. Do you see how doing that becomes
an indulgence? It takes courage to stand up and say: "I regret
this action. I ask for forgiveness, and I will correct it in the physical if possible. But I'm not going to let it define who I am." Judas
did not allow his betrayal of Christ to define who he was in the
ultimate sense. He balanced that karma and had his victory.

Let us accept in every atom of our being that we are worthy.
God is in our temple, and he would not be there if we were not
worthy. An antidote to this self-created prison is a greater
development of our heart through Saint Germain's heart meditation. It will expand and expand the heart and dissolve the
constricting energies of unworthiness.

5. Guilt and Self-Condemnation

What is so diabolical about guilt is that it can stop our forward progress and trap us in a prison of defeat and despair.

The Great Divine Director teaches:

> *There is a certain abjectness about conditions of guilt whereby individuals continue to multiply those undesirable conditions within their feeling and thinking worlds rather than to multiply the spirit of Christ-victory.*[217]

In other words, when we consider ourselves guilty, it can become a self-fulfilling edict because we multiply it in our worlds instead of focusing on a spirit of Christ-victory. Like attracts like. If you focus on negativity, that is the magnet you establish in your being. So focus on who you want to be like and what qualities you want to embody. Focus on El Morya, Saint Germain, Mother Mary. Focus on the qualities of joy, of kindness, of giving. You will become what you put your attention on.

If we focus on guilt, shame, unworthiness, and self-condemnation, that defines who we will be. That is the world we will live in. You can see how dangerous it is to the soul and how the condemning demons will amplify and expand those negative energies unless we challenge them and take a stand saying: "Thus far and no farther! Lord I am worthy, make me worthier still."

The result of indulging in negative feelings is especially sobering in God Meru's description of someone who engages in self-condemnation:

> *Some of you sit in the seat of the scornful. You are scornful toward yourselves. You condemn yourselves because you think you are not what you ought to be, that you have not made a great enough effort....*
>
> *Finally, the end result of self-condemnation is rebellion against the Deity. For man cannot live in self-condemnation, and thus he must throw off that which he imagines to be the*

angry God who is condemning him. Therefore he can only find his freedom by totally denying God. But who has created this God of condemnation but man himself, through his dissatisfaction with himself! [218]

Isn't that intense? We rebel against God when we engage in self-condemnation. We need to challenge that momentum in our world.

One final thought on this. Many of us have made a renewed determination to put on our Christhood following Saint Germain's admonition to set a date for bonding to our Christ Self and to work on the top five habits or behaviors we want to overcome. (This topic is covered more fully in Chapter 13.) He also informs us that on this path the light can also bring up darkness—something important to remember! He says:

Do not respond to the sudden impetus to guilt all over again when the light exposes more that can be overcome! After all, we have exposed the levels of your attainment. May we not, then, be privileged to expose a few more faults without your falling into the trap of guilt and shame? [219]

We should not be surprised if faults we thought we had mastered appear again. These could be coming from our unconscious mind where they may have been lurking for thousands of years. We cannot allow ourselves to be overwhelmed by them but should see them as another opportunity for achieving wholeness as we go after eliminating them.

Even after fifty years of bearing the stigmata, Padre Pio had doubts about himself and asked a brother if he thought he was saved! We will keep on no matter what comes up, knowing we can do what others have done and overcome this darkness.

A Joyous Desire for Excellence

While we can accept the concept of worthiness, how do we make it a reality in our day-to-day living? If we are burdened by our mistakes and the pain we have caused others, the first place to start is confession and calling on the law of forgiveness. I have found that writing letters and burning them is a powerful tool when you want to address a master, the Karmic Board or our Father-Mother God. Confessing to God or the masters allows the karma of our actions to descend and be balanced more quickly.

When we ask for forgiveness, we must first forgive ourselves. The problem for many of us is that even though God may have forgiven us and the karma may be balanced, we tend to continue to be weighed down by our mistakes. Kuan Yin speaks of this:

> As long as mankind are mindful of their sins and iniquities—of which God has said, "I will remember them no more... though they be as scarlet I will make them as white as snow"— so long will they continue to relive those experiences which in the past have caused them so much grief.[220]

Whenever we feel the condemnation of past errors coming upon us, we can use fiats to affirm God's forgiveness and our worthiness. Omritas puts this in perspective for us:

> There is a time for self-correction, which has nothing to do with self-condemnation! A mistake begets a joyous desire for excellence, for self-overcoming, for reaching the star, for being like El Morya. It is not a question of guilt. It is not a question of sin. It is not a question of self-flagellation. It is a realization of limitation: "I will conquer! I see this. I will cut through it. I will put it behind me."[221]

Have you ever thought of a mistake as "*a joyous desire for excellence?*" We are going to make mistakes. When we do, we can see it as a joyous opportunity to overcome, affirming that we will balance the karma. We can assume a victory stance rather than fall into a "woe is me" trap.

And what of our karma from previous lifetimes, both recent and distant? Jesus reminds us that we cannot take upon ourselves the burden of guilt for something we might have done twenty embodiments ago. We are not the same person who made those mistakes.[222] That allows us to look at past errors more objectively. Though we have the karma associated with our actions, we would not do the same thing again because we have grown in our Christhood. We will get on with the business of righting these wrongs by balancing the karma associated with them. Then we will move on.

I was very excited when I found El Morya's dictation that will be played today. It's titled "Rejoice, O People of God! *Be Grateful for the Gift of Violet Flame.*"[223] He reminds us just how powerful the violet flame is in transmuting karma. Of course we know that, but have we really pondered the miracle of the violet flame for our ascension? When the weight of current or past mistakes comes upon us, we know with a certainty the karma can and will be balanced by the violet flame. We have many good reasons to reject falling into the traps of guilt, shame and unworthiness, and the violet flame is number one!

God's Perspective

A big danger for chelas on the Path is losing perspective—the perspective of the reality of our God-being and the nonreality of our human ego, the perspective of ever moving toward our ascension and that there are forces of darkness that will do everything they can to prevent our victory. If we lose perspective and get caught in a sense of unworthiness, self-condemnation, guilt and shame, we cannot make progress. So every day I say this prayer, "El Morya, please give me perspective so I can see what is real, what is unreal, how to order my life and how to act."

Overcoming the sense of unworthiness, guilt and shame takes work, even with the violet flame. Such problems could be caused by a pattern of thinking that we have held for so long that we must work daily to see it and change it. It takes fiats. It takes affirmations. It takes a love of God and the fire of determination to forge our victory. For some, the intensity of certain experiences may require the help of a therapist.

The Great Divine Director reminds us:

> Your victory is not won by lamentation or despair or a feeling of unworthiness, but it is won because you continue to seek to express the fullness of the Presence.[224]

Who do people see when you come into the room? Do they see someone who is burdened and weighed down? Or do they see someone who may be dealing with many issues, but approaches them in a higher way? People often assume that someone who has the joy flame is not burdened with as many problems as others have. Often, that is far from the truth; rather, they have chosen the joy flame as an affirmation of who they really are in God—*despite* their problems.

While self-correction and balancing karma are key elements of our path, they are not the means to our ultimate victory. We *must* put on our Christhood and express the fullness of our Presence. The human will never be worthy no matter what we do. Let us understand that we can pursue our Christhood with a zeal not polluted by the weight of unworthiness, guilt and shame. I believe that many of us are closer to our victory than we think. The forces of darkness can see this and are pulling out all the stops to derail us. We cannot and, by God's grace, *will not* let that happen!

Just think what a victory it will be when we are no longer vulnerable to aggressive mental suggestion! It may still come, but we can defeat it by our calls and rebuking the devils that bring it.

Gautama Buddha offers this help for us:

> ...*as I see the capacity for you to break through the consciousness of limitation and mortality, I tell you, there is such an opportunity waiting for you just around the corner—yes, for you who have made those mistakes and who wallow in the sense of guilt!*
>
> *O give [that sense of guilt] to me this day!...*
>
> *I say to you, put all [human consciousness of guilt] in the flame of my heart this day; for [this day] is indeed an open door, as we have told you. This is a wondrous day for new beginnings.*[225]

What an offer from the Lord of the World! It can be a day of new beginnings if we choose it! He won't *take* our guilt; we have to *give* it to him. We must be the active part of this exchange.

As we give Gautama our guilt, we know that, should it reappear in the future, we can give that to him as well. And we know our guilt is intricately interwoven with shame and the sense of sin and unworthiness. Therefore Gautama is essentially offering us freedom from the traps they all entail and the freedom to win our victory.

So I'd like to just take a moment here in the quietness of our own being to take advantage of the offering of Gautama Buddha, and if we desire, to offer our guilt to him this day. [32 sec. pause]

The crown of victory awaits us when we overcome. Let us believe in the promises of God and our worthiness in Christ to wear that crown. Let us claim it now, for it is truly a day of new beginnings.

ONE WITH
GOD-DESIRE

*A man without desire is one whose fires are
not only banked but also nearly gone out.
Desire need not be suppressed but tethered
by a higher vision to a higher goal.*

—KUTHUMI

NINE

One with God-Desire

As a baby-boomer, I was part of the first generation to grow up with TV and shows like *Romper Room*, *Howdy Doody*, *Davey Crockett*, and my favorite—*Robin Hood*. I won't sing the theme song for you but, believe me, I could. In imitation of my hero, I had a bow and arrows with rubber tips. But there was something else I wanted that I did not have—a quiver like the leather cylinder Robin carried on his back to store his arrows. I informed my mother that I needed one, and *soon*.

My poor mother! I was nine or ten years old when this happened. She looked at me wondering, I'm sure, where in the world she was going to find a quiver. Back in those days there was no internet or big-box toy stores, and toy selection was generally very limited.

"Mom, I *REALLY* want a quiver!" I became obsessed with it. I truly wouldn't be happy until I got my quiver. I remember her saying that she just wasn't able to find one, but I wasn't concerned with any reason she might have—I *WANTED* it! I think I must have focused so much energy on getting it that it finally materialized in front of me. I never knew what my mother had to go through to find one, but there it was. I was overjoyed—I had the object of my desire!

I don't know how many times I actually played with it, as there was no real demand for me to draw multiple arrows from my quiver. So it was only a few days before it was laying in a pile of toys in my room. Though I got what I wanted, my happiness was fleeting. I don't know for sure what my dear mother might have felt, but I can almost hear her sighing when she saw the quiver's fate.

Beloved Nada may have been thinking of children like me when she said:

> ...beloved hearts, the world and all that's in it has programmed the desire body to want this, want that, and want the next—through visuals of advertising, through all kinds of things that delight the eye. And the child reaches out and says, "I want! That's mine. Give me this!" And thus, the child early learns that it can use the desire body to get those things of its wants, its absence of wholeness in God.
>
> And therefore, life is a game of acquiring. And therefore, a success cult is built up so that individuals may acquire more and more of those things.
>
> You have heard people say, "I've always wanted this, and here it is!"— "I've always wanted that, I've always wanted this." Well, the always wanting has tied up an enormous quantity of God's energy until the very Law itself has fulfilled the want, bringing it to one's feet, as in the proverbial story of Midas. ...
>
> Therefore, once entwined by a tight coil of desire, it is most difficult for individuals to free themselves. For I think we all know, who have walked this earth, that desires can be the most overpowering momentums in our lives.[226]

Think of that: *"Desires can be the most overpowering momentums in our lives."* No wonder we struggle! Lanello warns us that wrong desire *"is the single factor that takes people from the path of initiation."* [227] He also explains: *"Karmas themselves beget wrong desire."* [228] Wrong desires can be so strong that they pull us away from those things that we need to do and want to do. The Apostle Paul put it succinctly in Romans 7:19 when he said: *"For the good that I would, I do not: but the evil which I would not, that I do."*

Desire vs. Desirelessness

Gautama Buddha teaches that desire is the cause of all unhappiness. Does that mean that to be happy and please God we must be without desire? Yes and no. However, as long as we desire only the "quivers" of the material world, we will never be fulfilled.

Jesus gave a profound teaching on the balance of desire and desirelessness:

> *I come to proclaim the freedom of mankind. I come to proclaim the freedom of souls! But it is a freedom that must be invoked by desire on the one hand, by desirelessness on the other. The action of desiring to be Godlike must be balanced by desirelessness, wanting nothing of this world or of the next but only to be God.*
>
> *The state of Being is not the state of desiring. For the state of being the fullness of God, I AM, is the Buddhic state—a state of comfort, completeness, wholeness. That is the state of Being.*
>
> *But the state of desire is one of discontent. This, also, is a healthy state. For in order to obey the fiat to come up higher,*

you must be discontent with the planes where you have rested, with the morass of human life.[229]

Jesus not only said it is lawful to desire to be Godlike, but it's also lawful and healthy to have discontent because it can motivate us to do things differently.

Didn't we all start to seek a higher way because of the feeling that something was missing in our life? We desired to have a deeper understanding of life, to know more of the truth, and to become more than we were.

In other words, discontent can be good for a soul. It's like the story of Midas who turned everything he touched to gold. Then after he saw the folly of his choices, he turned and served God. Sometimes human desires must be satisfied to clear the way for higher desires.

Now, we also understand that there is lawful desire and unlawful desire, or another way of saying it is that there is ordinate desire and inordinate desire. Kuthumi teaches that:

...a man without desire is one whose fires are not only banked but also nearly gone out. Desire need not be suppressed but tethered by a higher vision to a higher goal. Men must learn the glorious system of reactivating the fires of their beings and redirecting them Godward.[230]

The Power of Our Desire Body

Without desire we would not have started on the Path. It is *wrong* desire that has gotten us into trouble!

We all have an emotional body or what is called a desire body. King Midas's desire body was obviously rather large, and perhaps many of us have a large one as well. Djwal Kul tells us about the desire body:

*The desire body, as we have said, is anchored in and releas-
es its energy through the solar plexus and the throat chakra.
The desire body of mankind contains a greater amount of
God's energy than any of the other three lower bodies.*†²³¹

Some desires may not be wrong in one sense, but sometimes
those desires can tie up our energy and keep us from doing the
things we need to do. And, unfortunately, people can get caught
up in the most mundane things. Take Beanie Babies, for example. Do any of you remember them? They were toys released in
the early nineties that soon became the rage. Certain Beanie
Babies were very rare, and some people felt it was a sign of success to collect every one of them. It seemed harmless in some
ways, but it wasn't harmless in the sense that it tied up people's
energy, their thoughts, their consciousness and their supply.
And for what—who wants to buy a Beanie Baby today?

Yet God made sure people had their fill of Beanie Babies—
according to cosmic law! Mother taught about this:

*When we have desire, by cosmic law God surfeits us in
the filling of that desire, because it's one means of getting
us through with the desire and beyond it. And so, unfulfilled
desires are always ticking time bombs waiting to go off. When
you keep desires in your subconscious...sooner or later you
will attract the object of your desiring.*²³²

Haven't we all experienced having a desire, whether it's a
quiver or another desire we focus our attention on, and God
eventually brings it into our world? Mother once commented
that if people would put the same energy into the pursuit of

---

† The four lower bodies are four sheaths consisting of four distinct frequencies that
surround the soul—the physical, emotional, mental, and etheric—providing vehicles for
the soul in her journey through time and space.

God that they put into material success, the world would be a very different place.

Here's an example of putting a lot of energy into the pursuit of material things. Some years ago my family took a summer vacation at Lake Tahoe. We were hiking along the beach and came upon a beautiful house overlooking the water. There was a couple sitting at a patio table being served a meal by a butler in a full tuxedo and white gloves. The flagpole in the yard had a white flag with a large dollar sign flying atop it.

The scene conveyed the fulfillment of what this couple's goal in life was—the "good life" of money and material possessions. They apparently measured their identity and success by the symbols of wealth and pledged their allegiance to a flag with the almighty dollar on it. You can just imagine them looking forward to everything they finally enjoyed that day: talking, planning, working, striving and envisioning it with such power that it finally came to pass.

I am sure they did work hard toward their goal, and the universe gave them the object of their desire. From one perspective, it could be very easy to criticize their choices as leading to nowhere and certainly not to true happiness. From another perspective, one can hope that by having their desires fulfilled they soon saw the emptiness of their choices and looked to higher goals. If there's a positive note to that story, it's the fact that they achieved their desire in the physical octave, so it did not lurk in their subconscious for lifetimes to come.

Unfulfilled Desires

Now, what happens if we don't fulfill our desires in our lifetime, but we still have them in our desire body? Well, we take them with us when we pass on. And where do people go in that case? Sometimes they go to devachan.

The ascended masters teach that devachan is the first three levels of the etheric octave. It is the place of wish-fulfillment, where the soul may be assigned between embodiments to play out unfulfilled desires and prepare for the next incarnation.

Many souls—lightbearers—end up in devachan when they make their transition because of their unfulfilled desires. Such desires are clearly a sidetrack that takes us far from what we want to do and where we want to go. Yet it's ordained that we must go to devachan if we will not surrender them. And even if we are fulfilling our human desires in devachan, it is delaying us—for who knows how long—from fulfilling our spiritual desire to be one with God.

In some cases our unfulfilled desires don't even get us to the lower etheric octave. For example, many years ago a woman in our community who was a singer was killed suddenly in a car accident. When Mother looked for her, she found her singing in a night club on the astral plane because an unfulfilled desire took her there.

Some of you may remember an old TV show called *The Twilight Zone*. It was an early presentation of science fiction and a predecessor of some of the more bizarre shows aired today. There was one episode where a gangster was killed, and when he opened his eyes, he was in a gambling casino. He thought it was great! It was his version of heaven: he got whatever he asked for; the liquor flowed freely; he was surrounded by beautiful women; when he gambled, he won *every* time. At first, he was excited by all this, but then he realized there was no real happiness in getting everything you want all the time. Finally, he became so frustrated that he said to his spiritual guide, "I want to go to the *other* place," and the guide replied, "You *are* in the *other* place."

What God Desires for Us

Sorting out our desires can be complicated unless we understand what God desires for us. Do you ever wonder what God desires? In the Summit University course "The Teachings of the Cosmic Christ," Mother shared this perspective:

> *God has no attachment to a golden age per se. He is unattached, desireless. He has only one desire, that you become God. But he will not impose that desire upon you, he will give you the opportunity to choose to fulfill his desire.*
>
> *That is the explanation for the occurrence of calamity and cataclysm. People cannot understand why God lets suffering happen, yet it is because he values the life of your soul and the integrity of his commitment to you, his covenant of free will, more than he values the end result.*[233]

It's hard to fathom God in our limited capacity, but God's greatest desire is for us to become one with him. That shifts things into a higher perspective, doesn't it? So, if God's only desire is that we become God, what should our desire be? Obviously, our desire needs to be the same! Therein lies the rub. It's very easy to say that we want to become God and be truly sincere about it. Yet the minute after we speak our vow and go about our daily life we are often faced with conflicting desires.

However, before we look at how we can be freed from lesser desires or wrong desires, let's look at other lawful desires we may have. The concept of lawful desire may seem rather Zen or contradictory to the statement that we can desire to be God but be desireless about everything else, but it's not. Saint Germain teaches:

...it is not wrong to desire happiness, to desire the family of God, to desire your own fulfillment or education or God-success. Truly, no thing will God withhold from you when you use legitimate means of arriving at the goal. ...

You see, beloved ones, all desires of the human that you may have in this world can be surrendered. And when they are surrendered, the divine desiring comes into your life. For every human desire there is a divine desire that is legitimate, that is fulfilling, that will give to you whatever you thought you might get through human desiring but truly could never have or keep and much, much more. But it takes courage.[234]

We demonstrate our faith and trust in God by giving him our desires. Some people may perceive a risk in doing that, thinking they may lose something. And while he might not give all our desires back to us, God has promised to return all the legitimate ones.

We don't want to be entangled and weighed down by our unfulfilled human desires, but what do we do? We know they won't magically disappear. We don't want to sublimate them. We can't pretend we don't have those desires. We have to be honest with ourselves by being honest with God. God knows it anyway. So, it takes courage, faith and trust to surrender every desire we have to the will of God.

Human Desire and Divine Desire

There is a difference between human desire and divine desire. When George Washington showed up at the Continental Congress meeting that was going to choose the commander-in-chief of the American forces, he arrived wearing his military uniform. Not so subtle, was it? Was this human desire or divine desire? For the vast majority of people, I believe it would be the reflection of a human desire for power, for prestige, for fame. For Washington, it was the desire to serve his country, to fight for freedom, and even if he didn't realize it on the outer, to fulfill his divine destiny.

Perhaps Washington didn't think of it in terms of human or divine desire, but his steadfastness and his endurance unto the end of the ensuing eight-year war proved it was divine desire. And what did he do when the war was over? He surrendered his sword and returned power to Congress. An unprecedented action! What military conqueror in history ever did that? In fact, when King George of England heard about it, he commented that Washington must be the greatest person in the world to surrender power when he didn't have to. Clearly, he followed divine desire in carrying out his role.

Yet divine desire cannot be passive. It must be put into action. As Morya said:

> You cannot sit on the sidelines and be a spectator, waiting [to be perfected so that you can begin your mission]. You know that you have a mission. You must be up and doing! You must be up and doing, beloved![235]

And what of the need to follow Buddha and be desireless? Mother explained:

> The path of desirelessness does not take from us our God-desire. And when we contain the desires of God, in effect, we are desireless because all other desire is neutralized by our very containing of the desire of God.[236]

Isn't that interesting? When we have God-desire our human desire is neutralized. Doesn't that sound like a great liberation and freedom from wrong desire? We struggle when we want both God and the things of the world. And when we contain the desires of God, the other desires fade away.

Learning the teachings on desire is a first crucial step. Now what do we do next? Well, there are some challenges that we need to master. One challenge is facing and conquering desires that we don't really want to give up.

I don't want to make light of the challenges involved in surrendering some desires. In order to serve the Brotherhood, many talented chelas have sacrificed careers in the world where they would have been very successful and made a lot of money. Some have surrendered marriages and family relationships to put God first. In fact, we have all surrendered something or we wouldn't be here today.

Saint Germain has asked us to give him this one lifetime in service and he promised to give us the opportunity to fulfill our lawful desires in the future. Whether you desire to be a musician or an artist or anything for that matter, he essentially told us that if we give him our life, we would have all the time in eternity to pursue other desires we might still have.

The question then arises, "What do we love most?" Do we love God and following his will above all else or do we love other things more? Unfortunately, we are often quite good at rationalizing why it is okay for us to keep certain desires, even when we know we should give them up. But we are sincere chelas and we eventually reach a point on the Path where we really do love God more than anything else, more than whatever unfulfilled desires we have. At the same time, we have been taught that the closer we get to our ascension the more burdened we become with the remainder of our human substance and human desires. So we must persist in putting God first because the battle is not truly over until we have finally won our ascension.

Dealing with Wrong Desires

What do we do when a thought or desire that is base or impure comes into our mind, whether through human desire or as a projection? Gautama Buddha gives us a dispensation to help us deal with this very thing:

> It is my desire for you to feel yourself free of extraneous feelings and thoughts, most blessed hearts. ...where there is not understanding of how to untangle the mass of threads of feelings—let all of this simply be released to me, that it might be examined and then transmuted...
>
> Do not hesitate, blessed one. Release them. For I will not, cannot, take from you that which you desire to keep. But let your innermost thoughts pass to me, that you for a while might know the freedom of dwelling within my own desire body and the essential feeling of perfect peace.[237]

What a wonderful key! We can dwell within Gautama Buddha's desire body that is a place of perfect peace. I think that will teach us what we'd like our desire body to be. He continues:

> Be not dismayed, for I am not dismayed. Be not ashamed, for I am not ashamed—not of you or to be with you or of the most base feelings that you have allowed, not only to pass through the astral body but to remain there.
>
> I come in love. I come to assist you to fulfill the innermost desire of your heart.[238]

Isn't that sweet and encouraging? And for those who prefer a more direct approach, just remember that Mark Prophet told us, *"As the Master said, 'You can't help it if a bird lands on your head, but you don't have to let him build a nest in your hair!'"* [239]

Are there physical ways to get free of wrong desire? As I mentioned earlier, one way is to simply be honest with ourselves and God. "God, I've got this desire; it's not going away. I want to surrender it, but it doesn't seem to be working." A prayer like that can open the door to grace and help move us toward releasing the desire.

Another way to clear desire is to use mantras. Some years ago, a friend of mine shared with me a short mantra that I really liked and took as my own: "I AM one with God-desire. I AM one with God-desire. I AM one with God-desire." That addresses the problem, doesn't it? We are affirming oneness with what God desires for us and what we desire in our innermost being. It is simple, yet profound in its implications. Whenever I felt a desire arise that I didn't like, I would rebuke it by repeating this mantra.

When I worked in downtown Minneapolis, I used to walk a mile from my parking space to my job, and I got into the habit of repeating the mantra over and over as I was walking along: "I AM one with God-desire." I don't know how many times I would give it during the course of that mile, but it was a lot! Though I wasn't quite sure how to get rid of my desires, I chose to affirm God-desire within my being and prayed that God-desire would replace the human desires from this life and other lifetimes.

The God and Goddess Meru gave us still another way to purge ourselves of untoward desires:

If you do not approve of or like the desires that you see in yourself, then "fast and pray" and call to God and demand that Archangel Michael bind the untoward desires. Let them be cast into the sacred fire and the violet flame. The Archangels are yours to command, in the name of Christ, to come forth and bind the human elements...[240]

The bottom line is that when we are plagued with wrong desires, we need to roll up our sleeves and go to work on them. As Mother taught, it is dangerous to sublimate wrong desire, as it is a ticking time bomb waiting to go off. And it always seems to go off at the most inopportune time. Therefore, because wrong desires can be so powerful, we need to be bold in challenging them with our calls and decrees. Freeing ourselves from wrong desire should always be part of our dweller calls and our calls to beloved Astrea. And, of course, the violet flame is the great eraser, helping to transmute wrong desire.

In the process of clearing wrong desire, we cannot indulge in either condemning ourselves for wrong desires or in not striving to free ourselves from them. Sometimes we use self-condemnation as an *excuse* not to do more, though we probably don't do it consciously. But think about it. When you affirm within your being that you are not capable of doing something, it lets you off the hook, doesn't it?

Well, as chelas of the ascended masters we must be accountable. We need to accept accountability for our desires, our karma and our actions going forward. And it takes courage to face wrong desire and be accountable.

Help from the Divine Mother Durga

When I select a topic for a Sunday service, it is often a dictation that inspires me and then I write the sermon based on that. In this case, it was the other way around. I researched teachings on desire and found a number of dictations and lectures about it. Though I have shared many of those today, none of those dictations seemed quite right for a service on God-desire.

As some of you may know, I grew up in a Pentecostal church, and in the Sunday services they often had a time for people to "testify." Hands would go up—"I want to testify! I want to testify!"—and people would get up and share some spiritual experience of what Jesus or God had done for them. The congregation loved it. So, if you'll indulge me, I want to give my testimonial.

My personal experience has been that I often need an intense fire to help me change and make progress. And frankly, there is no better way to get that fire than with the fierceness of the Divine Mother! Thinking back, I remembered a dictation from Durga given New Year's Eve 1991 that could help us with establishing God-desire. As you hear it and experience it for yourself this morning, I believe you will understand how I was struck by the power and intensity of it.

We had recently moved to Minneapolis, and the teaching center played Durga's dictation a while after it was given. It was one of those dictations where you felt like you had to wear a seat belt lest the fire blow you over. She challenged us to accept or reject the help that she was offering. The title says it all: "The Power of Confrontation. *How Shall the Quickening Come? Who Has the Will to Change?*"

It was the day after I heard the dictation and I had been pondering it ever since. I was dealing with a particular spiritual challenge at the time, and I decided to give Durga a try. The intensity of Durga or of Mother Kali is really different from what we are used to in Christian churches. But I was convinced enough by her dictation to accept her challenge regarding who has the will and the courage to let her help them change.

I was walking down the street and stopped and made a call

to her to help me. I can't tell you exactly what happened, but I instantly felt a response. Something in me was different. And from that day forward, I felt free from the particular issue I had asked for her intercession on. It was such a powerful experience that I got a focus of Durga for my altar to remind me of what she had done for me.

Durga is ready to be with you. She is definitely a Divine Mother you can call upon! I got an email yesterday from someone who saw the bulletin for this service. They told me that a friend of theirs had mentioned to them that they write letters to Durga all the time and claim they have gotten some amazing results. If you choose to accept Durga's help, your experience will be uniquely yours, but you can rest assured that she *will* respond!

The Journey from Human Desire to Divine Desire

Saint Germain teaches that it is a journey to go from human desire to divine desire:

> *Thus, you see, between the human will and the human desire and the divine will and the divine desire, there is an abyss to be crossed. Its name is time and space. It is governed by the law of mortality. You can take the route of the labyrinth. You can spend another thousand or ten thousand years or a million gingerly stepping in and out of the caves and caverns, underground and through the astral plane, seeking earthly treasure and not realizing that the divine is practically on the tip of your nose.*[241]

I think we all have a sense that *now* is the hour we want to move beyond seeking earthly treasure and make the right choices. We want to continue serving life through our sacred labor because that's one of the reasons we're in embodiment. But we also need to remember that the first person we need to save is ourselves and that putting on our Christhood and winning our ascension is the most important thing we can do for this planet.

There is no better way to deal with issues on the path to our victory than with the fire and intensity of the Goddess Durga! We know we can't do this on our own. Jesus asked the sick person if he wanted to be healed. Seems like an obvious question, doesn't it, but he asked it, "Do you want to be healed?" Similarly, we can ask ourselves, "Do we want to be freed from the darkness of wrong desire or whatever else is plaguing us?"

Well, we cannot truly be free until we let go of all that keeps us from God. Durga is offering herself. Do we have the will to change and the courage to accept her help? Just knowing about her offer won't make a difference.

Take a person who needs to exercise more and so he goes out and buys a treadmill. That's a commitment to exercise, isn't it? But he somehow equates buying the treadmill with physically exercising, though the treadmill sits idle.

It is the same thing with dispensations. Knowing them does no good unless we avail ourselves of them. As we hear Durga today, let each one of us make a conscious decision to accept or reject her offer of help. And she says if we do accept, we can all become "little Durgas."

I found it was important for me to open myself up to Durga. In other words I had to actually say, "Yes, Durga, I accept your dispensation." When we do this, we acknowledge that we have nothing left that we want to hide from ourselves or God.

Let's give it all to God. Let's take advantage of every dispensation, every opportunity. Our souls need us to do that. The world needs us to do that.

The Lasting Happiness of Desiring Only God

We can never achieve true and lasting happiness by pursuing human desire. There is a beautiful simplicity in desiring only God and trusting him to fulfill all our needs. It is hard to try to live with both divine and human desires. It is much simpler to trust in God and his desire for us to be one with him!

Why do we walk the Path? Why do we work so hard on our chelaship, on such seemingly mundane things as desires, while the world sees it only as foolishness? A few days ago, I was reminded why.

I was wrapping some Christmas gifts and I had Christmas carols playing in the background. One of the songs was "I'll be Home for Christmas." Interspersed between the lyrics of this particular version were messages from soldiers serving in Iraq. They talked about missing their children and spouses and the Christmas traditions. There were also some messages from children sent to the parent who was serving. Suddenly, I was flooded with memories of the past twenty years: the terrorism and wars in Afghanistan and Iraq; the losses and maiming of our precious soldiers, many of whom were very young; the pain to families, especially children, that seems almost incomprehensible.

So why do we diligently strive to free ourselves from karma and our human creation? Of course, it is because we want to fulfill our divine destiny and return to God. But it is also because we can *do more* for others in the world, we can *give more* when we are spiritually free. We can lift people up, as we have been lifted up by God and the ascended masters! Mother said if we win our ascension and don't save this planet it will be like ashes in our mouths.

Is there a link between saving this planet and the lightbearers and our work on wrong desire? Is there a link between giving more and opening ourselves to Durga and accepting her help? Yes, there is! It may seem small at first, but it is most assuredly there. When we strive, it sends a message to the Brotherhood that we are serious about our chelaship and serious about doing our part to save the earth and the precious lightbearers, wherever they are.

It is our privilege today to choose the right way, to choose God-desire.

What better time than now?

HUMILITY AND
HAPPINESS

Humility is the absolute sense of Self in God.

—PEACE AND ALOHA

✺

Humility is the displacement of self
by the enthronement of God.

—REV. ANDREW MURRAY

TEN

Humility and Happiness

Our scriptural reading today is from 2nd Corinthians 12, verses 1-10 from The New Jerusalem Bible. Paul is speaking: *"I am boasting because I have to. Not that it does any good, but I will move on to visions and revelations from the Lord. I know a man in Christ* [he's referring to himself here], *who fourteen years ago— still in the body? I do not know; or out of the body? I do not know: God knows—was caught up right into the third heaven. And I know that this man—still in the body? or outside the body? I do not know, God knows—was caught up into Paradise and heard words that cannot and may not be spoken by any human being. On behalf of someone like that I am willing to boast, but I am not going to boast on my own behalf except of my weaknesses; and then, if I do choose to boast I shall not be talking like a fool because I shall be speaking the truth. But I will not go on in case anybody should rate me higher than he sees and hears me to be, because of the exceptional greatness of the revelations.*

Wherefore, so that I should not get above myself, I was given a thorn in the flesh, a messenger from Satan to batter me and prevent me from getting above myself. About this, I have three times pleaded with the Lord that it might leave me; but he has answered me, 'My grace is enough for you: for power is at full stretch in weakness.' It is, then, about my weaknesses that I am happiest of all to boast, so that the power of Christ may rest upon me; and that is why I am glad of weaknesses, insults, constraints, persecutions and distress for Christ's sake. For it is when I am weak that I am strong."[242]

Who among us seeks out humility that we may be stronger in our weakness? Paul learned this lesson by having a thorn in his flesh. We don't know what it was, but it was enough for him to plead with Jesus three times to have it removed. Once Jesus told him that his grace was sufficient, Paul realized that his weakness was the price he must pay so that the power of Christ would remain with him.

Many may not want to embrace Paul's understanding of paying the price. Andrew Murray, a late 19th century minister put it this way in his book *Humility, The Journey Toward Holiness*:

> *Many Christians fear and flee and seek deliverance from all that would humble them. At times they may pray for humility, but in their heart of hearts they pray even more to be kept from the things that would bring them to that place.... There is still a sense of burden connected with humility in their minds; to humble themselves has not become the spontaneous expression of their lives.*[243]

A Humility Mindset

If we are completely honest with ourselves, I suspect that humility hasn't become the spontaneous expression in most of our lives. Our perspective, at least in part, is probably that being humble or being humbled is not something to be desired, but something to be avoided. That's the natural response of the human ego.

None of us would desire humiliation without a purpose, and even then it can be a hard test. In a previous sermon, I shared about the week I asked God to teach me some lessons in humility. However, I didn't ask a second time because I was in a very high-pressure, competitive job, and I feared not being able to compete with others and maybe even being humiliated by losing my job. I clearly didn't understand true humility and that, in essence, I was favoring my human self over my Christ Self. I didn't consider that Jesus' profound teachings to Paul on humility were also important to me—not only to my spiritual path but also to my secular path, and even to the goal of being happy.

If we were playing a word association game and the word humility came up, I doubt that "happy" would be the first word that came to mind! Perhaps we should consider that humility might be a key to happiness that has been right in front of us that we haven't been able to see. Our Christ Self does not fear or avoid humility but rather is the embodiment of it. So who is it that fears being humbled? Our dweller-on-the-threshold, of course.

It's time we developed a humility mindset. To do that, let's dig deeper into our understanding of humility, how it affects our happiness, and—most importantly—what part it plays on the path of our Christhood.

What Does Humility Look Like?

St. Augustine wrote, *"Should you ask me: What is the first thing in religion? I should reply: the first, second, and third thing therein is humility."*[244]

Why is humility so important? Reverend Murray puts it this way:

> Humility is the only soil in which virtue takes root; a lack of humility is the explanation of every defect and failure. Humility is not so much a virtue along with the others, but is the root of all, because it alone takes the right attitude before God and allows Him, as God, to do all.[245]

Rev. Murray also wrote, "humility is the displacement of self by the enthronement of God." [246] What a wonderful image—God enthroned in our temple! And enthroning God in our temple begins with humility.

We can ask ourselves "Who's in charge in my temple?" If we are strutting around in our human consciousness, God cannot enter our temple because the dweller is in charge. So we must develop humility so our Christ Self can eventually replace that dweller.

Jesus is the foremost example of humility for us to follow. From a very young age, he demonstrated his attainment by his humility. In *The Dossier on the Ascension* you get a sense of awe in Serapis Bey's description of Jesus' humility:

> I recall full well when the Master Jesus came to Luxor as a very young man, that He knelt in Holy Innocence before the Hierophant, refusing all honors that were offered Him and asking to be initiated into the first grade of Spiritual Law and Spiritual Mystery. No sense of pride marred his visage—no sense of preeminence or false expectation, albeit He could have well expected the highest honors. He chose to take the low road of Humility, knowing that it was reserved unto the Joy of God to raise Him up.[247]

Remember the apostles wanting to know who would sit at the right hand of Jesus in heaven? They obviously weren't coming from a place of humility!

What Was I Thinking?

Similarly, we might ask ourselves, "Am I content to wait for God to raise me up, or do I feel the need to do it myself?" I'll tell you a personal story of what that might look like. I was attending a seminar Mother held at Camelot in the late 1970s. I have no recollection of what the subject was, but I remember very clearly the lesson I got. This comes under the category of doing something that seemed right at the time, but afterwards left me wondering, "What in the world was I thinking!"

In my zeal and enthusiasm I determined that I would come early to every session and sit in the very front row right next to the center aisle. Only the right side of the chapel was being used, so I was as close to the altar and the messenger as possible. I sat there for every session—morning, afternoon, and evening—and no one ever said anything to me. But on the last day of the seminar as I was perched as usual in the front row, I could see Mother looking in my direction. She then asked everyone in the front row to please move to the last row and everyone in the last row to move to the front. I had been dethroned, and every eye could see me going from being first to being last! Even at that time I had to smile at the initiation, and from that day forward I have always tried to be careful not to put myself first.

When seeking to be humble, we can begin by asking ourselves, "Do I want to identify with God or with my human consciousness?" El Morya made the choice quite clear. He told us, *"Become zero that God may become the one-hundred percent of Being where you are."*[248]

We have been taught that pride goes before the fall.[249] When we are humble, pride has no place in our being. As Sanat Kumara teaches:

> *That is why you must enter into the point of humility of the saints and recite often to yourself the mantra, "Thou the All; I the nothing." Proclaim the nothingness of yourself and the Allness of your Holy Christ Self and your Lord and Saviour Jesus Christ and you will not make the mistake of falling into a pit of pride.*[250]

Andrew Murray conveys this same concept in different words, "*True humility comes when before God we see ourselves as nothing, have put aside self, and let God be all.*"[251]

While it might be easy to affirm our humility in words and say, "Thou the All; I the nothing," it's not so easy to put that into action in our lives. The real test comes each day as we interact with others. We have each developed a human persona over the ages that comes with a prideful vibration and attitude that we must surrender and overcome in order to truly live and act from moment to moment and day to day as if we are nothing and God is the All. And, of course, this is what the Path is all about.

Although I didn't realize it at the time, when I was seeking truth as a teenager, I was really seeking holiness. When I found the Summit Lighthouse, I found holiness, and I knew I was home. What I understand now but didn't recognize in those days was the link between holiness and humility.

We have been told that Alpha is the most humble being in the universe, and we know he is certainly the holiest. As Andrew Murray wrote:

> *There is none holy but God: we have as much holiness as we have God. And according to what we have of God will be*

our real humility, because humility is nothing but the disap-
pearance of self in the vision that God is all. The holiest will be
the humblest.[252]

Elohim Peace and Aloha put it this way:

Humility is the highest virtue. And it does not exclude
being firm—as Jesus was, casting the moneychangers out of
the temple. No, humility is this; I will define it for you: Humility
is the absolute sense of Self in God.[253]

Two Kinds of Humility

There are two kinds of humility that we practice, whether
knowingly or unknowingly. The first is humility before God
and the second is humility before others.

Humility before Jesus, the masters and angels is not hard.
We respect and honor the light that they bring. I love what
Lord Maitreya says about humility:

For I know well what is humility. And I can tell you, beloved
hearts, humility comes when you sit at the feet of Sanat Kumara.
Humility comes when you hear his heartbeat within the cham-
ber of your own heart and then you hear his heartbeat as the
great magnet of Almighty God magnetizing your own heart.[254]

While it's not hard to be humble in the presence of such immense light, what about being humble in the presence of the
light in our neighbor? Andrew Murray explains:

... the only humility that is really ours is not the kind we try to
show before God in prayer, but the kind we carry with us, and
carry out, in our ordinary conduct. The seemingly insignificant

acts of daily life are the tests of eternity, because they prove what spirit possesses us. It is in our most unguarded moments that we show who we are and what we are made of.[255]

As we examine ourselves and the way we live each day, let us not be overcome by a perceived lack of humility or the subtleties of pride that are exposed. We can ask ourselves, "Are my motives pure? Do I desire to be thought well of or am I serving and giving for the sheer joy of it?" Such reflection is the work of preparing our temple for the fullness of our Christhood.

We can learn a lot about our behavior patterns as we observe ourselves. For example, notice what you think of the person that sits next to you on the bus or that you work with every day.

In her teachings of the Elohim Peace and Aloha, Mother commented:

> *Be humble. This is a wonderful state of being, the state of being humble and of having humility. "Be humble before your God. Don't be a know-it-all but...have a sense of holiness in the presence of one another's Christ Self and a sense of the holiness of the flame that burns in the heart of the one that sits next to you."*[256]

Do you ever stop to think that the magnificent presence of the living God is in the soul of the one next to you? Shouldn't we bow before the light of God in each person, and shouldn't that be reflected in the way we treat them, the way we talk to them, the tone that we use? Our tone conveys so much. Do you ever catch yourself saying something that sounds rather harmless but you know the tone is not of the Christ?

I recall visiting a teaching center some years ago and we ended up in a prayer circle to make calls on a certain issue. The woman next to me clearly had a medical issue and her appearance was that of someone who didn't have much abundance. In short, it was easy to make certain judgments about her at first glance. We tend to do this almost automatically, without even thinking. In any case, we all started making our calls on the issue, and I couldn't help but hear what this woman next to me was saying. I soon stopped making my own calls as I was amazed at the power and purity of hers. Other than the messenger and a few dedicated chelas, I don't think I have ever heard anyone make calls like that. Whatever my judgments about her had been, I recognized I had clearly been wrong. And I was chagrined. At that point, I was able to honor the Christ flame of this dear soul next to me instead of judging her on appearances.

Though we know the way of the world is not our path, we have to be alert to habits that can cause us to slip and act in a worldly way. I have found that every time I make a conscious effort to work on my path it always brings a response from the ascended masters. I believe they're waiting to help us in any way they can, and they can help us even more when we actively take the first step. Passivity has no place in chelaship.

So where do we start? Well, we start somewhere: changing a thinking pattern, decreeing to transmute a past mistake that's burdening us, working with a therapist, and the list goes on. The point is to just start somewhere! Engage the Path, and when you engage the Path, you engage the ascended masters. And if you ask them for help in learning the lessons of humility, rest assured they will answer you! Such a grace!

Mother Teresa's Guide to Humility

Mother Teresa, in her book *The Joy in Loving: A Guide to Daily Living,* gave some practical guidelines for living humbly.[257] They sound simple but are powerful if we put them into practice.

1. To speak as little as possible of one's self.

We all know a person who, once you say hello, is off and running talking about themselves, their aches and pains, their family, their this and that. It's not malicious behavior, it's just a habit that likely stems from an insecurity or inner pain in their psyche.

If you have something to share with a person, ask their permission first. In general, we should listen to others and talk little about ourselves. A good listener can do much for someone by just listening, without doing anything else.

2. To mind one's own business.

Good reminder! We tie up a lot of energy getting involved in things that are not really our business, and that is a proven way to make karma. So don't get involved in things that aren't your business, except to make calls for God's will for people and situations.

3. Not to want to manage other people's affairs.

Isn't it funny that the easiest test to pass is always someone else's? It's so tempting to think we know exactly what another person should do in a situation, but that can be prideful. We don't know the karma involved in what is happening. So even when we think we know the solution, we shouldn't impose it upon them because we may unintentionally compromise the test they're going through.

One thing a minister learns is to never give advice or recommendations unless they're asked to. Basically, we all need to be very careful to let people walk their own path.

4. To avoid curiosity.

Curiosity can lead to gossip—something to be avoided at all costs! Some of you may remember the story of the Keeper of the Flame who passed on and Mother found her on the astral plane gossiping with three other ladies. When she saw Mother, she recognized her, and Mother told her she must come with her. The other ladies said, "Oh, you won't be happy up there," acting as if they could spend eternity gossiping. Fortunately the lady went with Mother and was taken to the retreats.

5. To accept contradictions and correction cheerfully.

Although it seems natural to be defensive when our words and actions are questioned or criticized, we need to pause long enough to discern the best reaction! Accepting corrections and contradictions cheerfully can be a learning experience and an act of humility.

I love this quote from Epictetus, a Greek Stoic philosopher: "*If anyone tells you that a certain person speaks ill of you, do not make excuses about what is said of you but answer, 'He was ignorant of my other faults, else he would not have mentioned these alone.'*" [258] Doesn't that sound like the voice of humility?

6. To pass over the mistakes of others.

That's the kind thing to do. The author of another guide to humility put it this way, "*There's a saying I like which goes something like this, People will always forget what you told them, but they will never forget how you made them feel.*"[259]

Overlooking mistakes is an opportunity to be magnanimous in the spirit of Lanello. Most mistakes are unintentional, and the person probably already knows they made a mistake. Let's not add to any weight of condemnation they might be feeling.

7. To accept insults and injuries; to accept being slighted, forgotten and disliked.

This can be a tough one for any of us. As lightbearers we are sensitive, and the slights often come from a friend or someone in the community. Practicing Buddhic non-attachment and affirming who we are in God will help to heal the pain that we feel from these things. Reverend Murray puts it this way: *"Accept every humiliation: look upon every person who tries or troubles you as a means of grace to humble you. God will see such acceptance as proof that your whole heart desires it."* [260] Giving it all to God and forgiving everyone involved can bring peace.

8. To be kind and gentle even under provocation.

This is the opposite of the typical "fight or flight" response to aggression. At the same time, this doesn't mean being a door-mat to someone's abusive energy. Rather, it is the response that comes from integration with our Christ Self. When we don't feel the need to defend our ego or human self, we can become the instrument of our Higher Self. Proverbs 15:1 reminds us: "*A soft answer turneth away wrath: but grievous words stir up anger.*"

9. Never to stand on one's dignity.

I believe Mother Teresa is referring to our so-called human dignity and not the dignity of our Christ Self. Human dignity is prideful and can trap us if we are not wary. Our dweller-on-the-threshold has *no* dignity in God!

10. To choose always the hardest.

Words to live by—if we choose to do so. The hardest things to do are the most likely to keep us humble and to be more dependent on God to do them. This will bring us greater joy when the task is completed.

As you can tell, striving to put on true humility is not a weekend project! It takes constant effort and striving based on a love of God that is greater than the momentums of your human consciousness. Though you may not change overnight, with continued effort you will definitely make progress. Be aware of your daily routines and take time to reflect on how you are doing on your path of humility.

Humility Brings Happiness

If you asked a hundred people what they want out of life, I suspect the vast majority would say that being happy is one of their goals. Most would associate happiness with abundance, a satisfying job, romantic love, and things of that sort. Some might associate it with a spiritual path as well, but how many of those would even think that humility is a key to true happiness? Yet the bible says, *"God resisteth the proud but giveth grace unto the humble."*[261]

Serapis Bey teaches that the greatest prize that a chela or seeker for God can have is humility.[262] The prize of humility is freedom from our human self. As Reverend Murray wrote, *"It is indeed the deepest happiness of heaven to be so free from self that whatever is said of us or done to us is swallowed up in the thought that Jesus is all and we are nothing."*[263] That is the freedom our soul is seeking.

Murray further says:

> *Humility is perfect quietness of heart. It is to expect nothing, to wonder at nothing that is done to me, to feel nothing done against me. It is to be at rest when nobody praises me, and when I am blamed or despised. It is to have a blessed home in the Lord, where I can go in and shut the door, and kneel to my Father in secret, and am at peace as in a deep sea of calmness, when all around and above is trouble.*[264]

To be *"at peace as in a deep sea of calmness"* takes work in today's world. But isn't that a lovely description of happiness?

Freedom from pride also brings happiness. Humility will keep us from falling into the *"pit of pride"* as Sanat Kumara describes it.[265] Since I started working on this sermon I have looked more closely at my actions and the perspective I bring to my daily activities and challenges. Self-observation can be sobering but also illuminating as to how we tend to think about and view ourselves and is especially revealing regarding our continual identification with the human self.

Defending our human consciousness and our dweller-on-the-threshold is a losing battle that takes us far away from the peace and happiness of God. It is a battle that cannot be won and only brings strife and sorrow as its ultimate fruit. As we daily make the call for our dweller to be bound, we can practice and affirm our human nothingness and the allness of God within us. It certainly becomes easier to turn the other cheek when we practice humility and stop defending our ego.

Changing Our Perspective

Some years ago I did a sermon on pride and during it I read a Catholic prayer called the "Litany of Humility." What is so striking about this litany is that the prayers in it are the exact opposite of the way 99 percent of the world lives. While we may not view some of these ideas as the Catholic tradition would, the litany gives a powerful perspective of the path of becoming zero so God can become the All where we are.

Its list of fears can seem overwhelming considering how many might still be lurking in our consciousness. However, as we meditate on this prayer, it can help us change the way we think about ourselves. It can reorient our thinking about who we are and who God is by reinforcing right desire within us and asking for deliverance from fears that are clearly holding us back. So I'd like to re-read a portion of this prayer to you as we meditate on desiring humility.

> O Jesus! meek and humble of heart,
>   Hear my prayer.
> From the desire of being esteemed,
>   Deliver me, Jesus.
> From the desire of being loved,
>   Deliver me, Jesus.
> From the desire of being extolled,
>   Deliver me, Jesus.
> From the desire of being honored,
>   Deliver me, Jesus.
> From the desire of being praised,
>   Deliver me, Jesus.
> From the desire of being preferred to others,
>   Deliver me, Jesus.
> From the desire of being consulted,
>   Deliver me, Jesus.
> From the desire of being approved,
>   Deliver me, Jesus.
> From the fear of being humiliated,
>   Deliver me, Jesus.
> From the fear of being despised,
>   Deliver me, Jesus.
> From the fear of suffering rebukes,
>   Deliver me, Jesus.
> From the fear of being slandered,
>   Deliver me, Jesus.
> From the fear of being forgotten,

Deliver me, Jesus.
From the fear of being ridiculed,
Deliver me, Jesus.
From the fear of being wronged,
Deliver me, Jesus.
From the fear of being suspected,
Deliver me, Jesus.[266]

To further change our mindset and how we think, view and act on a daily basis, we should affirm that God or Jesus or our Holy Christ Self are the All and we are the nothing. But what is it going to take to truly change our perspective on who we really are so that that reality manifests in our lives? While it is easy to make a fiat saying God is the All and I am the nothing, living that truth without having to think about it is another matter.

Remember, the path of humility is just that—a path. We put on the garment of humility as we gain mastery in its many aspects. If we begin with a change in perspective about ourselves and begin to think, affirm and live as if God is the All and we are the nothing, then progress will come.

One way I have found that helps me to focus on a particular virtue like humility is to write small notes to myself as reminders, put them where I will see them, and change them periodically. You might have another way that helps you. One reason doing something like that is important is because when we are truly engaged, it allows the masters to intercede in a greater way, reinforcing our efforts and bringing us ever closer to oneness with God.

The Power of Humility

True happiness is one of the fruits of humility, but there are many others. One of them is being given greater access to the power of God. My favorite example of this is Igor, the humble Russian peasant whose prayers and devotions saved millions of lives during the Russian revolution. His humility allowed God to grant him the power to change history. I've mentioned him in sermons before to encourage us—one soul, who was looked down upon by everyone in the village as simple minded, saved millions of people! God gave him that power because he had the humility to use it correctly.

As we view what appears to be the crumbling of western civilization around us, it is good to remember that our humility can change the outcome of events because God will be able to use us in a much more powerful way. And being of greater service to God would surely raise us to a new level of peace and happiness.

"Humility Within and Boldness Without"

Besides our human ego opposing our happiness in humility, the conspiracy of dark ones will do everything they can to stop each of us individually from this happiness and to thwart such happiness in all the lightbearers on this planet.

I read something recently that seems ridiculous on the surface but illustrates the extent of opposition to true happiness in God. As you may know, psychologists and psychiatrists both use a diagnostic manual to classify the many conditions that an individual may be experiencing. This is required for insurance claims, and so it's used almost universally by professionals.

Richard Bentall, writing in the Journal of Medical Ethics in 1992, proposed *"that happiness be classified as a psychiatric disorder...under the new name: major affective disorder, pleasant type. In a review of relevant literature it is shown that happiness is statistically abnormal...is associated with a range of cognitive abnormalities, and probably reflects the abnormal functioning of the central nervous system."*[267]

While this view was not included in the diagnostic manual, nevertheless, I believe such thinking is a reflection of someone who has no God consciousness within them. Such people can't ever be happy, so they don't want us to be happy either. They want to condemn people's happiness as a mental disorder! And when the so-called authorities of the world say such things, it's no wonder the lightbearers are confused about who they are and what their goal in life is!

By God's grace, we have the masters' perspective to align ourselves with Reality. In 1974 Lanello wrote:

> The greatest lesson I find that I have learned from Jesus, from the great Masters down through the ages, is the lesson of humility. Humility is a candle that burns with fervor and is aware of its identity as the Identity of God—not a thing apart, but a thing within.... This I would pass on to you—that humility within and boldness without, boldness for the Law, for God, for Hierarchy, will carry you far in the march across the earth and into eternity.[268]

We straddle two worlds: the world of our human consciousness and the world of our Christ consciousness. We have one foot in each and it's a difficult place to be. We want to remain in our Christ consciousness and that will take devotion and concerted effort on the Path. We need to recognize that our dweller-on-the-threshold is strong, humble ourselves before God and seek his help in casting it out.

The victory will be ours, but we freely acknowledge that we could not do it without God. When we remain humble, put forth the effort, strive on a daily basis, laugh at our human foibles and work to overcome them, God and the masters will bring us what we need to help solve our dilemma.

To reiterate, we can walk this path to our victory if we make the effort, if we strive. Let us embrace humility as the key to having God reign supreme in our temple and to walking the earth as a Christed one.

Humility *will* bring happiness.

THE ONE
THAT HAS
GONE ASTRAY

*Defend all souls. Go after them! Pursue them
as if you were the hound of heaven! And realize that you
are in embodiment for one reason: to be the defender
of souls who cannot at this point in time defend
themselves before the Lords of Karma.*

—ARCTURUS

ELEVEN

The One That Has Gone Astray

Our first scripture reading today is from John 10:11-16: *"I am the good shepherd: the good shepherd giveth his life for the sheep. But he that is an hireling, and not the shepherd, whose own the sheep are not, seeth the wolf coming, and leaveth the sheep, and fleeth: and the wolf catcheth them, and scattereth the sheep. The hireling fleeth, because he is an hireling, and careth not for the sheep. I am the good shepherd, and know my sheep, and am known of mine. As the Father knoweth me, even so know I the Father: and I lay down my life for the sheep. And other sheep I have, which are not of this fold: them also I must bring, and they shall hear my voice; and there shall be one fold, and one shepherd."*

The next reading is from Mathew 18:12-14: *"How think ye? if a man have an hundred sheep, and one of them be gone astray, doth he not leave the ninety and nine, and goeth into the mountains, and seeketh that which is gone astray? And if so be that he find it, verily I say unto you, he rejoiceth more of that sheep, than of the ninety and nine which went not astray. Even so it is not the will of your Father which is in heaven, that one of these little ones should perish."*

In 1866 Emperor Theodore of Ethiopia made a big mistake. He continued to hold three English envoys as prisoners for several years, often keeping them in chains. Despite repeated British efforts to get them released, Theodore refused, all but inviting the British to do something about it.

The challenge for Her Majesty's government was two-fold. The first obstacle was Theodore himself. Author Alan Morehead described him as *"a mad dog let loose, a sort of reincarnation of Ivan the Terrible"* considered a megalomaniac by some.[269] The second obstacle was the land of Ethiopia itself. The ancient Christian country was isolated behind high mountain ranges, over 400 miles from the sea with virtually no roads and plagued by almost constant tribal wars.

Despite these challenges, England had to do something. One might ask, "Why? Wouldn't it have been a lot easier to keep trying diplomacy and hope the problem would resolve itself or be forgotten by the public? After all, the British Empire had far greater challenges than three people held hostage in an inaccessible part of Africa." Nonetheless, the British determined to rescue the three because the honor of England was at stake. They believed that the world must know the consequences of defying the Crown and that the empire would protect and defend every single person who represented them. This is an example of how a tiny island ruled the largest empire the world had ever known. So the decision was made: the hostages would be rescued.

Moorehead continues:

> There has never been in modern times a colonial campaign quite like the British expedition to Ethiopia in 1868. It proceeds from first to last with the decorum and heavy inevitability of a Victorian state banquet, complete with ponderous speeches

at the end. And yet it was a fearsome undertaking; for hundreds of years the country had never been invaded, and the savage nature of the terrain alone was enough to promote failure.[270]

An engineer, Lieutenant-General Sir Robert Napier, was chosen as commander of the expedition. By August 1867 he estimated the immensity of what would be required: *"about 12,000 fighting men with roughly twice as many followers, at least 20,000 mules and other transport animals...artillery of all kinds and a fleet of 280 ships...to carry the force to its destination."*[271] In addition, *"forty-four elephants were to be sent from India to carry the heavy guns. A railway, complete with locomotives and some twenty miles of track was to be laid across the coastal plain, and at the landing place large piers, lighthouses and warehouses were to be established. Two condensers to convert salt water to fresh were needed, and a telegraph line several hundred miles in length was to maintain communications with the base on the coast."* Even this proved to not be enough—the campaign to rescue three individuals ended up with 32,000 men and 55,000 animals![272]

After all that effort, everything they had built was torn down when they left. One writer described the action as *"one of the most expensive affairs of honor in history."*[273] And, oh yes, the campaign was a success; all three hostages were rescued.

If this is what a secular government did for the honor of an empire, what are we willing to do for the honor of God, for the one sheep held hostage by their karma and the other millions that have gone astray?

The answer, of course, is that we are already doing a lot. Our embracing the science of the spoken Word and giving daily decrees has accomplished and continues to accomplish quite a bit—much more, I am sure, than we shall know this side of heaven. Yet I believe we would all like to be doing more, even though the personal challenges many are facing can seem overwhelming at times.

What we will be considering today is exciting because, in spite of the constraints of our personal lives, it is something we can *all* do that even the ascended masters cannot do by cosmic law. So don't ever doubt your value to God and the masters when you live the teachings they have given us.

We Are Sponsored

We are sponsored. A simple phrase, but behind it is the reality of every spiritual opportunity we have had in this and, no doubt, many other lifetimes. We have been told that none of us would have had the opportunity of contacting these teachings without the sponsorship of an ascended master. Indeed, at a very basic level, we know that the Maha Chohan has said he will keep the flame of life for us until we are able to keep it for ourselves.

A friend recently reminded me of a story Mother told about a chela who was sponsored by *seven* ascended masters but subsequently lost his great opportunity by leaving the Path. You wonder just how much it may have cost the masters that sponsored him, and how long it may take him to get sponsorship again. Interestingly, the fallen ones also sponsor each other. El Morya taught that Modred, the betrayer of Camelot, had one million fallen ones as his sponsors.[274]

When I did a search for the word "sponsor" in *Pearls of Wisdom* online, I was surprised at the page after page of references to our sponsorship. The following quote from Archangel Jophiel in his 1973 dictation "To Sponsor the Children of the Sun" is indicative of just one opportunity for sponsorship we have been given:

I ask you to submit your applications for the Ascended Master University. For I desire to sponsor you! And I, Jophiel, have stood before the Lords of Karma this day; and I have said to them, whatever number among this group desire to attend our university—even if they be found wanting, even if they are not wholly prepared—I will sponsor them. For I am determined that mankind shall have the wisdom of the Mother. And I shall lay before the Lords of Karma this day the yellow diamonds of my attainment as collateral for those students; and if they fail, I shall willingly forfeit those diamonds. For this is my gift; this is my faith in these students; this is my faith in mankind and in the God in man.

Therefore I come as your sponsor! Golden children of the Sun, I stand to sponsor you! [275]

Likewise, all of us who have gone to Summit University have been sponsored!

Sponsorship Is Part of the Brotherhood's Work

It is also evident that some ascended masters sponsor other ascended masters in their efforts to help the lightbearers of earth. For example, El Morya was benched when some of the chelas misused his light, and when a portion of that karma was balanced, Kuan Yin and Mother Mary interceded which allowed him to be unbenched. [276]

Sponsorship seems to be a part of much of the Brotherhood's work, not just on earth but throughout cosmos. So the pursuit of some dispensations by the masters requires the sponsorship of the Great Karmic Board and the various governing bodies of the cosmos. Even Sanat Kumara needed sponsorship!

In the case of individuals, some are sponsored because they

have earned it, others because of their sponsors' hope that they will come up higher, and still others because they have needed it acutely.

Archangel Michael in his dictation given at the 1992 Freedom conference expounded on this for us:

> I tell you, beloved ones, every single one of you has been handpicked as a ripe apple from the Tree of Life. By and by, after you had suffered long enough and become fed up with the world and the human consciousness, you were drawn to this Path and this Teaching....
>
> Do not think it is because you are special in the sense of attainment, but simply assume that it is because you are special in the sense that you have an extraordinary need for an extraordinary help from those of us of higher octaves. And because you have that need, beloved, and can make it [back to your home of Light in] no other way except by our Intercession, we have called you to be the firstfruits of those who should receive the Light from the altar.[277]

So, we of all people, who have been so blessed, should be the most humble because we could make it "in no other way except by [their] Intercession."

In that dictation Michael also promises that anyone who gives at least twenty minutes of calls to him *daily* will have a mighty blue-lightning angel assigned to be with them at all times. A wonderful dispensation!

Reflecting on the numerous opportunities we have had in the past and still have today, I can only think that *all is grace.* I recall Mother saying that the Great White Brotherhood would do all that they did through the messengers for *one* soul, just one of Jesus' precious sheep that has gone astray.

Sponsorship of an Archangel

The following is a powerful excerpt from the same dictation where Archangel Michael describes what it means for us personally to have the sponsorship of an archangel.

I AM Archangel Michael! I stand for your eternal victory! And I will tell you one thing: There are days (as I count the days) when for one single one of you, I and my legions, in order to defend you, will slay ten thousand demons. [This we will do] on behalf of one Keeper of the Flame! Now understand how heaven goes to war for you! These are not small skirmishes. These are the wars against the ultimate fallen ones, who know you, who have your number and would see to it that you are put out of embodiment.

Blessed ones, when we come home from these battles, we are happy! We are happy to see you rejoicing. We are happy to see you in your recreation and in your dedicated service and [we are at your side strengthening you when the] hours are long. We would like you to know, however, what it takes on our part and on the part of your Mighty I AM Presence to keep you in embodiment on the Path. And we would like you to know that if you should apply just a little more effort to your dynamic decrees, we could help others like you who are not able to decree, for they know not of the science of the spoken Word.

Therefore we ask you to think of us each day out of God-gratitude for our service as we lay down our lives for you daily. And we ask you to manifest your gratitude by laying down some portion of your life in decreeing for the Lightbearers who are at the very next ring and the next and the next— three rings out from the Inner Retreat—whom you must go and find and save and defend.

We say, be ourselves in form! Defend them as we defend you! And see how you will meet your comrades of all ages and systems of worlds.[278]

It is also important to note that we are part of a mandala of souls who have been together for untold ages. I recall a master commenting that there are souls who are closer to us than our current families and friends that we have not seen since Atlantis. Not to mention our twin flames or soul mates that we may still be separated from as well. What we do can truly change the destiny of more souls than we can imagine.

We Are Called to Sponsor Others

Along with being called to be defenders of the lightbearers, we are also called to be sponsors of others. We can become *co-sponsors* with the ascended masters. In his Wesak address in 1998 Gautama Buddha told us:

> *Thus, in the endless chain of the figure-eight flow, sponsorship must extend; and when you become co-sponsors with us of the next rung of Lightbearers on the rung of the ladder beneath you, then those in embodiment who cannot see or understand us will embrace the path of the Seventh Ray of Aquarius because they see you and they see that though you may not be perfect or without fault, you are humble before your God, a joyously obedient servant, one who does not neglect the creative fires of Being on the altar of the heart.*[279]

Isn't it inspiring to think that by earnestly and humbly walking the Path we can be co-sponsors with the ascended masters?

I remember when attending early conferences in Pasadena and at Camelot how greatly I was affected by the students and their devotion. Their shining faces were a testimony, and I wanted to be like them. Now it's our turn to be the living testimony.

The Importance of Sponsorship

Now, just how important is sponsorship? In the dictation we are hearing today, Arcturus implores us not to take it for granted. It's quite simple: without sponsorship we wouldn't be here; we wouldn't have the violet flame; we wouldn't have the incredible support of archangels, Elohim and masters. With sponsorship we have sat at the feet of the embodied guru, if not physically then in videos and lectures; we have traveled in our finer bodies to high levels of the etheric that some souls haven't been to for thousands of years.

Because we are sponsored we have these teachings. We know who we are and who we are not. We have the fountain of eternal youth before us. We have the knowledge, the tools and the support to win our ascension and get Home to God if we choose.

In the dictation referenced earlier, Archangel Michael said he had observed us caught in the astral plane for decades between embodiments and he could not help us because of our free will choices that had taken us there. Sponsorship is the greatest gift for our greatest need. As Archangel Michael said, we "*have an extraordinary need for an extraordinary help.*"

Sponsorship can truly be a matter of life or death for a soul. Without sponsorship, the law acts without mercy. The compelling story of Sanat Kumara and the 144,000 who came with him to earth reveals the sponsorship of an entire planet and people.[280]

One way we can honor the sponsorship that we have received

is to sponsor others. But who do we sponsor? Or perhaps another way to ask that is: Who is worthy of sponsorship?

We know that God loves us all equally. However, there are souls who by cosmic law cannot be sponsored by the ascended masters at this time due to their heavy karma. There are also souls who have lost their threefold flame due to intense anger or pride and cannot be sponsored until they regain it, which can take centuries. We have been asked to make calls for those who have lost their threefold flame or are on the verge of losing it. And when we make the calls for those on planet Earth, why not expand the call to apply to every one of these souls throughout cosmos? It is doing something for souls that the masters cannot do.

On another note, think about the first thing that comes into your mind when I mention the laggard evolutions.[281] Do you have positive feelings about them? Well, interestingly enough, in the early 1970s when I was rather new in the teachings, I remember that the Karmic Board approved a proposal made by a Keeper of the Flame for the sponsorship of some of the laggard evolutions by individual Keepers! *Yes,* the laggards.

Many might ask, "Haven't they been 'written off' by the Brotherhood?" On the other hand, we might ask ourselves, "Are we being prejudiced against the laggards and other evolutions on earth whom we consider beyond the realm of salvation?" Jesus thinks we might be. In his Thanksgiving address 1994, he admonishes us and helps us realign our thinking and attitudes:

> *Oh, let there be the binding of the sense of sin and of the condemnation upon those who stray from the law. Have I not forgiven thee—forgiven thee and forgiven thee again and again? And have I not admonished you to forgive seventy times seven?* [282]

...We speak of prejudice against this Church or against this or that race, but do we know (and I speak for you as I am one of you) when we are unlawfully prejudiced against others? Do we automatically define this group and that group, these others and those others?...

This is not to say that you look down upon those who do not have the light of the eye or of the aura. But it is to say that at the very moment when by sheer mindless, unthinking habit you would be prejudiced against those whom you deem to be of lesser attainment on the Path, you turn to the beautiful face of my Father Maitreya and you remember his eternal kindness and his eternal compassion. And your heart then overflows with love for a soul, any soul, for here is God encased in mortal form....

The fact remains that I am the Lord and the Saviour of every lifestream upon earth, even those whom you would consider to be of the seed of the Wicked One or of the fallen angels or mechanization man, et cetera....

Understand, then, that inasmuch as God has given life to a soul, that soul shall have salvation through me, shall have my support until the LORD God himself declares that the hour of the final judgment of that one is come. It is only then that I let go of my service to set that lifestream free.[283]

Compassion for the Christ Potential in All

In that dictation, Jesus also used a tragic example to teach us what this is in practice. He referred to an event that occurred on October 25, 1994. Susan Smith of Union, South Carolina, reported that a man had hijacked her car at a traffic light and forced her to drive 10 miles at gunpoint. She told police that he then ordered her out of the car and took off with her two sons, Michael, 3, and Alex, 14 months.

On November 3, nine days after the alleged abduction, Smith confessed that she had killed her sons in desperation over money problems, her failed marriage and disappointment in romance. She told authorities she had set her car rolling into a nearby lake with her children strapped in the back seat. In her confession letter, she wrote: "I wanted to turn around so bad and go back, but I knew it was too late. I was an absolute mental case! I couldn't believe what I had done."

Public reaction to Smith was angry and intense. One person said, "She betrayed her children and the entire country." A woman at the nearby airport said, "She's slime, just slime." A woman whose daughter worked with Smith advocated "stringing her up right in the middle of the courthouse." As Smith left the courthouse following her arraignment, the crowd jeered and hissed. Her lawyer, David Bruck, said, "She is heartbroken."[284]

Perhaps you remember when this incident happened. I think probably most of us felt a similar condemnation of this woman and her actions. This is why many were shocked when Jesus made reference to it when he said:

> Think of the mother who in desperation took the life of her two little boys. How the nation is disgusted with this mother. Severe crimes are being committed every day in every nation. Shall we toss this one or that one onto the rubbish heap and say, "This one is no longer worthy of kindness or compassion. His sins are too great"?
>
> No, we shall not, beloved. For one day that one who receives kindness and compassion, together with the violet flame of the Holy Spirit, may surely be converted to the real and living Christ, who I AM. And I do not exclude souls from my Church or ministry based on human prejudice or on the darkness of their deeds.[285]

I recall Mother commenting about a prisoner who had killed a man in a fight who wrote to her and asked if he could become a Keeper of the Flame. She asked Jesus, and he told her the man could do so in one year. Mother said she wondered if all of us would have the same compassion that Jesus had. We can think of Mother Teresa as an example of someone who mastered this compassion for the Christ potential in all.

Compassion does not mean that we embrace the same philosophy that The Rolling Stones rock group promoted in their album entitled "Sympathy for the Devil." Nor does it mean we compromise the light that God has given us by somehow allowing ourselves to get entangled with people we should not.

Be Non-Judgmental

So how do we know when we encounter a lightbearer and when we face a person *"who is of the Evil One?"* [286] We know by the gift of discernment, the most important gift from the Holy Spirit. Jesus continues:

> But if you see by the gift of discernment of spirits that there is evil at the core of an individual, do not hesitate to call for the binding of that one's dweller-on-the-threshold that the soul might be liberated to fulfill her mission. [287]

I remember an experience I had in an elevator at the State Department in Washington, D.C. An individual came into the elevator who, though a professional dressed in a well-tailored suit, had the greatest manifestation of evil in his aura that I have ever experienced. I could hardly look at him, he was so dark. I believe that that was no accident, and I was able to make calls on the darkness he was manifesting. Even the judgment call is an act of love because we call for the judgment of actions not individuals.

This is illustrated quite clearly in verse 9 from the book of Jude: "*Yet Michael the archangel, when contending with the devil he disputed about the body of Moses, durst not bring against him a railing accusation, but said, The Lord rebuke thee.*" In the New Jerusalem Bible it reads: "*Not even the archangel Michael, when he was engaged in argument with the devil about the corpse of Moses, dared to denounce him in the language of abuse; all he said was, 'May the Lord rebuke you.'*"[288]

Michael did not condemn even the devil when talking to him about the body of Moses. He simply rebuked him but dared not denounce him in the language of abuse. God may send his wrath on the fallen ones, but our job is just to be the instrument to make the calls that need to be made.

God is the arbiter and judge of souls, not us. We can see through this teaching how non-judgmental we need to be. That doesn't mean we condone wrong action at any level. It does mean we cannot pronounce a soul lost until God himself makes that determination. This does not make us weaker; it makes us stronger as we are obedient to our calling. This does not mean we lesson the fire or intensity of our calls for the judgment of darkness and the saving of souls.

Some people hate rock musicians. Though it may be lawful to hate rock music, if we hate rock musicians at a personal level, a tie is created and we make karma with them. This could even prevent our ascension until it is resolved.

Our I AM Presence Can Sponsor Souls

As we refine our perspective on souls in need of sponsorship, one thought that may come to us is, "What is the cost to us if we sponsor others?" After all, when we are striving to balance karma, can we afford to put our "diamonds" of attainment on the altar as Jophiel did. We might also ask, "Aren't we ourselves the first person we need to save?" True, no doubt. But according to Arcturus, we can sponsor souls through the power of our I AM Presence. By doing so, he says we "*will lose nothing because the I AM Presence is infinite and has infinite glory and power and dominion.*"[289]

We can ask to sponsor souls all over the world through the I AM Presence—a million or even ten million souls. There is no limit to what God can do! I can hear some people thinking, "Sounds simple. What's the big deal? Can't we just make a quick call or write a note to the Karmic Board and ask to do it?" I'm not sure we can dismiss it so blithely.

There is a science to sponsorship based on cosmic law. I was pondering how it might work, and I thought of two decree inserts that appear to be based on the same principle as the opportunity Arcturus is speaking about. The first is 707B, "In the Name of My Mighty I AM Presence, I Go Forth to Heal Millions of Elementals in the Earth." It was dictated by Oromasis and Diana and makes very precise reference to what percentages of our I AM Presence can be allowed by the Lords of Karma for the liberation of elemental life.

This teaches us that we need to ask for the intercession of the Lords of Karma to adjudicate our request to sponsor souls. This is a great protection that allows us to safely ask for the maximum percentage of our I AM Presence allowed by the Great Law for the sponsoring of souls. And no doubt we could also balance karma that we may have with some of these individuals.

Oromasis also requested we make stickers of his call and place them where we would see them to remind us to give it frequently. Extrapolating from this, we can clearly understand that the use of our God Presence also requires the giving of specific calls daily or more frequently.

The second decree insert is entitled "Empower the Great White Brotherhood."[290] It came from a dispensation by Saint Germain and El Morya. The insert gives the "Great White Brotherhood the authority of my mighty I AM Presence to act in my name," giving them carte blanche to use our causal bodies in situations that are of "vital and urgent necessity." This call is magnificent, and if we would all give it daily, just think what the Brotherhood could do!

These inserts and the request by Arcturus to sponsor souls give a hint of the incredible power of our I AM Presence and causal bodies. I was talking to a friend about this request from Arcturus and wondering how it seems to have escaped notice for so long. She reminded me that sometimes the dictations came so fast there was hardly time to assimilate them before another and another came. Now we have the time to seek out and find these incredible teachings and, more importantly, the time to implement them.

Take Advantage of Arcturus's Dispensation

A dispensation and opportunity like this only works if some take advantage of it. If some will, in the words of Arcturus, *"deliberate profoundly"*[291] and *act*, incredible things can happen. It is one thing to intellectually acknowledge what this can mean, and quite another to wholeheartedly do it.

The cover of this week's bulletin has a quote from Arcturus's dictation as a reminder for us to make the calls. I'm sure many of you have a good way to organize your calls, but you might want to take this page and put it where you will see it every day and can make the call.

What I have found works for me is to have a file folder filled with prayer requests and items for calls, otherwise I simply forget to give some of them. Going through the folder is like turning the pages of a book and summoning the fire to make calls for immediate needs as well as some of the ongoing challenges on the planet.

This type of attention to detail can make our work so much more effective. And as we learn to pour more love and fire into our decrees, the difference can be dramatic. As we heard today in the children's story about the ascended master Igor, lives will be changed, lives will be saved. Why? Because some loved enough to take advantage of dispensations and make the calls day after day, month after month.

Sponsor Souls!

What you will also hear from Arcturus today is a plea to remember those who do not have sponsors. What if we could help make the difference for souls by sponsoring them just as we have been sponsored? What a profound opportunity to respond to the call of Elohim and help others. Can't you imagine the excitement of a soul without hope who suddenly has possibilities in their lives that they never had before!

Let us remember our own path and what sponsorship has meant to us. I literally get chills thinking about it. This incredible opportunity to help souls without sponsorship was almost lost in the thousands of dictations we have available to us. Now that we know about it, we can do something!

Arcturus pleads with us to *"rise up in a certain dominion, a certain selflessness, a certain sense that* you must *be there for the Divine Mother. You must be there for the angels of God."*[292]

The ascended master Igor encourages us with this viewpoint:

Now, precious hearts, know that heaven is not far, but so very close. Know, then, that all that you are required to give in this hour of giving is but a fragment, a morsel of all that God has given to you, and that in your giving, billions of souls will go free. In your withholding, an evolution may be lost.[293]

And Arcturus charges us:

Be ye therefore intercessors on behalf of all people!...
Defend all souls. Go after them! Pursue them as if you were the hound of heaven! And realize that you are in embodiment for one reason: to be the defender of souls who cannot at this point in time defend themselves before the Lords of Karma....
Thus we, as Elohim, come as the champions. We enlist you as champions. You have the knowledge. You have the tools. You have the voice!...
I say to you, become sponsors of souls who do not merit the sponsorship of an Ascended Master. Sponsor souls! Bring them along on the Path until they come to that level where an Ascended Master may apply a portion of his Causal Body in sponsorship. Sponsorship is the key, beloved.[294]

We may even ask for the opportunity to sponsor millions of souls. If it is hard to think of millions, think of one. Have a picture of a child or a soul without hope that can represent the millions.

Imagine a time in the future when, by the grace of God, you are ascended, and a soul approaches you who has also won their ascension because they had opportunity through your sponsorship—who could have easily been lost forever without it. What will that mean to you? What will it mean to God? Can you imagine the gratitude for this one victory or one of many? While acknowledging God is the doer, we can do our part by making ourselves available to him to do what no ascended master can do.

We can make the difference *"as to whether a single soul— and millions of souls—shall have everlasting life or go through the second death."*[295] We are not overwhelmed or made proud by this because we know that God is the doer—so we make ourselves available daily in his service.

It is a high and holy calling—one that we were born for. It is our Father's business and our Lord's. For did he not say, *"it is not the will of your Father which is in heaven, that one of these little ones should perish."*[296]

God in us, our I AM Presence, can be the sponsor of one soul or of millions of souls. Let us rejoice in this opportunity as we affirm this mantra with Arcturus,

"I AM the sponsor. I AM the sponsor. I AM the sponsor."[297]

DEFEATING THE
LAST ENEMY

Fear not, then. Death is the last enemy.
Defeat it now! Get it out of the way!
And accept the glory of your eternal Life.

—JUSTINIUS

Defeating the Last Enemy

Our readings today are from 1st Corinthians Chapter 15: *"For this corruptible must put on incorruption, and this mortal must put on immortality. So when this corruptible shall have put on incorruption, and this mortal shall have put on immortality, then shall be brought to pass the saying that is written, Death is swallowed up in victory. O death, where is thy sting? O grave, where is thy victory?"*[298] Verse 26 is short and clear: *"The last enemy that shall be destroyed is death."*

For those who have chosen the path of the ascension and their reunion with God, these verses tell us that defeating death is an inevitable part of our path to victory. We can review in our minds what that victory will look like as we prepare for our ascension at the conclusion of this life.

The Day of Our Victory

When we come to the day of our transition, we will stand alone in the honor of God. We have stood alone and experienced aloneness many times before in this life and others. It might have been the aloneness we felt when our I AM Presence withdrew for a season or the aloneness of standing before the courts of men, accused because of the light in our hearts. We have all known the feeling. But putting on immortality is an aloneness unlike any other. It is an *all-one-ness*.

Imagine you are standing on the dais at Luxor just before you ascend, anticipating the moment you have striven for since your first incarnation in matter. At times it seemed like an impossible dream, yet here, by God's grace, you stand. As the ascension flame, the honor flame, starts to rise beneath your feet, the joy of victory fills your entire being.

Oh, if you could only tell all who would listen—every test, every trial, every sickness of the mind and body, every failure that brought new determination, the many times of despair or loneliness, the loss of those we loved, the emptiness of times without God—it was all worth it!

Paul echoed this when he wrote: "*For I reckon that the sufferings of this present time are not worthy to be compared with the glory which shall be revealed in us.*"[299] And I love how Mother Teresa put it, even though her perspective didn't include reincarnation: "*In the light of heaven, the worst suffering on earth, a life full of the most atrocious tortures on earth, will be seen to be not more serious than one night in an inconvenient hotel.*"[300]

Serapis Bey gives us a vision of our day of victory:

Have you not heard the trumpets of Luxor, the angel choirs singing the victory, the triumphal march—the march of your triumph? For that is the song of the ascension flame, and that is the march of candidates marching from the four quadrants to the flame. They march in time and space. They march across Cosmos. They march to the place where time and space are no more and death is swallowed up in victory.[301]

In the depths of our being we know our victory is by the grace of God, the sponsorship of the ascended masters, the violet flame and the many things that made this moment possible. But it is not a passive victory. It is also the result of our striving, our service, and our determination to overcome every obstacle before us—our karma, our psychology and the forces of darkness arrayed against us. It is the result of our determination to never give up, no matter what the pain.

We have been taught that pain is the portal to bliss, that it is part of our path to freedom. We also know that God will not bring us any more pain than is necessary and that it will pass as we win our victory.

We Must *Win* Our Ascension

The ascension is a real possibility for students of the masters, but that victory is not won until it is won. Until we step down from the dais in Luxor as an ascended master, the victory is not finally won.

Let us free ourselves from everything within us that makes us vulnerable to the wiles of the fallen ones. As we move forward with courage, God will help us be victorious. And many of us still have one major battle that we must win before we ascend. We must, as Saint Paul said, defeat the last enemy—death.

How could we possibly ascend if we have not defeated the darkness of death within our being? Our Saviour defeated death and showed us the way. Now we must defeat it too. Though it might seem overwhelming, we cannot dismiss the need to prepare for and engage in this fight.

Understanding what death is and what it isn't defines the battle in terms we can relate too. Lanello and the masters have brought us the wisdom and understanding we need to win. In a dictation not long after his ascension, Lanello reflected:

> *There comes a time in the life of every initiate when he must face the temptation to believe that death is real....*
>
> *Somehow, somewhere, through habit and indoctrination, mankind have accepted the concept that the laying down of the physical body, the cessation of life and consciousness and heartbeat in the material form, is the definition of death. This definition is neither scriptural nor is it founded in cosmic law. As we, then, intensify our effort to merge our consciousness with your own, we can do aught but challenge the record, the memory, and the consciousness of death that lurks as the enemy within the camp at subconscious levels of humanity's awareness.*[302]

From the earliest days on my path, I can remember the admonition to make calls to clear "records of death." I didn't totally understand the concept and, at my young age back then, I didn't really consider the ramifications of those records. However, as we mature on the Path, we recognize the importance of clearing these records. I heard an estimate that we have had one hundred thousand lifetimes on planet earth! Whatever the number, we know it is a lot. And for each lifetime there was a physical death and, therefore, a record of death.

How many times did we die in battle or from some terrible disease? How many times did we die in our beds? How many times were we murdered? How many times did our loved ones die? How many times did we die and leave them behind? All these things leave records of death in our consciousness. So much grief and sorrow and pain! In this life, I deeply felt the early passing of my father to cancer, and I know how my whole family was affected. That's just one lifetime. If we consider these various records and multiply them by the tens of thousands of lifetimes we have had, it's no wonder we need the violet flame to help transmute them!

As we explore defeating the last enemy, let us be merciful to ourselves considering the records we carry. Our souls have been on an arduous journey, and we have made a lot of mistakes along the way. But now we are on the cusp of our victory. We are so close. And even though we must still win this victory, we have the preparation from this and other lifetimes, along with the knowledge of the steps of the Path, the violet flame and all the spiritual tools the masters have given us. It is possible to succeed! When we do our part as we have been taught, God in his mercy and love for us will do the rest.

Defining Death as the Last Enemy

Aside from rare exceptions, we know that we will all experience a physical death as the gateway to our ascension. As Lanello puts it, *"Clearly there is a death which must be welcomed as the edict of the Lord and a death which must be overcome—and this, too, is his edict."*[303]

Serapis Bey outlines some requirements for our victory in the ascension:

> *I say then, God-mastery is the requirement, and God-obedience. You must have dominion over death in order to inherit immortal Life. You must transmute the planetary death consciousness. Death that has come out of Egypt as the perversion of the ascension spiral in the great pyramid must be consumed now—ahead of time, before you face death. Before death comes knocking at the door—that is the time to consume it in the flame of the ascension current.*[304]

We cannot accept the world's consciousness regarding death. Hopefully, none of us suffers from "thanatophobia" which is anxiety caused by fear of death. I recently came across an article about death meditation which is described as a "mindfulness meditation process centered around thoughts of a person's death [that] has taken social media by storm, with 2.5 million views on TikTok."[305] One of the latest aspects of this has people wrapping themselves up as mummies and picturing their dead bodies to imagine and come to terms with their eventual death. Isn't that strange? A psychologist quoted in the article said, "*You recognize that death is a real thing. We're not immortal, and having that recognition is important so that you make the most of today.*"[306] These things affirm death instead of life, and that's the opposite of what the masters teach about the soul's path to immortality.

Though we must challenge the consciousness of death in ourselves and on this planet, we should do it in the way the masters have instructed us. We have been asked to make calls for the arresting of the spirals of death and hell on the planet. This assignment, of course, begins with arresting the spirals of death and hell within ourselves.

That which God has made cannot die, whereas all that is unreal *will* die. As Lanello puts it:

> *In this context we define death as the cessation of being. Neither God nor his creation—his offspring, the Christ—can die. But the creation of unreality, of darkness and sin, of the Liar and the lie, is doomed to death from the moment of its inception.*[307]

While we accept that we will go through the change called death as we leave this physical octave, we must not accept the world's view of death. Instead, we must realize that death is a transition to our true home of light.

Death Is Not Real

While death is our entrée into the heaven world, the fallen ones know at some level of their being that their time of opportunity is up and that they will pass through the second death.[308] So to them death is final.

I remember when Nelson Rockefeller died Mother informed us that he went to the second death. Henry Kissinger (who Mother told us was embodied as Caiphas at the time of Jesus) gave the eulogy at his funeral. He was crying throughout, perhaps for Rockefeller and perhaps partly for himself and his future fate.

The fallen ones work to perpetuate a culture of death on the planet. They seek revenge against God by going after his children. It is incumbent upon us to overcome the consciousness of death in ourselves and set the example for other lightbearers that they might free themselves as well.

This culture of death can enter our being in very subtle ways. Archangel Michael and Kuthumi explain one way this can happen:

Often those of elder years conclude by voices or premonitions that their time is spent. More often than not, these are the voices of entities that speak from out of the decay within the body that is not clean, that has not pursued the paths and ablutions of self-purification. Thus, there is the tempter who is the false-hierarchy impostor of the angel spirit who comes to take the soul to other years and other spheres at the hour appointed.[309]

In contrast, Mother once told the story of a very elderly woman in our community who was suffering from a fatal illness. The woman fought valiantly for months to defeat it, but it was clear that it was a losing battle. She wrote to Mother and asked permission to surrender to the inevitable and Mother told her she was free to go. She had won the battle!

Mother Mary makes it very clear that we must do the same:

> Love not your lives unto the death, for death is but a chimera. It is not real; it was not ever real; it never shall be real!....
>
> Our Son, Jesus, proved beyond the shadow of a doubt that there is no death. And he has asked me to ask you this day, would you not like also to prove the unreality of death in this life? [310]

Where do we start to prove Mother Mary and Jesus' declaration that death is not real?

Death as Doubt and Fear

Ray-O-Light gives us a clue. He teaches, "Death has two components: doubt and fear." [311] As we all know, doubt and fear go hand in hand, and every one of us has fear at some level of our beings. Fear of death has so permeated life on this planet that, even with all that we know, we still need to work on freeing ourselves from it.

Archangel Michael elaborates on what we must do:

> Banish doubt! I say: It is the enemy of your certain victory. Banish fear! I say, for it displaces all love of God's holy will.
>
> And, beloved, see to it that [you challenge] all records of Death and Hell that challenge [your] eternal faith in God's

law and will, see to it that you arrive each Friday night at our services until you have vanquished every record of death that has accrued to your lifestream and your electronic belt in the past two and a half million years. Blessed ones, let no record of death remain nor of hell itself! [312]

What a key—fear *"displaces all love of God's holy will."* In other words, implicit in loving and following God's will is having absolute trust in him, and that trust can never include fear!

An excellent way to work on momentums of fear and doubt is to challenge them as they come up. For example, if you feel a fear regarding some part of death, you can challenge it right then and there. You might give a fiat something like: "My Saviour defeated death and, with his help, so can I!" Or "In the name of Almighty God, be gone fear! Be gone doubt!" Or as Ray-O-Light taught, "Strip us of all doubt and fear." Fiats like that can roll back and neutralize any fear or doubt. It's important that we don't let any energies tied to death and hell go unchallenged when they crop up in our consciousness.

Mother's Victorious Battle with Death and Hell

Saint Germain told us about an incredible encounter that the messenger had with death and hell before she left Los Angeles to move to the Inner Retreat in Montana. He said:

Blessed ones, I will tell you of the final initiation of the Messenger in Los Angeles. It was to deal with a confrontation of Death and Hell. It comes to all, beloved. It is well that you know of the Messenger's initiation, for you must have a keen vision.

You must know that the last time she left here in late fall to return to Los Angeles, descending into the city and into the airport she saw [through the eye of an Archangel and said to herself], "This is a city of death and all whom I see are the living dead." And it was so, as far as those who happened to be in the airport at that time. For I did portray vividly a panorama of the dead/wounded dying, that she might know, by stark contrast to the Inner Retreat and the spiritual life, the challenge that remained. And so she saw clearly through my heart that this "death" and the "city of death" would seek to devour her ere she should leave. And so, praying earnestly, she went about the business of concluding my book and others.

Blessed ones, you should know of the projections of Death that were played upon her by masterminds of the false hierarchy twenty-four hours a day, waking and sleeping. These projections were vivid as movies, as though on film, portraying a blow-by-blow account of what her demise should be in the coming weeks. Having scarce the time to separate herself from the writing of the books, there grew in her an inner resolve of resistance to Death and a transmittal to the decree tags[313] *of the understanding of this force and its modus operandi that I gave to her.*

And this is the key, beloved—whether it is the death wish of the various sects of religion on earth wishing and willing the death of the Messenger, whether it is Russian psychics or KGB agents who have masterminded the ability to probe the human mind and penetrate it, whether it is from Mars or Pluto or the moon or Hell itself, those embodied or disembodied, Death yet exists in the astral plane and it will come knocking at your door one of these days as surely as Death knocked clearly and loudly at the bedroom door of your Messenger in Los Angeles.

And this occurred at the hour of 4:00 a.m. And at that hour the loud rap came twice—a physical sound bringing her to the awakened state and then the instantaneous knowledge that though the sound were physical, the presence was astral.

After moments and minutes of silence assessing this knock, which came only days before her departure, and assessing the astral vibration and all of the compounding of these projections of Death, there began to be heard in the farthest star, where angels waited breathless for the response, the cry and the call that went forth: "Archangel Uriel, enter this house and bind Death and Hell!" These calls of the Messenger continued unabated beyond an hour until the Peace of the Archangel had devoured and bound the enemy.

Blessed hearts, within twenty-four to thirty-six hours of that event, the Messenger with her daughters seated here experienced a carefree return to youth, of joy and laughter and fun and jokes. Beloved, it was the victory over Death, whose victory is always the Lord's if only the one assailed will make the Call.[314]

Saint Germain said death and hell will come knocking at our door one day, but we can be prepared to be victorious over them! We need to take his words to heart. Every one of us has experienced projections that were sent against us. Mother was not exempt from them, but she developed a strong *"inner resolve of resistance to Death,"* and we can all pray for that same resolve. Following her example again, we can also make the call for the binding of death and hell!

I am familiar with experiences of death energies that individuals have had similar to Mother's before they embarked on a major commitment to the Path, such as attending Summit University or joining the Church's staff. Dealing with death energies is a hard test, but as Mother demonstrated, making the call can be key to the victory. All that one of these individuals could do was call to Jesus to help him, repeating Jesus' name over and over. He made the call and that was enough to displace the intense darkness, proving that God is greater than any evil that may assail us.

Practices to Help Overcome Death Energies

So what is the death energy that must be defeated so we can have our victory? Lanello explains:

> *The death that is overcome is the sense of death, the fear of death, even the second death and the dissolution of worlds. The death that is overcome is finality and the force that would seek to rob the soul of its eternality.*[315]

Do we harbor the concept of finality when we think of our death? As we know, it is only the fallen ones that should fear the finality of death—the second death.

When we tackle specific energies within ourselves, we need to be as precise as possible in our calls. When we name a fear, it seems to lose some of its power, and we can work with the masters to clear it from our being. When you can name it, you can tame it!

The following are a few of the fears regarding death that we can make calls on. I suspect that each of us has other fears that we can also name.

1. Fear of fatal diseases
2. Fear of pain and suffering
3. Fear of dementia
4. Fear caused by records of death
5. Fear of leaving/losing loved ones
6. Fear of being taken out of embodiment prematurely

7. Fear we will not defeat our dweller-on-the-threshold
8. Fear we will get caught in the astral plane
9. Fear of standing before the Karmic Board for our life review
10. Fear we will not make our ascension because of all our "unforgiveable sins"
11. Fear we might have to reembody
12. Fear of prophecy and Armageddon

As students of the masters, we might have some of the fears in this list just because we have more knowledge of the spiritual realms than our Christian friends or most people. Most Christians are convinced beyond a doubt that they are saved and have nothing to fear, which is the reason many are angry when they die and find out the truth. How grateful we are that we know the truth and can work on being freed from our fears *now.*

Three of the best ways to free ourselves from death energy are: invoking the violet flame, binding our dweller-on-the-threshold, and calling to the Elohim Astrea. Even though that's hardly news to us, nevertheless it is important to be precise in our calls and decrees so we can receive the maximum benefit from them.

There is also a certain fierceness and intensity we must bring to our calls to clear the records that we haven't been able to touch before. Transmuting our records of death is vital to overcoming fears—conscious, subconscious, or unconscious. The most dangerous fears are the unconscious ones because they are so well hidden. I'm guessing that most of us have spent some time in the astral plane between embodiments and have had uncomfortable life reviews before the Karmic Board. All of us may also be dealing with the records of the sinking of Lemuria and Atlantis. It is understandable that we fear a repeat of those events since we have been told that some people are still not over the sinking of Lemuria—fifty thousand years later!

I like to make lists of things for my calls, including types of fear that may be lurking in my unconscious mind. That way I can make the calls without forgetting to name any of them.

Try making a list of fears and records from this life, and then you might even list records the masters have mentioned that affected us all, like leaving the Mystery School and the sinking of Lemuria and Atlantis. Again, be as precise and specific as you can. Remember, as mentioned before, if you can name it, you can tame it! As you are consistent with making the calls, I believe you will see a reduction or elimination of these fears. You will also be less vulnerable to aggressive mental suggestion from the fallen angels and dark forces.

The Part of Us that Must Die

If we are to defeat death, then that part of us that is not real and can never inherit eternal life must be defeated. It is the one part of us that must die. It is our carnal mind, our dweller-on-the-threshold, our synthetic self, our not-self. Whatever you want to call it, it *must* go. Of course, we know that on one level. But are we engaged at the intensity that is needed to be free of this unreality once and for all?

Even as we call for the transmutation of the fears around death, we also need to cast out those fears in our dweller calls. The dweller itself has a fear of death and will fight to the finish. We cannot defeat this darkness by ourselves but need the help of the angels and masters to surgically remove those portions of the dweller and cast them into the lake of fire.

Consistency is the key. Defeating death requires daily calls that are specific to our goal. The masters have given us a formula for success that includes daily calls to Archangel Michael and the violet flame, as a support for doing dweller calls. The dweller must be bound every day lest it vent its darkness into your world when you least expect it. The conclusion of the decree to cast out the dweller-on-the-threshold clearly emphasizes the importance of overcoming death: *"Lo, I AM, in Jesus' name, the victor over Death and Hell! Lo, I AM, in Jesus' name, the victor over Death and Hell! Lo, I AM THAT I AM in me—in the name of Jesus Christ—is here and now the victor over Death and Hell! Lo! It is done."* [316]

There will only be *one* victor in our battle with the dweller, and with God's help it will be us.

Glimpses of the Heaven-World

We have been taught what to expect in our chelaship, in our testing, in the fallen ones' challenge to our path of Christhood. We live the Path every day. Our goal is our ascension, and we have a foretaste of what it will be like from what the masters have told us. But, personally, I am not really clear what it will be like to be, in the words of Lanello, *"everywhere in the consciousness of God."* [317]

In this regard, I have found it helpful to read about near-death experiences or NDEs. As you know, NDEs happen when a person physically dies but comes back to life, often with a story of what they experienced. For the most part I think these individuals visited the lower levels of the etheric octave, but even so the descriptions are breathtaking. And though they don't describe being *everywhere* in God's consciousness, I wanted to share a few NDEs that paint a glorious image of the heaven-world and offer just a small glimpse of what we can expect when our victory is won.

There are dozens of books about NDEs but the one I will be reading from is *Imagine Heaven* by John Burke, a pastor from

Texas. The book is written from a very Christian viewpoint and has nothing about reincarnation in it. Nevertheless, I found many of the descriptions so compelling that I wanted to share a few with you.

I love the story by a gentleman named Ian McCormack who got caught in the astral plane and Jesus came to rescue him. Here is how he described what happened:

> *Directly behind Jesus was a circular shaped opening like the tunnel I had just traveled down. Gazing out through it, I could see a whole new world opening up before me. I felt like I was standing on the edge of paradise . . ..*
>
> *Through the center of the meadows I could see a crystal clear stream winding its way across the landscape with trees on either bank. To my right were mountains in the distance and the sky above was blue and clear. . ..*
>
> *Jesus asked me this question: "Ian, now that you have seen do you wish to return?" I thought "Return, of course not. Why would I want to go back? Why would I want to return to the misery and hatred? No, I have nothing to return for. I have no wife or kids, no one who really loves me. You are the first person who has ever truly loved me. . .."*
>
> *But he didn't move so I looked back one last time to say, "Goodbye cruel world I'm out of here!"* [318]

What happened next was that he saw a vision of his mother and others he knew and realized that there *were* people who loved him. And then he saw many others that he didn't know or love, but Jesus said that *he* loved them and wanted them to come to know him. So Ian went back to share the truth of heaven and hell and the afterlife.

The next story is by a gentleman named Dale who was the

only survivor of a small plane that crashed. He left his body and was escorted away by two angels dressed in seamless white garments woven with silver threads. He tells about his experience.

> *I was fast approaching a magnificent city, golden and gleaming among a myriad of resplendent colors. The light I saw was the purest I had ever seen. And the music was the most majestic, enchanting, and glorious I had ever heard. I was still approaching the city, but now I was slowing down. Like a plane making its final approach for landing. I knew instantly this place was entirely and utterly holy. Don't ask me how I knew, I just knew.*
>
> *I was overwhelmed by its beauty. It was breathtaking. And a strong sense of belonging filled my heart; I never wanted to leave. Somehow I knew I was made for this place and this place was made for me . . .. The entire city was bathed in light, an opaque whiteness in which the light was intense but diffused. In that dazzling light every color imaginable seemed to exist and—what's the right word?—played . . .. The colors seemed to be alive, dancing in the air. I had never seen so many different colors. . .. It was breathtaking to watch. And I could have spent forever doing just that.*[319]

He goes on to relate that the light didn't shine on things from an outside source but rather shone directly from things themselves—everything emanating its own light. He talks about the incredible beauty of the flowers in colors we have never seen, and picture-perfect homes. He describes a huge gathering of angels and countless millions of people outside the city moving in the light and worshipping God.[320]

Ahh, but what happens to people in near death experiences

is that everything is wonderful and great until *what*? Until they are told they have to go back to earth.

I think one of the reasons there are so many near death experiences is that it's a way for God to show someone that they have unfinished business to complete so that they will not have to embody again. And unless it is God's will, I don't think any of us want to come back. Jesus told us: *"Foreseeing the world as I foresee it, I do not recommend in all cosmic honor that you plan on reembodying again on this earth."* [321] Looking around the world today, I think we can understand that.

The final NDE story I want to share with you is by a woman named Crystal, reflecting on her experience in heaven. She admits that it's challenging to find the right words to describe everything she experienced in heaven, simply because human language is so inadequate that it doesn't even come close to conveying the reality. She says words like "beautiful," "brilliant," and "amazing" fall far short. The book details the following:

> *"What I experienced in heaven was so real and so lucid and so utterly intense, it made my experiences on Earth seem hazy and out of focus—as if heaven is the reality and life as we know it is just a dream."* Crystal describes being immersed in a feeling of complete and utter purity, perfection, unbrokenness, and peace, a kind of assurance she's never experienced on earth. *"It was like being bathed in love,"* she remembers. *"It was a brightness I didn't just see, but felt. And it felt familiar, like something I remembered, or even recognized. The best way to put it is this: I was home."* [322]

How long has it been since we left "home"? As Archangel Michael said, for many of us it's been two and a half million years! We have a home in heaven with our Father-Mother God, with the ascended masters and with others who have served the light. We've obviously been away a very long time from wherever we came from. Now is the hour of our return and we certainly don't want to come back into embodiment to take care of unfinished business and unbalanced karma.

Become the Example

Deep within our being is a compelling impetus to balance our karma, complete our mission, and return to the heart of God from whence we came. Obviously, we are not finished on earth since we are still here. And along with balancing our karma and fulfilling other requirements, we must defeat the last enemy.

Beloved Justinius makes our assignment clear:

> *Fear not, then. Death is the last enemy. Defeat it now! Get it out of the way! And accept the glory of your eternal Life. This is my message to you. Defeat Death and Hell today and get on with living the Life everlasting here on earth while you yet enjoy being in full health in physical embodiment yet caught up in resurrection's flame.*
>
> *Be the example! Let your Light shine!* [323]

Many people need our example. Mark and Mother were our examples. As we have been told, what man has done, man can do. As we win our victory, others will follow in our footsteps.

There will come a time when each one of us will answer the call from our Father-Mother God to move on to a higher dimension. Let our transition be not one minute sooner nor one minute later than God wills it. And let us complete the race that is set before us with patience, with determination, with fire, with love, and with gratitude and joy.

What happens to us next all depends on us. Saint Germain spoke of this:

> *Therefore it is good, it is well to contemplate one's mortality. I ask you to contemplate it, for you will see very quickly that you must do more if you are to guarantee your victory in this life. And do you know you are the guarantor of your own victory? Who else can guarantee your victory! It is your choice. It is your day.*[324]

So have no doubt that, with God's help, you can do it! Jesus showed us the way, the messengers showed us the way, and many in our community have shown us the way. Death can be defeated; *every* ascended master has done so! They are our examples. What they have done, we can do.

Is there any other choice to make?

"BE MY CHRIST"

*This is the day that the path of thy Christhood must
begin in earnest. Not [postponed] till tomorrow
but today, my Christ, thy Christ One.*

—JESUS

✳

*I AM your Jesus.
Now I say to you, Be my Christ!*

—JESUS

THIRTEEN

"Be My Christ"

It was a Sunday, not unlike many that came before and many that came after. It was the early 1980s and Mother was present almost every Sunday at Camelot, the church headquarters in Malibu, California. The congregation began decrees by 9:00 a.m. to prepare the forcefield so she could give her sermon and deliver a dictation. We would decree until it was time for the Sacred Ritual and then decree again afterwards. Between the Chapel of the Holy Grail and the Summit University classroom, there must have been several hundred people decreeing in anticipation of Mother's arrival.

By 11:00 or 11:30 that morning you could read the thoughts of the congregation wondering when Mother would come. Then shortly after noon the thought of lunch started to intrude, at least for me, since I knew that the service would take a while and it could easily be 2:00 or later before we ate.

Mother came out between 1:00 and 1:30. There was an almost audible sigh of relief when she appeared. She told us that she had been waiting for us to clear the energy of opposition to the service before she came out, and we still hadn't done so.

After telling us that, she turned to the altar and made a brief call. "There," she said, "the energy is cleared."

What a lesson! It was obvious that because Mother had been willing to pay the price for her spiritual mastery, she was able to accomplish in a few seconds what several hundred people had not been able to do in a few hours!

The Value of Christhood

Today America and the world seem to be plunging irreversibly into darkness. Hardly a day goes by that we're not shocked by something we see in our culture or in the world. It's an obvious burden on us and the masters.

While it's important to be aware of what happens on this planet, *just being aware is not enough.* We pray and make our calls. We wonder how things will ever change. In asking ourselves what is missing, we are faced with the questions: What is the equation for the victory of America and the precious lightbearers on earth? What are *we* willing to do to attain our Christhood?

What is the value of a Christed one? If there is one soul that can truly inspire us regarding this, it is the ascended master Igor. Lord Maitreya said:

> Remember Igor, the unknown saint who kept the vigil with the blessed Mother of Jesus during the Bolshevik revolution. Blessed ones, that single isolated saint keeping the flame and keeping the tie to the Blessed Mother did prevent untold millions [from perishing] who would have been engaged in bloodshed and would have [indeed] perished.[325]

One devoted soul and untold millions saved! It's incredible to think that a single Christed one can make such a difference.

If Mother could make one brief call and clear the energy that hundreds couldn't clear in several hours, if one humble saint of God prevented *millions* from perishing in the Russian revolution, isn't our path obvious in this hour of earth's darkness? It's time to become the Christ!

I believe that if earth's victory is to be won, we individually and collectively must decide that our human consciousness, our dweller and our karma will *not* prevent us from fulfilling our high and holy calling of being the Christ in embodiment.

Jesus Calls Us to Christhood

Putting on our Christhood is more than just a good thing to do. It is actually *required* of us. In his 1982 Christmas Day address, Jesus admonished us:

> *The years are hastening on. Soon two thousand years of Christmases will have been celebrated in my name. Heed, then, the Law. For in the conclusion of the cycle of this life, your Christhood is not only expected, it is demanded. And to fail to be that one, therefore, will result in untold setback and the discontinuation of assistance and intercession by the hosts of the LORD. You will then truly be on your own.*[326]

That's not only a sobering thought but a necessary one for each of us who may not be striving at the level we need to be. So we are humbly grateful for Jesus' admonition.

Then in 1987, Jesus gave the landmark dictation we will be hearing today. He told us, *"This is the day that the path of thy Christhood must begin in earnest. Not [postponed] till tomorrow but today, my Christ, thy Christ One."*[327] The mercy and grace of God is that we still have opportunity. Yet what's going to motivate us to fulfill Jesus' call given thirty-six years ago?

Thirty-five thousand years ago two million of us who had Christ mastery went with Jesus when he left Atlantis after he was rejected by the people. One million of our brothers and sisters made their ascension, but we are still here. Ernon, the Rai of Suern, explained why some didn't make it:

> *The one million who did not ascend, though they had Christ-attainment, did not have the sufficiency of love to sustain that level of devotion that would allow them to merit the ascension.*[328]

Thirty-five thousand years ago!! Even though we had Christ-attainment, we didn't have enough love to see us through to our victory. And we subsequently lost the attainment we had. Is it any wonder that God is demanding that we put on our Christhood once and for all? And if we don't take advantage of this opportunity, when will we have another chance?

Where are those who ascended thirty-five thousand years ago now? Where are they in their spiritual evolution? No doubt many are cosmic beings! That should awaken us to the realization that we need to do something differently. We have our spiritual practices. We're doing decrees, and a lot is being accomplished. But what's the equation that's going to truly turn this planet around? If we are not walking the earth as Christed ones right now, then we need to do something more.

We can't condemn ourselves, or belittle ourselves, or think ourselves unworthy. That's all human nonsense. However, we do need to recognize that the negative momentums we've been dragging around with us are like a ball and chain. In Jesus' dictation he speaks of *"becoming fed up with the old ways of the old man."*[329] Isn't that true? Aren't you fed up with the old ways?

I am. And that is an incentive to get rid of those patterns so we may be closer to our Lord, follow his example and his instruction to *"Love one another, as I have loved you."* [330]

Saint Germain's Challenge and Plan for Our Christhood

In 1991 Saint Germain challenged us to decide to put on our Christhood once and for all:

Determine that you shall be wed to your Holy Christ Self by a certain day and date and set a reasonable timetable for yourself. Then call for the initiations of Jesus Christ and ask that you might be made his very personal disciple and that he might anoint you this night. Set yourself to the task of rooting out, plucking out, line by line and hair by hair, every point that is out of alignment with that Christ-potential within you. [331]

When I thought about his challenge, I felt more than a little trepidation. Of course, we are striving to put on our Christhood and hopefully we are making progress. But setting a date definitely changed the equation and raised many questions for me: How could I know what date to set? What would I have to do differently than what I am doing now? Can I really become the Christ? Have I just been paying lip service to attaining Christhood while remaining comfortable in my daily routines? Suddenly, I saw Maitreya in the distance walking towards me and there was no place to hide!

True chelaship can make us uncomfortable—but it will certainly change us for the better. Isn't that what we want?

Saint Germain is the master alchemist. I don't believe he would have urged us to set a date for our Christhood if we didn't need to. His dictation was given in 1991, and by the mercy and grace of God we still have the opportunity to respond to it. It came almost four years after Jesus's dictation that we'll be hearing today.

Saint Germain outlined a practical, scientific plan for us to reach our goal:

> *Most individuals do not have more than five seriously bad habits in their worlds. You should isolate what you consider to be five [negative] practices or habits, character traits or momentums that you notice are repetitive in your life.*
>
> *Isolate them. Go after them. Call to the Five Dhyani Buddhas [to help you]! Call to Mighty Cosmos' five secret rays [to help you]! Go after the eradication of those points, beloved, perhaps points of density or ignorance or slothfulness or untidiness or unkindness, et cetera, et cetera.*[332]

Identifying the five habits and going after them takes courage and a strong self-identity that is willing to see our shortcomings, wants to be free of them, and does not see them as our ultimate reality.

As I went about this task, I was forced to look at things in my consciousness that I knew were there, but that I hadn't really known how to deal with. I also found that I had to remind myself that these habits were not really me, but only something I had temporarily allowed to be part of me. What a joy, what a freedom, I thought, to be liberated from them!

I knew I could work on these even if I did not set a date for achieving Christhood and wondered if it was necessary to do so. After all, how would I even go about setting a date? Would I even know for sure if I had put on my Christhood? What if I failed? Where would I be then? Did I really need that extra pressure on me?

Well, that certainly sounds like the carnal mind speaking, doesn't it? What would we lose by not setting a date? First of all, Saint Germain called for us to set a date. In my mind, that is reason enough to do so. It gives a sense of urgency to our work that has not been there for most of us. It demonstrates our seriousness and commitment to be the Christ. It also does something else for us—it makes our commitment very measurable.

Setting a date opens the door for the Brotherhood to help us accelerate. If we are bold and realistic and take a stand by choosing to set a date, then the Brotherhood will develop a plan for our chelaship, a plan for our testing, in short, a plan to get us there! We're not doing this alone. We obviously have to do our part, but they will work with us.

Saint Germain said:

> If you are determined and absolutely determined on this Path and you will not take a backward step but pass every test, I, Saint Germain, assure you that you can make rapid strides in the internal harmony of being and in the great fount of Love that wells up within you, even as a gift of the Sacred Heart of Jesus to you. [And I assure you] that you are [now] able to achieve that bonding much more quickly than you have anticipated.[333]

Isn't that encouraging? Maybe we're closer than we think. Who knows, it might even happen sooner than the date we set!

Getting Started

This commitment is not to be taken, as the marriage ceremony cites, "unadvisedly or lightly." This is not a game. It's not a fantasy. It's not an illusion. It's a serious work of chelaship on our homeward path. So let us be sober and mindful in approaching this and deciding this is what we want, what we *really* want! Isn't that why we are here?

It takes great love to win our Christhood, to make God's will supreme over ours, to be victorious over the ego patterns that have been with us for thousands of years. It takes a love greater than the challenges and opposition to bonding with our Christ Self.

The masters believe that we can achieve it. And Saint Germain outlines steps to help us:

> When you begin to analyze yourself and set a chart before yourself and write down when you pass or fail your tests, when you will go about this systematically as a grocery packer checks off that which he is packing, as the simplest of workingmen does keep account of what he has accomplished on an assembly line or in any place of work whatsoever—when you look at the spiritual path in these terms, you will find that it is possible [to tackle this] task with practicality, setting up systems for yourself and reminders [so that you can whittle away at the dead and dying momentums of your human consciousness]....
>
> Set yourself to the task of self-observation. Close your eyes and meditate and take a moment apart, even apart from your body, to look upon yourself as though you were another person. Observe yourself as others observe you. And if you are not able to do this so well, then ask others how they see you or ask to be taken to the Cave of Symbols or to the Royal Teton Retreat, where you may look upon yourself in the cosmic mirror under the guidance of myself or others of the Ascended Masters who shall tutor you....
>
> It is an age of science and nothing can be said to be more scientific than the plan that must be laid by each individual to

secure the victory in his individual life and for his nation and for the planet.[334]

Saint Germain is like a cosmic cheerleader urging us on to our victory. So the burning question is, "If we don't set out to become the Christ now, when will we?" Choosing a date gives us a level of accountability that we might never have experienced before. Maybe it's time to say, "God, with your help, I am prepared to face the initiations for my Christhood." It takes courage to do that because it will mean our lives will change, but it is the call of Saint Germain to each one of us.

If you decide to follow Saint Germain's guidance, then where do you start? One way is to write to the masters stating your commitment and specifically asking for help based on his instruction. Writing a letter with our commitment anchors it in the physical and opens the door for support from the masters. We can make a copy for our altar and then burn the letter as our covenant with the Lord.

Part of this alchemy is to decide what five habits or behaviors to work on. When I did this, I found that they seemed to be either exact reflections or derivatives of the five poisons that the Dhyani Buddhas antidote.

In a dictation given at the Freedom conference in 1993, Vajrasattva clearly enumerated the five poisons and their antidotes for us:

As you know, the five poisons are: (1) ignorance, antidoted by Vairochana's All-Pervading Wisdom of the Dharmakaya, (2) anger, hate and hate creation, antidoted by Akshobhya's Mirrorlike Wisdom, (3) spiritual, intellectual and human pride, antidoted by Ratnasambhava's Wisdom of Equality, (4) the passions—all cravings, covetousness, greed and lust—

antidoted by Amitabha's Discriminating Wisdom, and (5) envy and jealousy, antidoted by Amoghasiddhi's All-Accomplishing Wisdom, the Wisdom of Perfected Action.

And the sixth poison is non-Will and non-Being—fear, doubt and non-belief in God, the Great Guru—antidoted by Vajrasattva's Wisdom of the Diamond Will of God.[335]

How wonderful that we were given the antidotes—what a key to victory!

A number of masters have echoed a call to action going after our personal poisons. On Easter Sunday 1997, Jesus asked us to work on the greatest stumbling block on our path. He specifically identified pride:

Now, I say to all of you: Call for the encirclement of the boulder of your pride. You may think you do not have pride, but most chelas retain pride as the last element of the dweller-on-the-threshold to go into the flame unless they have sustained their humility for many lifetimes... Pride and anger go hand in hand. Where there is no pride, anger too is extinguished.[336]

Pride should obviously concern us. So many masters have talked about pride and how subtle it can be in the chela. How great that when we are free of pride, anger is extinguished too!

If you don't think you have pride, ask God to show you your points of pride. This is part of observing ourselves. We observe behavior and patterns. It's like we're standing outside of ourselves, hearing what we're thinking and saying, and seeing what we're doing. Once we notice what is out of alignment, we can go after it with our calls and self-correct.

Lanello taught us about observing ourselves when he said:

Be watchful. Watch, then, out of the corner of the mind's eye the behavior of the untransmuted self. Be the watchman upon the wall of your own citadel of freedom, your own manifestation in this octave, and be quick to snuff out the candle of that ego which is not the Divine Ego....

Thus, the way of the one who is becoming the adept is to make a list of all those things that one desires to work on in one's lifestream that are not pleasing to God or pleasing to oneself. In your mind you put each one on a separate piece of paper, or you may actually take a box and put in it all of your pieces of paper [on which you have written your faults].[337]

Of course, it can be a cardboard box or even an envelope. Simply write down the five habits, put them in the box and keep them there. Lanello then tells you what to do with it:

Each day when it is time for prayers and the recitation [of decrees] and rosaries, ...take, then, this [mental or physical] box. Open it. Draw one or more of these pieces of paper. [And as you commune with your Mighty I AM Presence], work on [your negatives] diligently by inner resolve, by will, by fire, by love, by gratitude to God for his mercy that these things might be consumed by the violet flame.

Give it your best, beloved! Make your calls and fiats and when your session is through, put all these "things" back in the box. Seal it tight, put it on the shelf of the mind and leave the altar with renewed joy and zeal, and walk in the footsteps of your Lord, Jesus Christ.[338]

Though we identify these issues, we do not see them as who we are because we walk in the footsteps of our Lord, each day putting on more of his consciousness. Wishful thinking won't help us become the Christ. We won't become the Christ through osmosis. It takes effort, it takes spiritual fire, it takes will. It takes sore knees, praying before our God. There is no doubt that seriously following the path the masters have outlined for us will lead us to our Christhood.

Challenging the Dweller

We have been given many powerful tools for our victory. "The Dweller-on-the-Threshold" decree is a perfect example. As we have been told, the dweller is our own sorcerer's apprentice. We have created it, and it has become more powerful than we are. We can only defeat it with the help of the angels and ascended masters, which is why we need to make the call. When given in conjunction with our calls to Archangel Michael, it can help free us from those things in our being that must be resolved for us to become the Christ.

When my wife and I were co-directors of a teaching center on the East Coast, there was a professional couple on the board who were very supportive of the center both financially and in their service. During that time the dweller call was given to us by Jesus in a dictation. This couple immediately rejected it, refused to give it, and eventually left the teachings. I believe what that decree triggered in them was one of the main reasons they left. What they failed to recognize is that the dweller call is a gift from God for our soul's victory.

Saint Germain gave us this inspiring instruction on giving the dweller-on-the-threshold decree. He said it doesn't only help us, it also helps many others:

> If you could know how you can bind this force among the people and see your children, whom you believe in, and so many who began as wonderful souls turn around and face

their God because you will give this call three or nine times
a day, I tell you, you would do it! And I promise you that if
you do not do it, it will be your greatest regret when you pass
from the screen of life and graduate with less than cosmic
honors.[339]

Graduating With Honors

Did you ever think of graduating with cosmic honors? You
might ask, "Isn't making my ascension enough?" While making
our ascension is a tremendous victory, we desire to graduate
with cosmic honors, not for ourselves, but to show our gratitude to God for these teachings, for the Path, for the light we've
been given, and to honor the masters for their sponsorship of
our souls across the millennia.

We can't just pay lip service to the path of our Christhood or
we will never attain it. Instead, we work at it one day at a time
and trust that God and the masters will bring to our awareness
those things that we need to be liberated from and the exact
things that we need to do to reach the goal. The key is to be
engaged at a level greater than the force opposing our victory!

Think of every force of anti-Christ that could be within you,
whether pride, anger, rebellion, self-pity, self-condemnation,
self-justification, self-delusion, et cetera. Don't be afraid to
stand with Jesus in going after the momentums of the dweller
that could be blocking your path.

As with any call, the more specific we get about various
aspects of our dweller the faster we can make progress. An
example of something specific is anger towards God. We all
recognize that as a no-no, don't we? Yet we've been taught that
we *all* have it at some level of our being. While it may be from
many thousands of years ago, such feelings can still be lurking
in our unconscious mind.

So we make the call for the clearing of all anger towards God within ourselves. We shouldn't condemn ourselves for it because it doesn't reflect who we are now. Of course, when we make a call like that, we don't want to identify with the error, nor do we want to defend it. However, we must make the call because the record must be transmuted and the energy must be freed.

Echoing a teaching from Jesus, Winston Churchill wrote: "*When there is no enemy within, the enemies outside cannot hurt you.*"[340] Because the enemy within often hides in the folds of our garments, dealing with our psychology is another key to our Christhood. A couple months ago a friend told me she had written a letter to Mother and Lanello asking for help in exposing and overcoming issues with her psychology. That idea appealed to me because I know the tender care the messengers have for us. So I wrote the same kind of letter, burned it, and promptly forgot all about it. But the messengers didn't forget!

Over the next several weeks two issues came to my attention that I needed to work on. What was interesting was that I suddenly saw them in a different light. I was aware of them before, but somehow I didn't make the connection that I should do something about them. It was an *aha!* moment, and I felt a wave of gratitude for having them pointed out to me. What was even better was that they were relatively easy to correct. It was my inability to see them properly that was a bigger problem than actually doing something about them.

So What!

We all know what happens when we undertake a greater commitment to our path, and we can anticipate what will happen when we make our goal the bonding with our Holy Christ Self. Lord Maitreya addresses this challenge:

And all who desire that Christ, all who have the capacity to see that Christ will love you and will come unto you because you raise it up. And then again, beloved, because you raise it up, all who have enmity with Christ, all who hate that Christ will revile you: they will persecute you, they will do it again and again.

And I, Maitreya, say to you, So what! [10-second applause]

Be tough! Be tough students of Maitreya and understand that this will continue until that Christhood becomes as fearsome as vajra! vajra! vajra! Vajra! [341]

We know the score by now, don't we? Anytime we try to do something for the Brotherhood or our path, opposition arises. But we have been taught how to deal with opposition! We don't pretend it's not there. We don't cower in front of it. We deal with it through our calls and prayers. Maybe we do have to bear a little persecution. Maybe we do have to bear a little pain to see if we will repeatedly stand for our Christhood, for the principle of the Christ, and for the honor of God. In the past, we have compromised the honor of God by things we have allowed into our consciousness or things we have done. Nonetheless, we can balance that karma and move on to gain our victory.

If we are diligent and follow the practices outlined by the masters, we do not need to be sidetracked by the fallen angels and their tactics. God is infinitely more powerful than they are! Nevertheless, let us be wise as to what we will be facing as we enter into this commitment "reverently, discreetly, advisedly, soberly and in the fear of God." [342]

This is spiritual graduate school, and we have been preparing for this, not only in this lifetime, but for many lifetimes. God would not have brought us to this point if we were not capable of winning our victory. It's up to us to summon the fire and the will to do it.

The Elephant in the Room

As we work on the five (or more) issues we have identified, the question arises, "Will I even know when I have put on my Christhood?" And, of course, the elephant in the room question, "What do I do if I don't make it by the date I set?"

I thought a lot about whether I would know if I had bonded to my Christ Self. I wasn't sure, so I decided to ask other chelas what they thought. Interestingly, most of them weren't sure they would know either. The consensus was that we would surely know at inner levels, but we weren't sure we would always know in our outer awareness.

One person suggested that we could know by what we do. We know that putting on our Christhood is a daily process, and we can often be in our Christ consciousness even before we are totally bonded to our Christ Self. As we observe ourselves, we can often know if we are doing what the Christ would do. Conversely, we can recognize human behavior and the motivation behind it. I decided to trust in the process and the master's plan to help us.

Overall, if we don't make it by the promised date, are we better or worse off than if we hadn't set a date? We can look at it in two different ways. If we don't make it and we have not made a sincere effort to keep going when we stumble or fall, allowing self-pity or failures to overcome us, then I can see where we might be worse off. Would we rationalize that since we didn't make it, the teachings don't work? God forbid.

On the other hand, if we give it our all and strive day by day, resolutely getting up every time we fall down, going after our wrong behaviors with the sword and the fire of our hearts, and still come up short, wouldn't we still be better off? Since we can only put on our Christhood incrementally, wouldn't we be closer to our victory?

That is not to say the date is unimportant because it *is* important. However, missing it need not be the end of our striving to become the Christ. We don't want to let ourselves off the hook, so to speak. Pursuing our Christhood doesn't mean we won't make mistakes or get discouraged. We know that sometimes the greatest mistake creates the greatest regret that stokes the fire and determination to keep going. Morya has said that to make your ascension you only have to get up one more time than you fall down.

The Warp and Woof of Christhood

The phrase *warp and woof* was widely used in the 1500s to describe the threads in a woven fabric, composed of the warp (threads running lengthwise) and woof (threads running crosswise) to create the texture of the fabric. From a colloquial perspective it can mean two different parts needed to create the whole.[343]

Our journey to Christhood will require at least two parts. The one where we identify and go after the five or more behaviors or habits that are holding us back. This can include our psychology, conquering wrong habits or thought patterns, or challenging indulgences that we have entertained for too long. It means facing the darkest parts of our karma, our electronic belt, and things hidden in our unconscious mind for longer than we may think possible. It takes courage, it takes spiritual fire, and it takes using the tools the masters have given us to defeat the enemy within.

But there must be another part to our striving. We cannot win our victory simply by the absence of wrong habit or behavior. That's a void to be filled. Once again, our father Lanello has the key:

*See, then, and understand that pleasing God does not re-
quire gymnastics of the mind or ultimate feats of this and that
but simply the gentle heart. Oh, the gentle heart, the heart of
kindness, the heart of Maitreya, the heart of Bodhisattva!...*

*Let the power of God that you love as God's holy will make
you humble—humble before your God and truly humble before the God in each and every one upon earth. Humility is the
key, beloved. Be humble and let God raise you up. Always remain humble.*[344]

The gentle heart, the kind heart, the humble heart. This is
the woof of our journey. What if we strove to focus on one
God-quality for a week, whether it be kindness or humility
or the like? Do we look for an opportunity to be kind? Do we
look for an opportunity to lift a burden from someone in our
household or someone we greet along the way? It's an extra
effort, but these seemingly little things are key to developing
the flame of loving humility that is necessary to have along
with being a spiritual warrior.

Preparing for Battle

If we determine that this is the path we want to follow, we
need to be prepared for what might come our way. We are
determined to answer the call of Jesus and Saint Germain to
accelerate our path of personal Christhood. We know it will
be challenging, but we are more committed than ever before.
We are not naïve about the opposition we will face, but trust
that by our efforts and with the help of the masters, we will
make it.

We write our letter to Jesus, we make our list of five things to
work on, we "gird up our loins" for battle, and off we go. It does

feel different this time and we are so sincere in our efforts. It may be a few days, it may be a week or two, but then the opposition hits us, often at a point of great fatigue. We might fail the simplest test, perhaps one not that important in the big scheme of things, but nevertheless important to our journey. The test could be how we react to someone cutting in front of us in a long line or to a bank teller being rude to us. We often don't think these seemingly minor encounters are tests, but they are. For how can God give us a bigger test of harmony or of anything else if we can't pass the little ones? So be on alert for such things and think of them as a test that you can pass.

We can also expect aggressive mental suggestion telling us that we are not worthy, or our karma is too great, or we have failed on the Path, and on and on ad nauseum. To become the Christ we must be prepared to deal with this force of anti-Christ. We must also affirm in the deepest part of our being that we are worthy, that many have victoriously walked this path before us and that we can do it too!

All of Jesus, All of Our Holy Christ Self

I recall visiting with a member of the I AM Movement who knew Godfre quite well. He said Godfre told him that when Jesus was with him, he would often hold Godfre's hand. Isn't that incredibly sweet?

Jesus is with us too. He has been our brother, our teacher, our very personal saviour longer than we can imagine. We have walked and talked with him. We knew him on Atlantis. Perhaps we saw him in Palestine and were known to him by name. We have seen him demonstrate the Path for us. He has held our karma in abeyance until we could bear it. When we have stumbled and fallen, he has kept the vision for us.

The refrain from the hymn "In the Garden" speaks of our intimacy with Jesus:

> And he walks with me,
> And he talks with me,
> And he tells me I am his own;
> And the joy we share as we tarry there,
> None other has ever known.[345]

With over two and a half billion Christians devoted to Jesus today, how could one individual share a joy with him that none other has known? Our beloved El Morya answered this question in his dictation as the Patriarch Abraham. Although he is referring to himself, I have no doubt what he said would apply to Jesus and all the ascended masters.

> Let us move forward together! Let us go hand in hand! I place my Electronic Presence with each one of you... I am exclusively and uniquely your own. It is a one-on-one relationship. You can have all of me to yourself, each one of you.[346]

It's true! Each master, including our beloved Jesus, can exclusively be our own.

Don't we yearn for that relationship deep within our souls? Isn't that what led us here? Didn't we come searching for God, searching for holiness, searching for the truth? Where Christ is, his disciples gather. And we are disciples of our Lord who desire to become initiates. That goes beyond just a friendship with the master. It goes to integration with the master, with our Holy Christ Self.

We have a tremendous opportunity before us. Yes, it's for the salvation of the planet. Yes, it's so that other souls might be saved and not lost. Yes, it's for the establishment of Saint

Germain's' great golden age and so that Earth can become freedom's star. But what will the effect of pursuing this opportunity be for us? Number one: we'll be free of those things, or a good portion of them, that have weighed us down for so long, that the forces of darkness have used to keep us from oneness with God. We have believed the lie of the fallen ones too long—the lie that we are unworthy.

Mark Prophet used to talk about the puny little demons that sit on people's shoulders and whisper in their ears and get them to do things they shouldn't do. We're not going to let that happen to us anymore. We're going to take a stand like Maitreya told us to and say: "Vajra!" When we make mistakes, when we fall down, we will get up, summon the fire and will of God, and we will keep on keeping on.

God is not asking a lot of us, and he's willing to give us his all—the all of our Holy Christ Self, of our Saviour, of eternal life. And we want to win our ascension with honors: the honor of the ascended masters, the honor of the messengers, the honor of our Holy Christ Self. We can do that by working to free ourselves from negative patterns and habits; whatever they are, they're not real. Though we have previously acted as if they were real in our world, with God's help we can be liberated from them.

Our Christhood can be won through our striving as a humble soul, a kind soul, a determined soul that loves God more than he loves his humanness. What does it take to be victorious? A greater love.

We're attached to ourselves and our human patterns. It's time to surrender and let it all go. Morya tells us, *"Become zero that God may become the 100 percent of being where you are."* [347] We have to put everything on the altar—*everything*. We trust God will replace it with the light of our Holy Christ Self and our very unique attainment in God.

Every ascended master has faced what we are facing. They have won their victory. We can also. When I wonder what the greatest tribute is I can give to Jesus, to Saint Germain, to God, the only answer I see is to put on my Christhood.

There are unknowns to this journey, but the great known is our love of God that can lead us through the labyrinth of our human creation.

Our Lord has called to us:

> *I AM your Jesus. Now I say to you, Be my Christ!*
> *With the sign of our Oneness and the Law of the Word, I AM with you alway—to the end of your tribulation in this age.*
> *AUM AUM AUM*
> *In the Oneness of the All, I AM thy True Self.*[348]

Let us honor him by our striving and, by God's grace, our victory.

Amen!

Dictations Played
After the Sermons

1 Choosing Joy

Beloved Mother Mary, 'The Chalice of My Heart," delivered April 9, 1971, published in *My Soul Doth Magnify the Lord* (Colorado Springs, CO: The Summit Lighthouse, 1974), p. 246.

2 Heaven's Perspective

Beloved Maximus, "I AM Maximus, I Maximize Light," *Pearls of Wisdom*, vol. 48, no. 49, November 27, 2005.

3 Trust and the Chela

Beloved Oromasis and Diana, "FREEDOM 1991 XI A Mighty Plan for Transmutation *The Mystery of Becoming God "In the Immaculate Heart of Mary, I Trust!" The Two-Way Street of Trust*," *Pearls of Wisdom*, vol. 34, no. 44, September 15, 1991.

4 The Largesse of Your Heart

Beloved Lanello, "The Ascension Process Is for Everyone," *Pearls of Wisdom*, vol. 45, no. 2, January 13, 2002.

5 The Path to Unconditional Surrender

Beloved El Morya, "The Gemini Mind For the Governing of Society and the Self," *Pearls of Wisdom*, vol. 24, no. 43, October 25, 1981.

6 Overcoming Self-Imposed Limitations on the Path

Beloved Jesus Christ, "FREEDOM 1991 VIII *I Love you!* My Heart/Thy Heart *'Jesus, I bid you enter my whole temple now'!*," *Pearls of Wisdom*, vol. 34, no. 41, August 25, 1991.

7 The Alchemy of Mercy

Beloved Kuan Yin, "Kuan Yin's Promise *The Crystal Sphere—Etheric Matrix for Earth's Seventh Age*," *Pearls of Wisdom*, vol. 31, no. 53, August 21, 1988.

8 The Power of Regret and the Trap of Guilt and Shame

Beloved El Morya, "Rejoice, O People of God! *Be Grateful for the Gift of the Violet Flame*," *Pearls of Wisdom*, vol. 24, no. 56, February 15, 1981.

9 One With God-Desire

Beloved Durga, "The Rapture of Divine Love V The Power of Confrontation *'How Shall the Quickening Come?'* Who Has the Will to Change?," *Pearls of Wisdom*, vol. 35, no. 5, February 2, 1992.

10 Humility and Happiness

Beloved Peace and Aloha, "We Bid You Keep the Flame of Peace," *Pearls of Wisdom*, vol. 45, no. 41, October 13, 2002.

11 One That Has Gone Astray

Beloved Elohim Arcturus, "Easter Retreat 1995 7 I AM the Sponsor *Be Ye Therefore Intercessors on Behalf of All People!*," *Pearls of Wisdom*, vol. 38, no. 22, May 21, 1995.

12 Defeating the Last Enemy

Beloved Lanello, "Speak to Them of Death and Life *A New Era for The Summit Lighthouse*," *Pearls of Wisdom*, vol. 48, no. 50, December 4, 2005.

13 "Be My Christ"

Beloved Jesus Christ, "Saint Germain Stumps America 17 The Day of Thy Christhood *Keep the Flame of Eternal Life*," *Pearls of Wisdom*, vol. 30, no. 74, December 13, 1987.

Notes

1. *My Soul Doth Magnify the Lord!* (Colorado Springs, CO: The Summit Lighthouse, 1974), pp. 249-50.
2. Beloved Gautama Buddha, "Practice Sainthood Daily Walk in the Footsteps of the Great Saints of East and West," *Pearls of Wisdom*, vol. 46, no. 40, October 5, 2003.

Choosing Joy

3. Alice Lady Lovat, *The Life of Saint Teresa* taken from the French of *A Carmelite Nun* (St. Louis, MO: B. Herder, 1912), p. 548.
4. https://www.azquotes.com/quote/347550, accessed March 24, 2022.
5. Beloved Archangel Gabriel, "The Joy of the Path," *Pearls of Wisdom*, vol. 27, no. 30, June 4, 1984.
6. Beloved Lanello, "How to Ascend *Score a Victory Each Day!* Ascension Day Address, Nineteenth Anniversary February 26, 1992 Drop by Drop Immortality Is Won," *Pearls of Wisdom*, vol. 35, no. 10, March 8, 1992.
7. https://www.goodreads.com/quotes/tag/joy, accessed February 5, 2022.
8. Ibid.
9. Beloved Jesus Christ, "The Point of Dazzling Joy *I Will Let No Man Take My Crown of Joy* The Secret of Keeping the Christmas Rose of Joy The Lord's Christmas Day Address 1992," *Pearls of Wisdom*, vol. 35, no. 69, December 29, 1992.

10. Beloved Elohim of Peace, "The Path of True Love *Legions of Peace March against the Astral Hordes of War* The Empowerment of Peace," *Pearls of Wisdom*, vol. 36, no. 21, May 23, 1993.

11. *A Joyride through History*, by Eileen Daspin, Time magazine, special edition, The Power of Joy, undated.

12. Beloved Jesus Christ, "It Is a Matter of Heart! *I Summon My True Chelas* I Can Save You Only If You and I Are One," *Pearls of Wisdom*, vol. 36, no. 26, June 27, 1993.

13. Proverbs 17:22.

14. "Finding Joy Is as Good as Gold in a Grim World," by Andrea Peterson, *Wall Street Journal*, March 21, 2022.

15. Beloved Jesus Christ, "The Point of Dazzling Joy *I Will Let No Man Take My Crown of Joy* The Secret of Keeping the Christmas Rose of Joy The Lord's Christmas Day Address 1992," *Pearls of Wisdom*, vol. 35, no. 69, December 29, 1992.

16. Book review by Richard Lea of Dr. Levy's book *Riding High Into the Sunset*, *Wall Street Journal*, April 11, 2022.

17. Beloved Lanello, "How to Ascend *Score a Victory Each Day!* Ascension Day Address, Nineteenth Anniversary February 26, 1992 Drop by Drop Immortality Is Won," *Pearls of Wisdom*, vol. 35, no. 10, March 8, 1992.

18. Ibid.

19. Beloved Saint Germain, "Be Free in This Day and Age! For Freedom Is the God-Intent of the Age Part 1," *Pearls of Wisdom*, vol. 60, no. 33, September 1, 2017.

20. Ibid.

21. Angels of the Cosmic Cross of White Fire and the Ruby Ray, "The Joy of Forgiveness," *Pearls of Wisdom*, vol. 40, no. 37, September 14, 1997.

22. The Ascended Master Phylos the Tibetan, "We Are Winners and We Win with Joy!" *Pearls of Wisdom*, vol. 34, no. 25, June 23, 1991.

23. Ibid.

24. https://www.goodreads.com/quotes/tag/joy, accessed February 5, 2022.

25. Beloved Elizabeth Clare Prophet, "Your Sorrow Shall Be Turned into Joy," *Pearls of Wisdom*, vol. 53, no. 2, January 15, 2010.

26. Ibid.

27. Rev. 10:10.

28. Beloved Elizabeth Clare Prophet, "Your Sorrow Shall Be Turned into Joy," *Pearls of Wisdom*, vol. 53, no. 2, January 15, 2010.

29. Beloved Jesus Christ, "The Point of Dazzling Joy *I Will Let No Man Take My Crown of Joy* The Secret of Keeping the Christmas Rose of Joy The Lord's Christmas Day Address 1992," *Pearls of Wisdom*, vol. 35, no. 69, December 29, 1992.

30. 2 Cor. 12:9.

31. Beloved Archangel Uriel and Aurora, "Command Ye Me to Bind the Fallen Angels! *Saint Germain Sends His Messenger and the Seven Archangels to South America to Inaugurate the Aquarian Age on Earth*," *Pearls of Wisdom*, vol. 40, no. 9, March 2, 1997.

32. Beloved Magda, "Roses from My Heart *Meeting Your Needs at Maitreya's Mystery School* The Sun of Righteousness Must Rise in You Today," *Pearls of Wisdom*, vol. 36, no. 27, July 4, 1993.

33. www.merriam-webster.com/dictionary/Pollyanna, accessed April 9, 2022.

34. Beloved Jesus Christ, "The Point of Dazzling Joy *I Will Let No Man Take My Crown of Joy* The Secret of Keeping the Christmas Rose of Joy The Lord's Christmas Day Address 1992," *Pearls of Wisdom*, vol. 35, no. 69, December 29, 1992.

35. Ibid.

36. Ibid.

37. Ibid.

38. https://www.spiritbutton.com/joy-quotes/, accessed February 15, 2022.

39. Beloved Jesus Christ, "The Point of Dazzling Joy *I Will Let No Man Take My Crown of Joy* The Secret of Keeping the Christmas Rose of Joy The Lord's Christmas Day Address 1992," *Pearls of Wisdom*, vol. 35, no. 69, December 29, 1992.

40. Mark L Prophet and Elizabeth Clare Prophet, *My Soul Doth Magnify the Lord* (Colorado Springs, CO: Summit University Press,1974), pp. 246-250.

41. Beloved Archangel Gabriel, "The Joy of the Path," *Pearls of Wisdom*, vol. 27, no. 30, June 4, 1984.

Heaven's Perspetive

42. Beloved Maximus, "I AM Maximus, I Maximize Light," *Pearls of Wisdom*, vol. 48, no. 49, November 27, 2005.

43. Ibid.

44. Ibid.

45. Ibid.

46. Ibid.

47. Beloved El Morya, "I Bring You a Heightened Sense of Your Own Immortality Accelerate in the Fires of the Holy Spirit," *Pearls of Wisdom,* vol. 44, no. 50, December 16, 2001.

48. The Beloved God and Goddess Meru, "Why One Is Taken and Another Left," *Pearls of Wisdom*, vol. 62, no. 26, July 8, 2019.

49. Wall Street Journal, "Old and Young Diverge on Values," by Chad Day, August 11, 2019.

50. Ibid.

51. Luke 12:49.

52. Archbishop Vigeron, quoted in *Domesticating the Divinity* by George Weigel, https://www.firstthings.com/web-exclusives/2017/08/domesticating-the-divinity, accessed September 16, 2019.

53. Beloved El Morya, "The Light and the Beautiful *A Line Is Drawn* Concerns for the Chelaship of My Own," *Pearls of Wisdom*, vol. 31, no. 77, November 13, 1988.

54. Ibid.

55. The Beloved God and Goddess Meru, "Why One Is Taken and Another Left," *Pearls of Wisdom*, vol. 62, no. 26, July 8, 2019.

56. https://www.lexico.com/en/definition/identity, accessed September 16, 2019.

57. Beloved El Morya, "The Light of the Guru and the Chela: Surrender for a More Perfect Love," *Pearls of Wisdom*, vol. 23, no. 45, November 9,1980.

58. The Beloved God and Goddess Meru, "Why One Is Taken and Another Left," *Pearls of Wisdom*, vol. 62, no. 26, July 8, 2019.

59. Beloved Saint Germain, "'May You Pass Every Test!'," *Pearls of Wisdom*, vol. 27, no. 49, October 7, 1984.

60. Beloved El Morya, "The Light and the Beautiful *A Line Is Drawn* Concerns for the Chelaship of My Own," *Pearls of Wisdom*, vol. 31, no. 77, November 13, 1988.

61. "Every man shall bear his own burden." Gal. 6:5.

62. Beloved El Morya, "The Light and the Beautiful *A Line Is Drawn* Concerns for the Chelaship of My Own," *Pearls of Wisdom*, vol. 31, no. 77, November 13, 1988.

63. Ibid.

64. Ibid.

65. Beloved El Morya, "'Where the Sea Meets the Land...'," *Pearls of Wisdom*, vol. 34, no. 28, June 26, 1991.

66. Beloved El Morya, "The Light of the Guru and the Chela: Surrender for a More Perfect Love," *Pearls of Wisdom*, vol. 23, no. 45, November 9, 1980.

67. https://aleteia.org/2017/03/24/why-do-we-kneel-down-to-pray/, accessed September 16, 2019.

68. Elizabeth Clare Prophet, *The Greater Way of Freedom* (Colorado Springs, CO: Summit Publications, Inc. 1976), pp. 73-74.

69. Beloved El Morya, "The Light and the Beautiful *A Line Is Drawn* Concerns for the Chelaship of My Own," *Pearls of Wisdom*, vol. 31, no. 77, November 13, 1988.

70. On Aug. 8, 1958, El Morya wrote a letter to "Chelas Mine," marking the founding of The Summit Lighthouse.

71. Beloved El Morya, "The Light and the Beautiful *A Line Is Drawn* Concerns for the Chelaship of My Own," *Pearls of Wisdom*, vol. 31, no. 77, November 13, 1988.

72. 1 Cor. 2:9.

Trust and the Chela

73. https://www.merriam-webster.com/dictionary/inscrutable, accessed April 12, 2021.

74. Beloved Saint Germain, "The Decision and the Vow," *Pearls of Wisdom*, vol. 29, no. 4, January 26, 1986.

75. Elizabeth Clare Prophet, "Fourteen-Month Cycles of the Initiation of the Christed Ones through the Spheres of the Great Causal Body," *Pearls of Wisdom*, vol. 27, no. 56b, November 25, 1984.

76. www.dictionary.com, accessed April 12, 2021.

77. Apollo and Lumina, "'Let the Floodgates of Wisdom Be Opened!' *Wisdom's Reward Is Not Withheld* How Much Do You Want El Morya's Sponsorship?" *Pearls of Wisdom*, vol. 36, no. 29, July 18, 1993.

78. Beloved Lanello, "Intensifying the Light Fires of the Heart Part 1 *Expanding the Capacity of Your Heart Chakra to Give and to Receive,*" *Pearls of Wisdom*, vol. 57, no. 3, February 1, 2014.

79. Ibid.

80. Archangel Chamuel with Covering Cherubim, "Open Your Heart to God *The Initiation of the Piercing of the Heart,*" *Pearls of Wisdom*, vol. 36, no. 9, February 28, 1993.

81. Beloved Lanello, "Intensifying the Light Fires of the Heart Part 1 *Expanding the Capacity of Your Heart Chakra to Give and to Receive*," *Pearls of Wisdom*, vol. 57, no. 3, February 1, 2014.

82. Elizabeth Clare Prophet, "*Darshan with the Messenger* The Guru-Chela Relationship 'Nothing Will Ever Allow Me to Stop Loving You' Part 4," *Pearls of Wisdom*, vol. 51, no. 23, October 15, 2008.

83. Prov. 3:5.

84. Elizabeth Clare Prophet, "*Darshan with the Messenger* The Guru-Chela Relationship 'Nothing Will Ever Allow Me to Stop Loving You' Part 4," *Pearls of Wisdom*, vol. 51, no. 23, October 15, 2008.

85. Beloved Mother Mary, *Pearls of Wisdom*, vol. 3, no. 42, October 14, 1960.

86. Beloved Hercules and Amazonia, "Know the Law and You Shall Conquer *In Defense of the Messengers of God* May You Pass Every Test of the Will of God! *Beware the Dweller-on-the-Threshold*," *Pearls of Wisdom*, vol. 36, no. 28, July 11, 1993.

87. Elizabeth Clare Prophet, "*Darshan with the Messenger* The Guru-Chela Relationship '*Nothing Will Ever Allow Me to Stop Loving You*' Part 4," *Pearls of Wisdom*, vol. 51, no. 23, October 15, 2008.

88. Serapis Bey, "Motivation 'What Is the Most Important Thing I Can Do to Become a Candidate for the Ascension?'," *Pearls of Wisdom*, vol. 33, no. 3, January 21, 1990.

89. Beloved Jesus Christ, "It Is a Matter of Heart! *I Summon My True Chelas* I Can Save You Only If You and I Are One," *Pearls of Wisdom*, vol. 36, no. 26, June 27, 1993.

90. New International Version, Biblica Inc., 2011.

91. Beloved Lord Maitreya, "The Kneading of the Dough The Living Guru as the Fountain of the Water of Life The Leap of Faith *Trust the Message of Metteyya and Simply Follow It*," *Pearls of Wisdom*, vol. 32, no. 37, September 10, 1989.

92. 2 Cor. 12:9.

93. Beloved Mother Mary, "The Mystery of an Initiation in the Secret Chamber of the Heart *Part 2*," *Pearls of Wisdom*, vol. 56, no. 8, April 15, 2013.

94. Ibid.

95. Beloved Saint Germain, "The Preservation of the Four Sacred Freedoms *Keep That Flame of Liberty Blazing over the Earth!* Part 2," *Pearls of Wisdom*, vol. 61, no. 38, October 8, 2018.

96. Ibid.

97. Rev. 1:6; 5:10.

98. Elizabeth Clare Prophet, "The Worship of the Goddess—The Path of the Divine Mother The Corona of the Brilliant Sarasvati and the Bountiful Lakshmi," *Pearls of Wisdom*, vol. 35, no. 38, September 20, 1992.

The Largesse of Your Heart

99. https://www.liveabout.com/heart-quotes-and-sayings-2832786, accessed April 22, 2022.

100. Elizabeth Clare Prophet, "The Magnanimous Lives of Mark L. Prophet Upon the Dedication of St. Mark's Church Universal and Triumphant of Livingston, Montana," *Pearls of Wisdom*, vol. 40, no. 14, April 6, 1997.

101. James Henry Breasted, Ph.D., *A History of Egypt* (New York: Charles Scribner's Sons, 1912), p. 392.

102. Henri Crouzel, *Origen* (San Francisco: Harper & Row, 1985), p. 25.

103. Will Durant, *The Story of Civilization: The Age of Faith* (New York: Simon and Schuster, 1950) p. 601.

104. Charles J. Rosebault, *Saladin: Prince of Chivalry* (London: Cassell and Company, 1930).

105. Ibid.

106. Herbert Thurston and Donald Atwater, eds., *Butler's Lives of the Saints*, rev. (New York: P. J. Kenedy & Sons, 1962), 3:98.

107. *Encyclopedia Britannica*, 11th ed., s. v. "Longfellow, Henry Wadsworth."

108. Beloved Lanello, "The Ascension Process Is for Everyone," *Pearls of Wisdom*, vol. 45, no. 2, January 13, 2002.

109. Ibid.

110. Ibid.

111. John 8:11.

112. Beloved Lanello, "The Ascension Process Is for Everyone," *Pearls of Wisdom*, vol. 45, no. 2, January 13, 2002.

113. Archangel Chamuel, "The Judgment of Mankind's Perversion of the Fires of Creativity," *Pearls of Wisdom*, vol. 18, no. 39, September 28, 1975.

114. Ibid.

115. Matt. 22:37-39.

116. Beloved Lanello, "The Covenant of Compassion Ascension Day Address, Eleventh Anniversary 1984," *Pearls of Wisdom*, vol. 27, no. 35, July 1, 1984.

117. Beloved Lord Gautama, "Help Me Hold the Banner of Peace," *Pearls of Wisdom*, vol. 10, no. 1, January 1, 1967.

118. Kuan Yin, "Beginningness and Its Ultimate Perfectionment Is an Act of Mercy," *Pearls of Wisdom*, vol. 12, no. 20, May 18, 1969.

119. Beloved Lanello, "The Ascension Process Is for Everyone," *Pearls of Wisdom*, vol. 45, no. 2, January 13, 2002.

120. Elizabeth Clare Prophet, "Sunday service, September 4, 1988, King Arthur's Court, Royal Teton Ranch." DVD "The Mysteries of the Holy Grail, New Year's Class 2011-12," available from summitlighthouse.org.

The Path to Unconditional Surrender

121. Matt. 12:25.

122. Matt. 26:36-39; 36:42; 36:44.

123. Beloved El Morya, "The Light of the Guru and the Chela: Surrender for a More Perfect Love," *Pearls of Wisdom*, vol. 23, no. 45, November 9, 1980.

124. Beloved Jesus the Christ, "'Almost Free!' The New Era of the Rising Son of Righteousness, *Pearls of Wisdom*, vol. 23, no. 47, November 23, 1980.

125. Beloved El Morya, "Teachings from the Mystery School *'And the Lord whom ye seek shall suddenly come to His temple.'* The Inner Temple Work of Serapis Bey In the Four Quadrants, 'Chariots', of Matter," *Pearls of Wisdom*, vol. 28, no. 43, October 27, 1985.

126. Beloved Archangel Jophiel and Christine, "How to Contact Angels—Your Guides, Guardians and Friends 2 Surrender to the Will of God Is the Key to Your Destiny *Make Your Statement in This Age* We Must Fight and Win the War against the Tobacco Industry!," *Pearls of Wisdom*, vol. 36, no. 10, March 7, 1993.

127. Ibid.

128. Gen. 25:32-34.

129. 1 Sam. 15:22.

130. Beloved Archangel Chamuel and Charity, "The Messenger Stumps South America 12 Prepare Yourself for Service *Saint Germain Sends His Messenger and the Seven Archangels to South America to Inaugurate the Aquarian Age on Earth* Part 1," *Pearls of Wisdom*, vol. 40, no. 3, January 19, 1997.

131. 1 John 4:1.

132. Beloved Hercules and Amazonia, "Easter Retreat 1993 9 Know the Law and You Shall Conquer *In Defense of the Messengers of God* May You Pass Every Test of the Will of God! *Beware the Dweller-on-the-Threshold*," *Pearls of Wisdom*, vol. 36, no. 28, July 11, 1993.

133. Ibid.

134. Beloved Gautama Buddha, "Claim the Earth for Light, for Victory *The Hour of Judgment of the Warlike Hordes Is Come* Only Make the Call Part 1," *Pearls of Wisdom*, vol. 45, no. 33, August 18, 2002.

135. Charity, "THE TRIPARTITE FLAME OF FAITH, HOPE, AND CHARITY *Man Shall Not Live by Bread Alone*' III

Charity—Third Step in the Externalization of the Divine Plan Out of Law, Order, and Reality—the Consciousness of Eden," *Pearls of Wisdom*, vol. 12, no. 6, February 9, 1969.

136. Elohim and Their Retreats: Cyclopea and Virginia https://pearls.tsl.org/1978pows/78CYCLOP.html, accessed February 15, 2024.

137. Luke 23:46.

138. Beloved Mighty Victory, "*The Victory Way of Life* 10 The Science of Life," *Pearls of Wisdom*, vol. 42, no. 52, December 26, 1999.

139. Beloved El Morya, "The Gemini Mind For the Governing of Society and the Self," *Pearls of Wisdom*, vol. 24, no. 43, October 25, 1981.

140. Ibid.

141. Beloved Godfre, "Total Victory by Total Surrender," *Pearls of Wisdom*, vol. 19, no. 26, June 27, 1976.

142. Ibid.

143. Ibid.

144. Beloved Archangel Raphael, "The Class of the Archangels God Has Sent the Seven Archangels for the Rescue of the People of Light on Earth XI Truth as the Foundation of God-Government in the Earth A Gift of New Perception," *Pearls of Wisdom*, vol. 24, no. 14, April 5, 1981.

Overcoming Self-Imposed Limitations on the Path

145. https://www.linkedin.com/pulse/self-imposed-limitations-davide-zaccariello, accessed July 31, 2021.

146. https://avemateiu.com/quotes/quote-343, accessed July 31, 2021.

147. Helios, "I AM In and Behind the Sun Part 1," *Pearls of Wisdom*, vol. 13, no. 29, July 19, 1970.

148. Beloved Jesus Christ, "*I Love you!* My Heart/Thy Heart 'Jesus, I bid you enter my whole temple now'," *Pearls of Wisdom*, vol. 34, no. 41, August 25, 1991.

149. https://www.linkedin.com/pulse/self-imposed-limitations-davide-zaccariello, accessed July 31, 2021.

150. https://breakingmuscle.com/fitness/overcoming-self-imposed-limitations-mind-training-strategies-from-gym-jones, accessed July 31, 2021.

151. Ibid.

152. https://en.wikipedia.org/wiki/Comfort_zone, accessed August 25, 2021.

153. Beloved Jesus Christ, "The Gift of Resurrection's Flame 'I Come as Your Friend and Comforter' The Guru-Chela Relationship," *Pearls of Wisdom*, vol. 33, no. 33, August 26, 1990.

154. https://blog.peoplefirstps.com/connect2lead/leaders-self-limitations, accessed August 20, 2021.

155. 1 John 4:18.

156. https://leaders.com/articles/personal-growth/limiting-beliefs/, accessed August 20, 2021.

157. El Morya, "We Shall Not Forsake Our Chelas," *Pearls of Wisdom*, vol. 14, no. 33, August 15, 1971.

158. Beloved Jesus Christ, "Be the Living Presence of the Holy Spirit," *Pearls of Wisdom*, vol. 45, no. 19, May 12, 2002.

159. Beloved Mighty Cosmos, "The Sword of Mighty Cosmos *Intercessor Before the Five Dhyani Buddhas*," *Pearls of Wisdom*, vol. 31, no. 63, September 25, 1988.

160. Elizabeth Clare Prophet, "Darshan with the Messenger, Reading from *The Masters and The Path*, Overcoming Negative Habits," December 11, 1996. DVD available from summitlighthouuse.org.

161. Mother Teresa, *Come Be My Light: The Private Writings of the Saint of Calcutta* (New York: Doubleday, 2007), p. 33.

162. C.B. Ruffin, *Padre Pio: The True Story* (Huntington, Indiana: Our Sunday Visitor Publishing Division, 1991).

163. Luke 19:13.

164. Beloved Jesus Christ, "*I Love you!* My Heart/Thy Heart '*Jesus, I bid you enter my whole temple now*'," *Pearls of Wisdom*, vol. 34, no. 41, August 25, 1991.

165. Ibid.
166. Ibid.
167. Ibid.
168. Ibid
169. Ibid.

The Alchemy of Mercy

170. *The Imitation of Christ*, re-edited into modern English by Wilfrid Raynal, O.S.B. (Mt. Vernon, NY: Peter Pauper Press, 1872), p. 67.

171. Beloved Mother Mary and the Seven Archangels, "Practical Spirituality: Love, Wisdom and Power in Action A Dispensation from the Seven Archangels," *Pearls of Wisdom*, vol. 44, no. 10, March 11, 2001.

172. *The Imitation of Christ*, re-edited into modern English by Wilfrid Raynal, O.S.B. (Mt. Vernon, NY: Peter Pauper Press, 1872), p. 124.

173. Beloved Kuan Yin, "The Mutuality of Self-Transcendence in Mercy's Flame," *Pearls of Wisdom*, vol. 23, no. 8, February 24, 1980.

174. Mark L. Prophet and Elizabeth Clare Prophet, Annice Booth ed., *The Masters and their Retreats* (Corwin Springs, MT: Summit University Press, 2023), p. 165.

175. Beloved Kuan Yin, "The Transcending Crystal Fire Mist *'Create Your Own Merciful Heart!'*," *Pearls of Wisdom*, v. 35, no. 16, April 19, 1992.

176. Matt. 5:45.

177. John 9:4; 12:35.

178. James 4:14.

179. Elizabeth Clare Prophet, *Forbidden Mysteries of Enoch, Fallen Angels and the Origins of Evil* (Corwin Springs, MT: Summit University Press, 1996), p. 12.

180. Beloved Kuan Yin, "The Transcending Crystal Fire Mist 'Create Your Own Merciful Heart!'," *Pearls of Wisdom*, v. 35, no. 16, April 19, 1992.

181. Lecture by Elizabeth Clare Prophet, April 3, 1980. Audio available online from Ascended Master Library.

182. Beloved El Morya, "The Light and the Beautiful *A Line Is Drawn* Concerns for the Chelaship of My Own," *Pearls of Wisdom*, vol. 31, no. 77, November 13, 1988.

183. Beloved Kuan Yin, "The Transcending Crystal Fire Mist 'Create Your Own Merciful Heart!'," *Pearls of Wisdom*, v. 35, no. 16, April 19, 1992.

184. Ibid.

185. Ibid.

186. Ibid.

187. Christianquotes.com, accessed January 18, 2023.

188. Beloved Kuan Yin, "The Transcending Crystal Fire Mist 'Create Your Own Merciful Heart!'," *Pearls of Wisdom*, v. 35, no. 16, April 19, 1992.

189. Ibid.

190. Ibid.

191. Ibid.

192. Beloved Kuan Yin, "Kuan Yin's Promise *The Crystal Sphere–Etheric Matrix for Earth's Seventh Age*," *Pearls of Wisdom*, vol. 31, no. 53, August 21, 1988.

193. Beloved Kuan Yin, "The Mutuality of Self-Transcendence in Mercy's Flame," *Pearls of Wisdom*, vol. 23, no. 8, February 24, 1980.

194. Lecture by Elizabeth Clare Prophet, April 3, 1980. Audio available online from Ascended Master Library.

195. Ibid.

196. William Shakespeare, The Merchant of Venice, Act IV, Scene 1.

197. Matt. 25:29.

198. Beloved Kuan Yin, "The Mutuality of Self-Transcendence in Mercy's Flame," *Pearls of Wisdom*, vol. 23, no. 8, February 24, 1980.

199. Beloved Kuan Yin, "The Transcending Crystal Fire Mist *'Create Your Own Merciful Heart!',*" *Pearls of Wisdom*, v. 35, no. 16, April 19, 1992.

The Power of Regret and the Trap of Guilt and Shame

200. Oxford Languages, Google Search, accessed January 18, 2023.

201. Daniel Pink, *The Power of Regret*, (New York: Riverhead Books, 2022) p. 8.

202. Ibid.

203. Robert Leahy, *If Only, Finding Freedom From Regret* (New York: The Guilford Press, 2022) p. 14.

204. Ibid., p. 2.

205. Beloved Oromasis and Diana, "FREEDOM 1991 XI A Mighty Plan for Transmutation *The Mystery of Becoming God* "In the Immaculate Heart of Mary, I Trust!" *The Two-Way Street of Trust*," *Pearls of Wisdom*, vol. 34, no. 44, September 15, 1991.

206. https://thewire.in/communalism/a-way-out-of-hell-forgive-them-for-they-know-not-what-they-do, accessed January 24, 2023.

207. Beloved Saint Germain, "The Inevitable Encounter *Keepers of the Flame Will Make the Difference*," *Pearls of Wisdom*, vol. 24, no. 521, December 25, 1981.

208. Beloved El Morya, "Rejoice, O People of God! *Be Grateful for the Gift of the Violet Flame," Pearls of Wisdom*, vol. 24, no. 56, February 15, 1981.

209. https://www.verywellmind.com/negative-bias-4589618, accessed February 4, 2023.

210. (Article II) Augsburg Confession of Faith (1530) https://www.theopedia.com/original-sin, accessed January 27, 2023.

211. *https://www.ascendedmasterencyclopedia.org/w/Original_sin, accessed March 6, 2024.*

212. Sponsors of Youth from Out the Great Central Sun, "Youth of the World: Rise and Take Dominion over Yourself and Your Planet *We Are Your Sponsors," Pearls of Wisdom*, vol. 46, no. 11, March 16, 2003.

213. Thomas More, *A Dialogue of Comfort, in The Complete Works of St. Thomas More*, ed. Louis L. Martz and Frank Manley (New Haven: Yale University Press, 1976) 12:155.

214. Beloved Astrea, "Freedom 1993 A GLOBAL CONFERENCE DEDICATED TO *Healing the Earth 3 "Here Am I. Send Me." Accept Your Seraph as Teacher, Initiator and Dearest Friend," Pearls of Wisdom*, vol. 36, no. 34, August 22, 1993.

215. Beloved Sanat Kumara and Lady Master Venus, "*Freedom Class of 1968* A Dispensation of Three Percent of the Energy of the Atomic Accelerator," *Pearls of Wisdom*, vol. 42, no. 35, August 29, 1999.

216. Beloved Mother Mary, "The Fusion of Your Heart with My Own You Must Overcome Every Concept of Limitation Christmas Eve Address 1990," *Pearls of Wisdom*, vol. 33, no. 48, December 9, 1990.

217. Beloved Great Divine Director, "Seek to Express the Fullness of Your Presence *A Mantle of Light for South America* Part 1," *Pearls of Wisdom*, vol. 49, no. 38, October 1, 2006.

218. Beloved God Meru, "What Is the Perfect Offering? The Mind of Christ Is the Mind of God in a State of Flow—the Quiet Flow of Wisdom Part 2," *Pearls of Wisdom*, vol. 62, no. 6, February 8, 2019.

219. Beloved Saint Germain, "The Inevitable Encounter *Keepers of the Flame Will Make the Difference,*" *Pearls of Wisdom,* vol. 24, no. 52I, December 25, 1981.

220. Beloved Kuan Yin, "The Consciousness of Noncondemna-tion," *Pearls of Wisdom,* vol. 15, no. 5, January 30, 1972.

221. Beloved Omri-Tas, "A Study in Christhood by the Great Initiator XLV A Saturate the Earth with Violet Flame! *Give the Violet Flame Fifteen Minutes a Day and It Shall Be Multiplied Ten Times* Send the Messenger to Deliver the Prophecy to the Nations," *Pearls of Wisdom,* vol. 27, no. 50a, October 17, 1984.

222. Beloved Jesus Christ, "Ascend to the Level of Your I AM Presence with Jesus Coming into Consonance with the Living Word of Your Own Being Ascension Day Address 1990," *Pearls of Wisdom,* vol. 33, no. 18, May 13, 1990.

223. Beloved El Morya, "Rejoice, O People of God! *Be Grateful for the Gift of the Violet Flame,*" *Pearls of Wisdom,* vol. 24, no. 56, February 15, 1981.

224. Beloved Great Divine Director, "Seek to Express the Full-ness of Your Presence *A Mantle of Light for South America* Part 1," *Pearls of Wisdom,* vol. 49, no. 38, October 1, 2006.

225. Beloved Gautama Buddha, "Thirty-Third Anniversary of The Summit Lighthouse VI I Deliver the Unconditioned Love *A Time for a Great Battle: A Time for a Great Victory* Take the Virtue, Take the Vow of the Bodhisattva," *Pearls of Wisdom,* vol. 34, no. 52, October 27, 1991.

One with God Desire

226. Beloved Nada, "Discover the New Age with Saint Germain II, El Morya's Plan for Prayer Vigils for the Nations Images of the Christ Mind," *Pearls of Wisdom,* vol. 26, no. 51, December 14, 1983.

227. Beloved Lanello, "How to Ascend *Score a Victory Each Day!* Ascension Day Address, Nineteenth Anniversary February 26, 1992, Drop by Drop Immortality Is Won," *Pearls of Wisdom,* vol. 35, no. 10, March 8, 1992.

228. Ibid.

229. Beloved Jesus Christ, "I Merge My Electronic Presence with Your Own Now and for All Time *The LORD God Has Said: The Hour Is Come for the Glorification of the Son of God in Man,* Thanksgiving Day Address," *Pearls of Wisdom,* vol. 55, no. 21, November 1, 2012.

230. Kuthumi, "The Nobility of Self-Effort," *Pearls of Wisdom,* vol. 13, no. 45, November 8, 1970.

231. Beloved Djwal Kul, "The Seven in the Seven and the Test of the Ten," *Pearls of Wisdom,* vol. 17, no. 44, November 3, 1974.

232. Elizabeth Clare Prophet, Summit University lecture on discipleship from *Corona Class Lessons,* given on March 17, 1983.

233. Elizabeth Clare Prophet, "Mother Teaches Summit University, The Teachings of the Cosmic Christ Part 4," *Pearls of Wisdom,* vol. 43, no. 42, October 15, 2000.

234. Beloved Saint Germain, "'May You Pass Every Test!'," *Pearls of Wisdom,* vol. 27, no. 49, October 7, 1984.

235. Beloved El Morya, "One Voice *The Cause That Is America* Let the People Return to the Liberty Flame *'Let the Troops March and Let the Bodhisattvas Appear!',*" *Pearls of Wisdom,* vol. 36, no. 5, January 31, 1993.

236. Elizabeth Clare Prophet, "The Law of the One from Morya/to Mother/to You," *Pearls of Wisdom,* vol. 25, no. 21a. NOTE: The text of "The Law of the One" is taken from a Community meeting held by the Messenger Elizabeth Clare Prophet on March 25, 1982, in the Sanctuary of the Holy Grail at Camelot.

237. Beloved Gautama Buddha, "Readiness in the Lord—The Power of Perfect Peace Thought Form for the Year 1981: The Right Hand of God over the Earth Extended in a Mudra of Peace, the Left Hand Beneath My Command: Establish the Teaching of Maitreya on Earth," *Pearls of Wisdom,* vol. 24, no. 11, March 15, 1981.

238. Ibid.

239. Mark L. Prophet and Elizabeth Clare Prophet, *The Lost Teachings of Jesus I* (Livingston, MT: Summit University Press, 1986), p. 177.

240. Beloved God and Goddess Meru, "Twin Flames on the Path at the Royal Teton Ranch 'Realize God Where You Are' A Summit University Lecture by the God and Goddess Meru," *Pearls of Wisdom*, vol. 28, no. 54, December 31, 1985.

241. Beloved Saint Germain, "'May You Pass Every Test!'," *Pearls of Wisdom*, vol. 27, no. 49, October 7, 1984.

Humility and Happiness

242. *The New Jerusalem Bible, Reader's Edition,* (New York, Doubleday, 1990).

243. Andrew Murray, *Humility, The Journey Toward Holiness,* (Bloomington, MN: Bethany House Publishers, 2001), p. 91.

244. Ibid., p. 89.

245. Ibid., p. 17.

246. https://www.goodreads.com/quotes/tag/humility, accessed August 5, 2023.

247. Beloved Serapis Bey, "Dossier on the Ascension 4 The Banner of Humility," *Pearls of Wisdom*, vol. 10, no. 16, April 16, 1967.

248. Beloved El Morya, "The Light of the Guru and the Chela: Surrender for a More Perfect Love," *Pearls of Wisdom*, vol. 23, no. 45, November 9, 1980.

249. Prov. 16:18.

250. Beloved Sanat Kumara with the Seven Holy Kumaras, "New Year's Class 1996: *The Convening of the Stars 2* Purge the Earth of Pride," *Pearls of Wisdom*, vol. 42, no. 11, March 14, 1999.

251. Andrew Murray, *Humility, The Journey Toward Holiness,* (Bloomington, MN: Bethany House Publishers, 2001), p. 55.

252. Ibid., p. 63.

253. Beloved Peace and Aloha, "We Bid You Keep the Flame of Peace," *Pearls of Wisdom,* vol. 45, no. 41, October 13, 2002.

254. Beloved Lord Maitreya, "Love of the Person and the Law of the Word: God and My Right The Ritual of the Great Interchange: The Sphere of My Chelaship under Sanat Kumara," *Pearls of Wisdom,* vol. 23, no. 51, December 21, 1980.

255. Andrew Murray, *Humility, The Journey Toward Holiness,* (Bloomington, MN: Bethany House Publishers, 2001), p. 53.

256. Elizabeth Clare Prophet, "Teachings of the Elohim Peace and Aloha Part 2," *Pearls of Wisdom,* vol. 44, no. 49, December 9, 2001.

257. https://www.goodreads.com/quotes/tag/humility, accessed August 5, 2023.

258. Ibid.

259. https://memlok.com/9-simple-ways-to-practice-humility, accessed November 6, 2023.

260. Andrew Murray, *Humility, The Journey Toward Holiness,* (Bloomington, MN: Bethany House Publishers, 2001), p. 85.

261. James 4:6; I Peter 5:5.

262. Beloved Serapis Bey, "Dossier on the Ascension 4 The Banner of Humility," *Pearls of Wisdom,* vol. 10, no. 16, April 16, 1967.

263. https://www.goodreads.com/quotes/tag/humility, accessed August 5, 2023.

264. Ibid.

265. Beloved Sanat Kumara with the Seven Holy Kumaras, "New Year's Class 1996: *The Convening of the Stars 2 Purge the Earth of Pride*," *Pearls of Wisdom*, vol. 42, no. 11, March 14, 1999.

266. https://en.wikipedia.org/wiki/Litany_of_humility, accessed August 5, 2023. This litany is commonly attributed to Cardinal Rafael Merry del Val (1865-1930), Cardinal Secretary of State of the Holy See under Pope Pius X. C.S. Lewis attributed its composition to Merry del Val in a March 1948 letter to Don Giovanni Calabria.

267. Quoted by Lori Gottlieb, *Maybe You Should Talk to Someone*, (Boston, MA: Houghton Mifflin Harcourt, 2019), following the title page.

268. Beloved Lanello, "The Torch Is Passed to a New Generation of Lightbearers Part II," *Pearls of Wisdom*, vol. 17, no. 10, March 10, 1974.

The One That Has Gone Astry

269. Alan Morehead, *The Blue Nile*, (NY: Harper Colins, 1962, 2000) p. 229.

270. Ibid., p. 258.

271. Ibid., p. 260.

272. Ibid., p. 263.

273. Marcus, Harold G., *The Life and Times of Menelik II: Ethiopia, 1844-1913* (Red Sea Press, 1995), p. 32.

274. El Morya, "'I Am Unbenched!' Lux Fiat! At King Arthur's Court on the Occasion of the Thirty-First Anniversary of the Founding of The Summit Lighthouse," *Pearls of Wisdom*, vol. 32, no. 33, August 13, 1989.

275. Archangel Jophiel, "To Sponsor the Children of the Sun," *Pearls of Wisdom*, vol. 16, no. 48, December 2, 1973.

276. Beloved El Morya, "'I Am Unbenched!' Lux Fiat! At King Arthur's Court on the Occasion of the Thirty-First Anniversary of the Founding of The Summit Lighthouse," *Pearls of Wisdom*, vol. 32, no. 33, August 13, 1989.

277. Archangel Michael, "'Meet Us Halfway!' Our Goal: Your Freedom from the Astral Plane *A Mighty Angel Assigned to Each Lightbearer 'Hold Fast What Thou Hast Received!',*" *Pearls of Wisdom*, vol. 35, no. 50, November 8, 1992.

278. Ibid.

279. Gautama Buddha, "Concerning Maitreya's Mystery School *The Line Is Drawn, the Standard Will Be Kept,* Wesak Address 1988," *Pearls of Wisdom*, vol. 31, no. 67, October 9, 1988.

280. See https://www.storyofsanatkumara.com/ for more information.

281. See https://www.ascendedmasterencyclopedia.org/w/ Laggards for more information.

282. Matt. 18:21,22.

283. Beloved Jesus Christ, "Close Communion *We Are Banking on the Victory!* Thanksgiving Day Address 1994," *Pearls of Wisdom*, vol. 37, no. 45, November 6, 1994.

284. Ibid., footnote 8.

285. Ibid.

286. Ibid.

287. Ibid.

288. *The New Jerusalem Bible, Reader's Edition* (New York, Doubleday, 1990).

289. Beloved Elohim Arcturus, "I AM the Sponsor *Be Ye Therefore Intercessors on Behalf of All People!,*" *Pearls of Wisdom*, vol. 38, no. 22, May 21, 1995.

290. In the name I AM THAT I AM, I give to the entire Spirit of the Great White Brotherhood the authority of my mighty I AM Presence to act in my name and by the full momentum of my causal body in those situations and areas that you deem of vital and urgent necessity. I give you carte blanche by the authority of my free will to act in the physical octave in circumstances of world treachery and intrigue. And I call for the forces of Hercules and legions of the first ray and of the God Star, Sirius, to take action, to checkmate any dark plot or cause of darkness on planet Earth.

291. Beloved Elohim Arcturus, "I AM the Sponsor *Be Ye Therefore Intercessors on Behalf of All People!*," *Pearls of Wisdom*, vol. 38, no. 22, May 21, 1995.

292. Ibid.

293. Beloved Igor, "A Simple Devotion to God," *Pearls of Wisdom*, vol. 57, no. 6, March 14, 2014.

294. Beloved Elohim Arcturus, "I AM the Sponsor *Be Ye Therefore Intercessors on Behalf of All People!*," *Pearls of Wisdom*, vol. 38, no. 22, May 21, 1995.

295. Ibid.

296. Matt. 18:14.

297. Beloved Elohim Arcturus, "I AM the Sponsor *Be Ye Therefore Intercessors on Behalf of All People!*," *Pearls of Wisdom*, vol. 38, no. 22, May 21, 1995.

Defeating the Last Enemy

298. 1 Cor. 15:53-55.

299. Rom. 8:18.

300. Quoted by John Burke in *Imagine Heaven*, (Grand Rapids, MI: Baker Books, 2015), p. 59.

301. Beloved Serapis Bey, "O Man, Receive These Fires and Be Free!," *Pearls of Wisdom*, vol. 16, no. 26, July 1, 1973.

302. Beloved Lanello, "The Putting-on of the Garment of the Lord III," *Pearls of Wisdom*, vol. 17, no. 22, June 2, 1974.

303. Ibid.

304. Beloved Serapis Bey, "O Man, Receive These Fires and Be Free!," *Pearls of Wisdom*, vol. 16, no. 26, July 1, 1973.

305. https://www.dailymail.co.uk/health/article-12394153/Want-feel-thrilled-alive-Try-death-meditation-involves-wrapping-sheets-like-mummy-imagining-looking-dead-body.html by Emily Joshu, accessed August 15, 2023.

306. Ibid.

307. Beloved Lanello, "The Putting-on of the Garment of the Lord III," *Pearls of Wisdom*, vol. 17, no. 22, June 2, 1974.

308. Rev. 2:11; 20:6; 20:14; 21:8.

309. Archangel Michael and Kuthumi, "Pierce the Veil, O My Soul!," *Pearls of Wisdom*, vol. 29, no. 46, October 5, 1986.

310. Beloved Mother Mary, "Communion Feast at the Temple of the Resurrection with Mary, Jesus, and Lanello Part II," *Pearls of Wisdom*, vol. 16, no. 30, July 29, 1973.

311. Beloved Ray-O-Light, "Easter Conclave 1982 VIII Concerning Those Things That Ought to Be Revealed and Are Not," *Pearls of Wisdom*, vol. 25, no. 29, July 18, 1982.

312. Beloved Archangel Michael, "The Sacred Fire in Winter IV A Countdown for Victory," *Pearls of Wisdom*, vol. 32, no. 4, January 22, 1989.

313. Groups of devoted students who take turns doing decrees to sustain the flame of God 24 hours a day keeping the vigil of Life in community and for the planet.

314. Saint Germain, "The Vow *A New Day and a New Covenant*," *Pearls of Wisdom*, vol. 30, no. 2, January 11, 1987.

315. Beloved Lanello, "Speak to Them of Death and Life *A New Era for The Summit Lighthouse*," *Pearls of Wisdom*, vol. 48, no. 50, December 4, 2005.

316. Mark L. Prophet and Elizabeth Clare Prophet, *Prayers Meditations and Dynamic Decrees*, (Gardiner, MT: THE SUMMIT LIGHTHOUSE, 1984), Decree 20.09.

317. Beloved Lanello, "Lanello's Mother's Day Address May 9, 1976 The Welcoming of the Mother into the Temple of Your Heart Part I," *Pearls of Wisdom*, vol. 19, no. 29, July 18, 1976.

318. John Burke, *Imagine Heaven*, (Grand Rapids, MI: Baker Books, 2015), pp. 262-63.

319. Ibid., pp. 102-103.

320. Ibid., pp. 103-104.

321. Beloved Jesus Christ, "Saint Germain Stumps America 17 The Day of Thy Christhood *Keep the Flame of Eternal Life*," *Pearls of Wisdom*, vol. 30, no. 74, December 13, 1987.

322. Ibid., p. 78.

323. Beloved Holy Justinius, "How to Contact Angels—Your Guides, Guardians and Friends 9 You Are Not Helpless! *You Can Defeat the Challenges of the Decade* Seraphim of God Establish an Amphitheater of Light over Chicago with the Queen of Angels in the Center *A Violet Flame Magnet to Draw More Violet Fire from the Great Central Sun*," *Pearls of Wisdom*, vol. 36, no. 17, April 25, 1993.

324. Beloved Saint Germain, "The Heart Is Everything *To Build for Eternity, Build the Threefold Flame*," *Pearls of Wisdom*, vol. 45, no. 45, November 10, 2002.

"Be My Christ"

325. Beloved Lord Maitreya, "To Restore the Christhood of America! *Return to the One God* The Question Is Not *Can* You but *Will* You Turn the World Around?" *Pearls of Wisdom*, vol 35, no. 42, October 11, 1992.

326. Beloved Jesus Christ, "Jesus' Christmas Day Address The Path of the Avatar," *Pearls of Wisdom*, vol. 25, no. 69, December 25, 1982.

327. Beloved Jesus Christ, "The Day of Thy Christhood *Keep the Flame of Eternal Life*," *Pearls of Wisdom*, vol. 30, no. 74, December 13, 1987.

328. The Ascended Master Ernon, Rai of Suern, "Lessons Learned *The Remnant of the House of Israel* Adeptship by Free Will," *Pearls of Wisdom*, vol. 34, no. 61, November 27, 1991.

329. Beloved Jesus Christ, "The Day of Thy Christhood *Keep the Flame of Eternal Life*," *Pearls of Wisdom*, vol. 30, no. 74, December 13, 1987.

330. John 15:12.

331. Beloved Saint Germain, "Light Cycles of the Decade *A Scientific Plan for Individual Victory* The Need for Personal Adeptship," *Pearls of Wisdom*, vol. 34, no. 64, December 8, 1991.

332. Ibid.

333. Ibid.

334. Ibid.

335. Vajrasattva: Spokesman for the Five Dhyani Buddhas, "Becoming the Gentle Ones *Vials of Antidotes for the Five Poisons* Certain Karmas Are Lifted from El Morya's Chelas," *Pearls of Wisdom*, vol. 36, no. 40, September 15, 1993.

336. Beloved Jesus Christ, "Embrace the Guru," *Pearls of Wisdom*, vol. 40, no. 35, August 31, 1997.

337. Beloved Lanello, "Points of Darkness *Oh, the Heart of Kindness!* Call to Lanello to Descend the Spiral Staircase 33 Days *I Have Broken the Chain of Mortality! Call to Me:*

I Will Show You How to Do It! Lanello's Birthday Address 1992 'The Christmas Wind!'," *Pearls of Wisdom*, vol. 36, no. 2, - January 10, 1993.

338. Ibid.

339. Beloved Saint Germain, "FREEDOM 1992 'Joy in the Heart' XIX For the Victory! *I Wield Archangel Michael's Sword to Cut You Free and Keep You Free* This Is the Ultimate Confrontation: Fight to Win!," *Pearls of Wisdom*, vol. 35, no. 44, October 18, 1992.

340. https://everydaypower.com/enemy-quotes/, accessed November 9, 2022.

341. Beloved Lord Maitreya, "To Restore the Christhood of America! *Return to the One God* The Question Is Not *Can* You but *Will* You Turn the World Around?" *Pearls of Wisdom*, vol 35, no. 42, October 11, 1992.

342. Church Universal and Triumphant Wedding Vow ceremony.

343. *https://en.wiktionary.org › wiki › warp_and_woof,* accessed November 29, 2022.

344. Beloved Lanello, "Points of Darkness *Oh, the Heart of Kindness!* Call to Lanello to Descend the Spiral Staircase 33 Days *I Have Broken the Chain of Mortality! Call to Me: I Will Show You How to Do It!* Lanello's Birthday Address 1992 'The Christmas Wind!'," *Pearls of Wisdom*, vol. 36, no. 2, January 10, 1993.

345. Words and hymn tune by C. Austin Miles.

346. Beloved El Morya as the Patriarch Abraham, "Friendship with God *Take the Leap in Consciousness!*," *Pearls of Wisdom*, vol. 35, no. 25, June 21, 1992.

347. Beloved El Morya, "The Light of the Guru and the Chela: Surrender for a More Perfect Love *Angels Gather Offerings of Resistance to the Will of God* Part 2," *Pearls of Wisdom*, vol. 51, no. 25, November 15, 2008.

348. Beloved Jesus Christ, "The Day of Thy Christhood *Keep the Flame of Eternal Life*," *Pearls of Wisdom*, vol. 30, no. 74, December 13, 1987.